Story Movements

*How Documentaries Empower People and
Inspire Social Change*

Caty Borum Chattoo

OXFORD
UNIVERSITY PRESS

OXFORD
UNIVERSITY PRESS

Oxford University Press is a department of the University of Oxford. It furthers
the University's objective of excellence in research, scholarship, and education
by publishing worldwide. Oxford is a registered trade mark of Oxford University
Press in the UK and certain other countries.

Published in the United States of America by Oxford University Press
198 Madison Avenue, New York, NY 10016, United States of America.

Library of Congress Cataloging-in-Publication Data
Names: Borum Chattoo, Caty, author.
Title: Story movements : how documentaries empower people and
inspire social change / by Caty Borum Chattoo.
Description: New York, NY: Oxford University Press, [2020] | Includes index.
Identifiers: LCCN 2019054872 (print) | LCCN 2019054873 (ebook) |
ISBN 9780190943417 (hardback) | ISBN 9780190943424 (paperback) |
ISBN 9780190943448 (epub) | ISBN 9780190943455
Subjects: LCSH: Documentary films—Political aspects—United States. |
Documentary films—Social aspects—United States. | Motion picture
producers and directors—United States—Interviews. | Social change
in motion pictures. | Social change—United States.
Classification: LCC PN1995.9.D6 B676 2020 (print) |
LCC PN1995.9.D6 (ebook) | DDC 070.1/8—dc23
LC record available at https://lccn.loc.gov/2019054872
LC ebook record available at https://lccn.loc.gov/2019054873

1 3 5 7 9 8 6 4 2

Paperback printed by LSC Communications, United States of America
Hardback printed by Bridgeport National Bindery, Inc., United States of America

For Elias and Simone

Contents

Preface

Documentary has played a central role in my career, and its value in my life has revealed itself in distinct waves and moments. In some ways, then, I have imagined this book for as long as I can remember being captivated by artistic nonfiction storytelling as a source of insight about the world and the people who inhabit it.

In the first moment, I was a fledgling viewer. In the mid-1990s, Kartemquin Films' intimate, emotional, entertaining film, *Hoop Dreams*, exploded onto the scene to critical acclaim, opening many eyes to contemporary documentary—including my own—and indelibly marching the form into the territory of thoroughly modern, independent cinema verité as it invited audiences into the lives of two Chicago teens as they navigated basketball passions and the messy details of life. Several years later, I saw one of Stanley Nelson's documentaries, *The Black Press: Soldiers without Swords*, a film that revealed the pioneering history of African American newspapers in the United States. For me, Nelson's lens helped illuminate the power of documentaries to correct inaccurate narratives and supply those that are often otherwise neglected. I was hooked.

The second wave in my documentary evolution happened years later in 2004, on the day I found myself on my first field shoot as a documentary producer after several years of other professional communication endeavors. Within the first minute of camera-roll, my job was to help hold our cinematographer—the accomplished documentarian Brian Knappenberger—steady as he filmed outside the open back window of a station wagon hurtling down the highway adjacent to St. Louis, Missouri. It was decidedly unglamorous, totally invigorating, and breathtakingly exciting. I had imagined how it would feel to be in the field, working with a creative crew and connecting with people, but nothing compared to being there and doing it. For that project, a short documentary that examined manufacturing job flight in the Midwest, my crew and I produced daily short films on a 10-day bus tour from Missouri to Iowa to Ohio to DC, stopping at remote FedEx locations to send mini-DV tapes to our editor. The experience was exhausting—physically and intellectually and creatively and emotionally—and hard. But it was deeply gratifying.

Starting that day, and several documentary films and TV projects later, I decided that producing nonfiction stories satisfied me more than watching them, although the lens and motivations matched my experience as an audience member—that is, shining a light on intimate human experiences to reveal societal challenges or perspectives often missing in the broader news or entertainment marketplace. And, by extension, through this spotlight, we—not simply audiences, but members of civically engaged publics who activate the public sphere from which democracy finds its life force—might have an opportunity to strengthen our communities, develop our own perspectives, and even to be advocates for change and justice.

In the ensuing years well past my documentary producer beginnings, nonfiction storytelling changed and exploded dramatically—in filmmaking technology in the digital age, in professional community, and in access to audiences. Documentary—and my specific interest, social-issue documentary—is in the midst of a legitimate heyday. Audiences are seeking and discovering and watching documentaries as perhaps never before. As a mechanism for democratic public engagement about social challenges, documentary is powerful. Situated in the participatory networked era—the age of streaming and social media—the rich early analog origins of this documentary tradition have evolved into a new generation's marketplace and civic participation practices.

And yet, although the transformation of cheaper digital filmmaking equipment and editing software has democratized creative access to new storytellers in many ways, documentary work can be difficult for makers. For many, to make a career in documentary, which is a form of art, is an economic struggle. It is often dangerous, mentally and physically exhausting work, unspooling over years and raising money along the way. Independent documentary in the United States, as well as many parts of the world, is shaped within a broader media system that is even more consolidated than ever before, at a time of digital surveillance and threats to free expression. These challenges provide opportunities for research and growth in the field.

This brings me to the third wave in my professional connection to documentary, which is my identity as a scholar focused on the intersection of documentary and democracy, or public engagement with nonfiction storytelling at the core. Between my first years of documentary production and the present moment, I also worked as a senior communication and philanthropy executive, researcher, and strategist specializing in social change. I came to believe that documentary storytelling, rather than being an outlier to that work, was the missing piece; even the most sophisticated, research-driven, social-justice communication strategy has little chance of success without the people-motivating role of narrative and creative culture. The more intimate the story, the better. Bringing these practices together is the focus of my documentary research and public writing.

As a hybrid producer, researcher, and professor who remains embedded within documentary practice and its professional field, I endeavor to contribute research and host convenings that enhance our collective understanding about how creative nonfiction storytelling sparks ongoing dialogue and pursuits for social justice. In this regard, I am constantly motivated to merge disciplines and sectors—academic, artistic, professional—toward the development of new insights. Years after discovering Kartemquin Films' pathbreaking work in *Hoop Dreams*, I am honored to serve on that organization's board of directors, along with the same appointment at the pioneering documentary organization Working Films, and on the East Coast board of advisors for the George Foster Peabody Awards, the oldest and most prestigious award for American broadcasting, which honors many seminal independent documentaries. These commitments, among other collaborations with the field, offer unique vantage points by which I continue to learn about the evolution of documentary filmmaking, as well as the study of its influence.

And thus, I arrive at the current moment.

Story Movements: How Documentaries Empower People and Inspire Social Change comprises the adventures, motivations, learnings, observations, co-creations, collaborations, and research projects that have taken place throughout this journey, along with the voices and perspectives of the memorable people I've encountered along the way. Most important, it aims to reflect the legacy and ongoing work of the artists, journalists, philanthropists, community members, and advocates who have so indelibly shaped—and continue to advance and bring to life—the intersection of creative nonfiction storytelling and democracy. Within these pages, I humbly attempt to offer something new, even while my effort stands amid tremendous bodies of brilliant work from many scholars, filmmakers, field leaders, and thinkers who came before and continue today, many of them cited and spotlighted here. For this foundation and these individuals, and the documentary and community engagement efforts that allowed me to craft such a volume, I am immeasurably grateful.

Acknowledgments

This book is the product of many conversations, acts of kindness, gestures of friendship, professional contributions and inspirations, for which I am deeply appreciative.

First, I thank my editor at Oxford University Press, Norman Hirschy, who enthusiastically encouraged this effort and furnished a wonderfully supportive, efficient process for this new book author. I also thank the anonymous peer reviewers for their crucial feedback, as well as Lauralee Yeary at OUP, for her guidance throughout the publication process.

In my current professional home, American University's School of Communication, I am indebted to faculty and staff friends and colleagues, beginning with Dean Emeritus Larry Kirkman, who shares my passion for this topic and offered invaluable early insights and introductions to like-minded thinkers. I thank former dean Jeff Rutenbeck for his support and friendship during our years of work together, and Dean Laura DeNardis for her kindness, impeccable integrity, and leadership. Pallavi Kumar and Leena Jayaswal, my dear faculty friends—fierce, inspiring leaders and role models—dispensed endless, unwavering encouragement throughout this project and beyond, and they contribute to my happiness on a daily basis. My former graduate student assistants Michele Alexander, Samantha Dols, Chandler Green, Sarah Huckins, Molly Page, and Hannah Sedgwick provided invaluable research and editorial support. Declan Fahy, my former faculty colleague, was the first reader of these abbreviated ideas years ago; his thoughtful critiques helped to sharpen them, and his enthusiasm made me believe they were possible to print. I am also grateful for the contributions of indefatigable scholar and passionate agitator Patricia Aufderheide, my frequent collaborator. Indeed, it's impossible to contemplate this book without the imprint of her years of service and scholarly gifts to the documentary field. Finally, none of my work at American University's Center for Media & Social Impact—from which this book draws in many ways—is possible without talented Varsha Ramani, my trusted colleague and friend who fuels our efforts in unfailingly cheery and diplomatic fashion.

My appreciation for documentary people is boundless. In addition to the many filmmakers, leaders, strategists, and scholars whose voices and perspectives are reflected in the pages that follow, I express special gratitude to Giovanna Chesler, Sonya Childress, Simon Kilmurry, Cara Mertes, Gordon Quinn, and Marc Weiss (and again, Pat Aufderheide) for their generosity and tremendous expertise as they shared formative insights that directly shaped this volume—and also patiently read early writing and provided vital feedback before this book went to print. In the documentary and civic storytelling sector, I am fortunate to learn from many trusted collaborators and friends, particularly Molly Murphy and Anna Lee and the team and board of Working Films; Amy Halpin, Tom White, and Carrie Lozano at the International Documentary Association; fellow board members and staff at Kartemquin Films; Jennifer Humke at the MacArthur Foundation; and public policy expert Will Jenkins, who co-authored the original reports and articles on which Chapter 7 (and the opening of Chapter 4) is based. Finally, media scholar and documentary champion Jeffrey Jones, director of the Peabody Awards, read early chapter drafts and offered invaluable critique, enthusiastic ideas, and inspiration for which I am profoundly grateful.

Much of my on-the-ground understanding of contemporary nonfiction filmmaking comes from my original documentary network in Los Angeles, circa 2004–2007—amazing storytellers and people for whom I feel long-standing admiration and affection (and with whom I share memorable stories from the field), especially the late Brian Gerber, Molly O'Brien, Rick Perez, Amanda Spain, Sarah Feeley, Kristy Tully, Carla Gutierrez, Brian Knappenberger, the late Jim Gilliam, and Robert Greenwald. Finally, no one person's values and contemplations are more richly embedded in this book than those of my dear friend and collaborator, the late Jeffrey Tuchman, who was not only an award-winning filmmaker who exemplified the documentary tradition of civic motivation and humanity and artistry, but a confidante and cheerleader whose brilliant mind and legendary kindness inspired me and everyone around him.

On a personal level, I offer deep gratitude to my former boss and lifelong mentor, the great producer and activist Norman Lear, who championed my early documentary and writing desires—and models the mix of passion, creativity, humor, curiosity, commitment, and connection to people that lives at the heart of authentic storytelling. Finally, no one deserves more appreciation than Larry Chattoo, who years ago waited patiently as I flew off for weeks at a time to produce documentary stories in the field, and years later ensured that our children remained happy and healthy while I locked myself away to write these pages; his love and support made this book possible.

To my amazing son and daughter, Elias and Simone, I offer heartfelt thanks for your patience, overflowing love, sweet and inspiring spirits, and funny personalities. I dedicate this book to you, with the hope that you will read it someday and contemplate why stories about how lives are lived—and your own voices—matter so much.

Parts of Chapter 5 originally appeared in "Anatomy of 'The Blackfish Effect,'" *Documentary* Magazine, March 23, 2016, used with permission from the International Documentary Association; and "Anatomy of 'The Blackfish Effect,'" Huffington Post (self-published), March 25, 2016. Some writing in Chapter 7 was previously published in: Caty Borum Chattoo and Will Jenkins, "From Reel Life to Real Social Change: The Role of Contemporary Social-Issue Documentary in U.S. Public Policy." *Media, Culture & Society* 41, no. 8 (November 2019): 1107–24. doi:10.1177/0163443718823145, used with permission from Sage Publishing; and appeared in "When Movies Go to Washington: Documentary Films and Public Policy in the United States" (2017), and "Movies and Grassroots Community Engagement: Documentary Films and State and Local Public Policy in the United States" (2018), public reports self-published by the Center for Media & Social Impact at American University, co-authored with Will Jenkins. Parts of Chapter 4 also were included in "When Movies Go to Washington: Documentary Films and Public Policy in the United States." Oxford University Press and I gratefully recognize these publishers.

Story Movements

Stories can entertain, sometimes teach or argue a point. But for me the essential thing is that they communicate feelings. That they appeal to what we share as human beings across our borders and divides. There are large glamorous industries around stories; the book industry, the movie industry, the television industry, the theatre industry. But in the end, stories are about one person saying to another: This is the way it feels to me. Can you understand what I'm saying? Does it also feel this way to you?

—Kazuo Ishiguro,
The Nobel Prize in Literature 2017[1]

This is the gift of documentaries: Going to a party you're not invited to, and it's not fancy and you don't have to dress up—you
come as you are. And the more you come as you are, the better the
shot at getting the good story.

— Sheila Nevins
Executive Producer, MTV Documentary Films[2]

1

Revealing New Reality

Documentary's Networked Era Arrives

2004 was not great for Walmart, despite its unrivaled position atop the Fortune
500 list. That year, the world's biggest company bore the paradoxical distinction of landing in *Fortune* magazine's "Most Admired Companies" issue,[3]
along with pro-consumer *Multinational Monitor*'s "Ten Worst Corporations
of 2004" list.[4] It was a curious perch, as *Fortune* mused at the time: "The more
America talks about Wal-Mart, it seems, the more polarized its image grows."[5]
A steady drumbeat of news coverage revealed stories of alleged worker discrimination, labor challenges, and other ills. Communities from Washington
to Oregon to California to Indiana forged alliances to keep Walmart out;
media captured these battles of grassroots resistance, a pattern that reverberated and picked up steam[6] (see Figure 1.1).

As a Los Angeles–based researcher and producer at the time, I did what
seemed natural: I wrote a documentary film treatment about Walmart, and
I shared it with everyone who would listen. It turns out I wasn't the only

Story Movements. Caty Borum Chattoo, Oxford University Press (2020) © Oxford University Press.
DOI: 10.1093/oso/9780190943417.001.0001

Figure 1.1. On July 21, 2004, protestors gather outside a meeting of the Chicago City Council as the council debates whether to allow Wal-Mart to build the second of their first two stores in the city. Photo by Scott Olson, courtesy of Getty Images.

one. By the end of the year, a meeting with another documentarian—Robert Greenwald of Brave New Films, a pathbreaking early adopter of grassroots online documentary distribution[7]—led me into a physical and virtual war room of filmmakers, civil society organizations, and community coalitions that were just beginning to shape a documentary film to push for change. I joined Greenwald's producing team immediately.

And thus, in early 2005, I began my journey traveling around the country—armed with a notebook, flip phone, audio gear, and copious extra batteries—working most of the time with a trusty cinematographer partner, Kristy Tully. We became a fast-moving two-woman team, arriving in small cities and towns, often working 12 hours a day in the field to connect with people from Arkansas to Ohio to North Carolina. We spent time with revered local business owners in Hamilton, Missouri, a Midwest haven of Americana where retailer J.C. Penney was born. In North Carolina, we gripped the sides of a racing speedboat captained by the joke-cracking Catawba Riverkeeper who had become an environmental advocate laser-focused on toxins leaking into the water supply. And we dimmed the camera lights to film with a former Walmart manager who could barely keep his emotions in check as he talked about his experience. These visits—revealing intimate human stories—would join others captured by our team of field producers to become the independent documentary, *Wal-Mart: The High Cost of Low Price*,[8] and the centerpiece of a national grassroots campaign to push for change.

We weren't simply concerned about one company's business practices. We, and many others, were worried about the race-to-the-bottom ripple effect on Walmart's distributors and supplier companies whose business protocols were forced to mold around the biggest corporate player on the planet. In such a moment, we reasoned, illuminating the struggles of ordinary people and community groups fighting back in the ultimate David versus Goliath story would provide a visceral lens and spark a meaningful, action-oriented public conversation.

Under Greenwald's visionary leadership, the team shaped the film as a living, in-the-minute exposé while simultaneously building a nationwide grassroots coalition of community and civil society groups. The list of unusual bedfellows included environmental groups like the Riverkeeper Alliance, progressive faith-based groups like Sojourners, labor unions, church groups, human rights groups, and neighborhood organizations. Through this network, we produced a documentary story to stand on its own but also to fit within a growing public cry for change in Walmart's business practices. *Wal-Mart: The High Cost of Low Price* (see Figure 1.2) premiered in November 2005 as the centerpiece of a nationwide grassroots mobilizing effort, "Wal-Mart Week." People around the country screened the film in homes, community centers, churches, classrooms, synagogues, and union halls.[9]

The Walmart documentary wasn't the first to leverage a coalition-based approach to raise awareness and mobilize publics around a social challenge. But the film was shaped and distributed in a meaningful juncture—in the crevasse between the early digital century and the looming revolution of the participatory networked media age. In retrospect, we can more clearly see the pivotal 2005 moment, marked by the transformation of digital filmmaking technology, the emergence of social media, and a new class of documentary makers engaging community through online platforms. At the time, YouTube was a curious fledgling novelty, people were just beginning to understand their new digital advocacy power, and social media networks—led by Facebook and Twitter—were a few years away from turbocharging the influence of activists in the first networked social movements, Occupy Wall Street and the Arab Spring.[10] And the visionaries at Netflix, the billion-dollar business that shifted media consumption habits and upended Hollywood business practices, were quietly planning the streaming entertainment uprising even while legacy news media prematurely—and amusingly—declared the then-mail-order DVD business dead.[11]

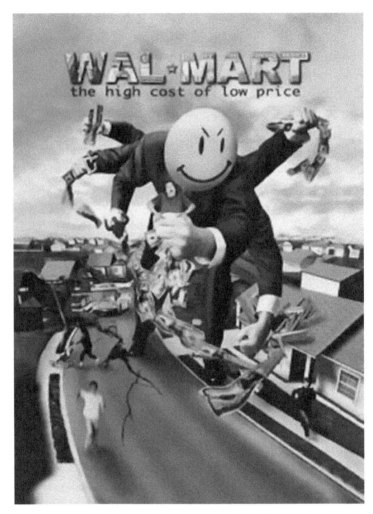

Figure 1.2. 2005 movie poster for *Wal-Mart: The High Cost of Low Price*. Image courtesy of Brave New Films.

As the century progressed, documentary's participatory networked era emerged. New organizations evolved from the practices and organizations established decades prior, designed to strategically leverage the intimacy, emotion, and depth of documentary storytelling to engage audiences in social challenges. New funding flowed into the work, fresh outlets for distribution launched, and fledgling storytellers arrived on the scene to take advantage of newly accessible production and editing gear. Audiences discovered documentaries in ways that seemed impossible a generation before. To the extent that media products, audience consumption behavior, and culture continue to transform in the post-millennial age, the present-day nexus of social-issue documentary storytelling and public engagement is simultaneously new but historically rooted in decades of cultural and technological change, shaped by pioneering filmmakers and activists. How we arrived here and how contemporary documentaries meaningfully reveal complex social issues and untold stories—and engage publics—is the journey of these pages.

This book explores the functions and public influence of contemporary social-issue documentary storytelling. Through the stories and ideas that follow, I argue that documentaries play a vital role in democratic functioning and social progress with a motivation toward justice and equity. In the present-day media environment, audiences experience the practice and output of documentary films that passionately interrogate topics like youth bullying (*Bully*), domestic violence (*Private Violence*), racial justice (*Whose Streets?*), and many other social issues. In a continuum of social change, documentaries have incited national and local conversations, set media agendas, provided intimate new lenses with which to see social problems and people, and sometimes contributed to changing laws and corporate policies. Publics can access the stories in a shifting, expanded media marketplace that ranges from theaters to streaming outlets to legacy public media and cable TV and community venues. Fueled by the possibilities of the participatory networked media age, the contemporary role and function of social-issue documentaries in the public sphere is embodied also in parallel community engagement practices—the active role of civil society groups, communities, and individual people speaking truth to power. Through the artistic lens of cinema and the integrity of journalism, documentaries showcase stories that disrupt dominant cultural narratives and contribute new ways for audiences to contemplate and understand the world around them.

What Is a Documentary?

For more than a century, documentaries have illuminated the messy, intimate human voyage and invited audiences to bear witness. Creative nonfiction stories—whether we experience them in theaters, on TV, online, in community centers, or classrooms—can delight, entertain, amuse, enrage, teach, shock, and mobilize; spark public and private conversations; fuel community solidarity; empower movements for change; provide new ways of seeing ideas we thought we knew; and introduce people and places we don't see at all. They proffer voyeuristic entry into lives, realities, problems, scandals, and intimate secrets, from poverty to sexual assault to drug addiction to racial discrimination. Along the way, documentaries contribute to the process by which we mold our perspectives of the world, and sometimes, the ways in which we reconstitute it. At their core, documentaries are a form of art that supplies the civic and narrative imagination that is vital—well beyond simply knowing facts and information—to shaping a culture that can understand and include the full spectrum of human experience and the lives we live. This cultural work embodied in stories is, in philosopher Martha Nussbaum's words, a required function for citizenship:

> Narrative art has the power to make us see the lives of the different with more than a casual tourist's interest – with involvement and sympathetic understanding, with anger at our society's refusals of visibility. We come to see how circumstances shape the lives of those who share with us some general goals and projects; and we see that circumstances shape not only people's possibilities for action, but also their aspirations and desires, hopes and fears. All of this seems highly pertinent to decisions we must make as citizens.[12]

The documentary tradition also has, over the course of its history, evolved from awkward propagandistic roots, as documentary scholar John Corner colorfully articulated: "At one time, it was thought that the most important thing to say about documentary was that it was a loose generic bundle of sham and trickery, grounded in technically devious schemes of expository or observational and authoritarianism and with a track record of political and social misinformation stretching back to the 1920s."[13] Documentary practices and forms have matured over the decades through the converged machinations of storytellers, technology, the marketplace, and demands for social reform.

How to define documentary as a mediated form of storytelling: Is it journalism? Is it entertainment? It can include elements of both. We find documentary within complicated, murky boundaries of practice and form, maker motivation and audience experience. In the words of British documentary luminary Nick Fraser:

> No body of theory exists to legitimise docs and I'm grateful for this. They have come to subsist at a crossroads of contemporary culture, somewhere between journalism, film narrative and television entertainment. They appear to thrive on contradictions, between the stubborn reality they purport to capture and their necessarily limited means, between the impositions of storytelling and the desire to interpret or analyse. They aren't fictional, ever, but they can seem in their attractiveness more real than reality.[14]

Documentary's origin stories trace back to the late 1800s with inventor and photography luminary Louis Lumière and his small, handcranked cinématographe camera,[15] but the genre stirred to life amid two paradoxical realities—the dizzyingly frenetic days of the early 20th century and the Great Depression, and the aesthetic artistry that emerged from fledgling Hollywood and motion picture storytellers around the world.. The Great Depression created tragedies of immense proportion—poverty and unemployment and starvation.[16] At the same time, from the cityscape of New York to the sunny paradise of California, the creative innovators in early Hollywood evolved motion pictures as entertainment for the masses.[17] Through their enthusiasm, moviegoers shaped the early aesthetic and artistic grammar of the visual entertainment narrative.

Both cultural realities—the innovation of motion pictures and the turbulence of the evolving 1900s—intertwined to position early documentary storytelling as artistic but educational, or at least societally useful beyond amusement. Documentary was shaped globally. Within this juncture, in the 1930s, John Grierson, a Scottish sociologist motivated by the desire for social improvement, articulated his enduring definition of documentary as a "creative treatment of actuality" in reference to a 1926 film, *Moana*, directed by Robert Flaherty;[18] Flaherty also directed *Nanook of the North* (1922), a portrait of an indigenous community widely recognized as one of the first documentary films.[19] For his part, Flaherty, an American filmmaker, echoed the aesthetic and narrative conventions seen in early fiction Hollywood motion pictures.[20] Considering Grierson's early focus on social responsibility, both social reform and the creativity of motion picture storytelling live in documentary's formative junctures.

Grierson's definition is flexible; a "creative treatment of actuality," a meaning that "leaves unresolved the obvious tension between 'creative treatment' and 'reality.' 'Creative treatment' suggests the license of fiction, whereas 'actuality' reminds us of the responsibilities of the journalist and historian," wrote documentary scholar Bill Nichols.[21] Grierson regarded socially conscious documentary imagery as a persuasive mechanism by which public opinion germinates and crystallizes, shaped in part by mass media.[22] Beyond his lasting definition, Grierson focused on a distinctive aspect of documentary— a social responsibility function. In his mind, echoed in the evolution of the artistic practice throughout future decades, the act of showing real life bore a certain responsibility. While well meaning, however, Grierson-style early documentaries—largely government-funded films—were characterized by a social reform approach that also rendered marginalized on-screen subjects as victims rather than individuals with full humanity and agency.[23] Critiques of Grierson's lens abound, but his early conceptualizations remain valuable.

Also reflecting documentary's early roots, scholar William Stott positioned 1930s "documentary reportage" by three primary composite elements: "direct quotation" (facts), "case history of an actual person" (lived experience of the subject), and "firsthand experience of the author" (the creative point of view of the filmmaker).[24] Although the form has evolved dramatically from the early analog days, a broad interpretation of the documentary reportage trifecta makes sense today: To show people's reality is to reveal their vulnerability and humanity—and to advocate improvement of the human condition. To render real life creatively and artistically, shaped by the point of view of the storyteller, is to draw people in. To locate case studies of social problems within larger frameworks of facts and information is to convey legitimacy and credibility. That said, documentary storytellers and communities today demand a more reflective interrogation of filmmakers' gazes and intentions; transparency and "naming the gaze" is explicitly discussed and embedded in much contemporary documentary practice.

Documentary is not, of course, solely a means to transmit information. Nonfiction storytelling packages and diffuses reality through artistic, creatively rendered narrative that evokes emotion, perhaps the most potent mechanism by which humans respond to the world. From the early roots of documentary, recognition about the underlying social power of emotion remains a dominant idea. When contemplating documentary's ability to spark motivated political action from an audience, for example, emotional response lies at the fore.[25]

Defining documentary—what it is, what it is not—remains an ongoing pursuit. Grierson's articulation and basic principles endure, embracing ongoing developments in media platforms and storytelling approaches. Both original elements—art and real life—are central to understanding documentary. And yet, given the complexities of reflecting truth through art, documentary definitions will continue to materialize, as historian and media scholar Patricia Aufderheide wrote: "A documentary film tells a story about real life, with claims to truthfulness. How to do that honestly, in good faith is a neverending discussion, with many answers. Documentary is defined and redefined over the course of time, both by makers and by viewers. . . . [W]e do expect that a documentary will be a fair and honest representation of somebody's experience of reality."[26] Documentary is not, however, fiction, despite its artistic license, as scholar and documentarian Michael Chanan asserted: "One of the crucial differences is that fiction addresses the viewer primarily as a private individual, it speaks to the interior life of feelings, sentiments and secret desires; whereas documentary addresses the viewer primarily as a citizen, member of civil society, putative participant in the public sphere."[27]

More than a century after documentary's early days, the basic equation of artistic nonfiction storytelling—reflection of truth shaped with creative freedom—and its broad social function remains durable, even while cultural and technology realities continue to shift. Documentary's dynamic evolution at the hands of each new auteur and platform ensures that it remains current and vital with each generation. No one definition, set of characteristics, or articulation of makers' motivations may ever satisfy all audiences or artists. As scholar Bill Nichols wrote, such fluidity gives cause to celebrate a unique form of cultural expression: "Fluid, fuzzy boundaries are testimony to growth and vitality. The amazing vigor and popularity of documentary films over the last 25 years is firm evidence that fluid boundaries and a creative spirit yield an exciting, adaptable art form."[28] Documentary is a living, breathing, evolving practice and product that comprises an array of genres and approaches, shaped by shifting cultural realities, media institutions, technologies, forms and sub-forms, and audience reception and interpretation. The post-millennial information age, however, presents a fresh and robust climate for social-issue documentary storytelling, as well as its role in public engagement with social problems.

Documentaries and Social Change: A Rich Foundation in Theory and Practice

Film scholars, historians, activists, and filmmakers have consistently recognized documentary's broad potential for positive societal intervention. Indeed, independent documentary, which largely characterizes the focus of this book—that is, produced and shaped by makers outside the confines of formal media institutions—"has always been driven by engagement, either political or social," wrote Michael Chanan.[29] In the pathbreaking historical work, *Documentary: A History of the Non-Fiction Film*, Erik Barnouw positioned documentary as a voice of art, societal critique and dissent.[30] Similarly, Bill Nichols canonized early Griersonian documentary as a "discourse of sobriety," a meaning that confers a nuanced depth and social-reform intent.[31] In his classic seminal documentary text, theorist Michael Renov referenced the functions of documentary as four modes: "1. to record, reveal, or preserve; 2. to persuade or promote; 3. to analyze or interrogate; and 4. to express."[32]

A more explicit connection between documentaries and social change is not new, even if semantics, practices, technologies, and marketplaces vary between then and now. One of the earliest labels, from the 1930s tradition of documentary reportage, is "the *expose*, which uses emotional reportage to persuade the audience to take action against men and evils that cause unnecessary suffering in the world."[33] Additionally, scholar Thomas Waugh examined similar principles in his 1984 work, *Show Us Life: Toward a History and Aesthetics of the Committed Documentary*. Waugh positioned social engagement practice and documentary against the backdrop of technological innovation and a changing analog media landscape. He saw "committed documentary" films as creative nonfiction works of art, but shaped with overt, "radical" social change objectives on the part of the filmmaker.[34] Further, cocreation with community was essential in Waugh's mind: "If films are to be instrumental in the process of change, they must be made not only about people directly implicated in change, but with and for those people as well."[35] More recently, documentary scholars Kate Nash and John Corner positioned the "strategic impact documentary" as "a transmedia practice that aims to achieve specific social change by aligning documentary production with online and offline communications practices."[36] My own writing locates contemporary social-issue documentary in the digital media landscape as an art form and mechanism for public engagement, but not an approach shaped explicitly—or solely—within movements:

> As audiences increasingly access documentaries in theaters, TV, online streaming outlets and social media channels, documentary storytelling plays an influential persuasive role, shaping public opinion and acting as centerpieces of strategic efforts to spotlight social issues. Documentary is increasingly leveraged overtly as an advocacy communication mechanism to raise awareness and advocate for change on challenging social justice issues.[37]

Today, in the midst of an expansive evolution often called a "golden era" for documentary,[38] nonfiction storytelling "has become the flagship for a cinema of social engagement" wrote scholar Bill Nichols.[39] Social engagement—activated publics who interrogate social issues discursively or physically in response to a documentary story—is both a legacy norm established by earlier documentary practice and a set of activities enabled by the possibilities of the internet's accessibility and participatory qualities. In this way, documentary fits within an invigorated contemporary understanding of entertainment that is, in the words of media scholar Jeffrey Jones, "just as capable of shaping and supporting a culture of citizenship as it is of shaping and supporting a culture of consumption."[40]

What might account for this documentary moment? In large part, digital media factors—newly accessible storytelling technology, viewers' expanded ability to find and watch documentaries, intentional social-impact strategy and campaigns, and vocal grassroots audiences who amplify critical messages through both physical gathering and digital organizing—have converged to support a sophisticated ecosystem that builds and enables social change with storytelling at the core.[41] The media marketplace for documentaries has expanded dramatically, including the entertainment streamers like Apple, Hulu, Netflix, and Amazon Prime, alongside outlets like Discovery, CNN, National Geographic, PBS, HBO, Showtime, Vice, and online offerings from legacy news brands like the *New York Times*.

Within this invigorated documentary juncture, contemporary industry professionals are ardent believers in the power of nonfiction storytelling as democratic discourse and art. Jenni Wolfson, executive director of the independent documentary production organization Chicken & Egg Films, notes that "documentary film can change the culture, conversation, policies, action, and behavior. Changing the conversation is social change itself."[42] Similarly, Ellen Schneider, founder of Active Voice Labs and pioneering architect of story-centered community engagement models, speaks about documentary as a mechanism for sparking community conversation and questions: "[Those films can] be the entry point for a much deeper conversation for what democracy can be like when people can learn, advocate, and are responsible for each other."[43]

Marcia Smith, Firelight Media's president, thinks of documentary as a vital corrective mechanism for people of color whose stories have been historically marginalized or unseen—and thus, in this way, "Documentaries are really concrete tools for liberation. It's more and more critical that people have access to documentary films that can be concretely useful in that way."[44] For Gordon Quinn, co-founder and artistic director of Kartemquin Films, the documentary production group behind form-creating social-issue films for more than 50 years, the nonfiction storytelling motivation has always been rooted in democracy and justice: "Our key values have always been focused on understanding what kind of role media can play in a democratic society— and how telling stories about the consequences of social policies in people's lives is a way to draw people into a story."[45] And yet, as the International Documentary Association's executive director Simon Kilmurry cautions, contemplating documentaries and social change also means casting a wary eye on reductionist thinking that can reduce documentaries to didactic tools:

> One of the things we have to be clear on in this field is the heavy burden we place on documentary films to have specific outcomes. We don't place that burden on any form of journalism and form of art. Documentary films don't live in a vacuum but live in political debate. To place that burden on them is a heavy one. It's been nice

to see the pendulum swing back. It's a bit of a naïve expectation for a film to have a measurable outcome for policy or legislation. Those films that have that are the outliers. I think films that go into production with that as the *goal* become didactic and preachy and less interesting.[46]

Despite seeming clarity about the symbiosis of documentary storytelling and social change, a warning is in order. In an attempt to describe, we might be tempted to summarize a kind of template. We might erroneously imply a dogmatic approach or formula for documentary storytelling that aims to illuminate a social challenge and activate members of the public. In the stories relayed throughout this book, I hope to dissuade this thinking and encourage the opposite—to show a broad range of artistic approaches that can shape a truthful story.

The rich ecology of contemporary documentary lends itself to many narrative styles that can encourage community engagement, as in the verité personal exploration of *Minding the Gap* (directed by Bing Liu, produced by Diane Quon), or the intimate first-person essay portrait of *Strong Island* (directed by Yance Ford, produced by Joslyn Barnes), or the investigative style of *Citizenfour* (directed by Laura Poitras, produced by Mathilde Bonnefoy and Dirk Wilutzky), or the true-crime revelation of a sexual assault case in *Roll Red Roll* (directed by Nancy Schwartzman, produced by Steven Lake and Jessica Devaney). Looking to documentary forms for precision does not supply a meaningful, complete understanding of the many nonfiction artistic approaches or the public engagement that emerges around them: Motivations of the makers matter.

Characteristics of Social-Issue Documentary in the Networked Era

What can we say about describing contemporary social-issue documentary practice in the networked era? What are the defining characteristics? Here, I offer a list of shared traits—located in the production practices, intent, and protocol of the makers, regardless of whether the stories are linear or interactive or three-dimensional, irrespective of the films' precise artistic approaches. These ideas live and breathe, informed by and evolving through professional practice and the perspectives of documentary industry leaders and makers; the case studies in this book illuminate these qualities more vividly.

I offer this overview of social-issue documentary as a practice: Contemporary documentary that engages social issues is a creative, entertaining, often investigative narrative mechanism—a process and a product—by which storytellers interrogate and reveal the human complexity of social challenges and lived realities, thus contributing to the revitalized public sphere, the cultural place where social problems are negotiated by motivated publics. In such a civic function and practice, the public's access to information is key, and its ability to act is central.

Contemporary social-issue documentaries generally exhibit the following values and traits through the practices of their makers and output of their work: editorial independence, commitment to truth and ethics, civic motivation, and entertainment value. Do all social-issue documentaries follow these contours precisely? They do not. Art is not a tidy business, after all; but, broadly speaking, these are shared characteristics derived from the interviews and analysis reflected in this book. As future chapters reveal, these characteristics integrate with documentary's civic functions in the digital public sphere.

Independence

Social-issue creative documentary films often are produced by independent storytellers outside the confines of media institutions. To be clear, creative independence does not preclude these films from being distributed in the commercial or public TV marketplace, from Netflix to CNN to HBO to PBS. Independence also doesn't mean that editorial notes from distributing media organizations are not expressed or incorporated, *or* that filmmakers commissioned to produce documentaries for media outlets do not retain a great degree of editorial freedom. Instead, editorial independence leaves the *primary* creative decision making in the hands of independent directors and producers who are not employees of media institutions that commission or distribute their work.

In related peer-reviewed work, collaborators and I have referenced this idea as "authorial documentaries," meaning those that are "produced by independent documentary producers who are not employed by the distributing broadcast network. These authorial works are then acquired and licensed by the distributing broadcast network to showcase publicly. Final choices about story, characters, and crew (directors and producers) are made entirely by the independent decision-makers (directors and, to a lesser extent, producers), not the distributing broadcast network."[47]

Creative editorial independence is meaningful to documentary's ability to reflect a perspective or community not often included in the mainstream of the increasingly consolidated media marketplace—and thus, it supplies a critical lens outside the status quo or dominant cultural narrative. As documentarian Stanley Nelson reflected, "Editorial independence of the filmmaker is key. In most documentary films, documentary filmmakers don't have complete editorial independence. In the new way we're working now, you do have an executive producer or you're producing for a show or there's somebody else looking at your work. But within that framework, you're given money to make a film or a grant or permission because of your sensibility—because you are wedded to the project because of something you have been thinking about or working on years before. So, there is a lot of editorial independence."[48] Sally Fifer, president and CEO of the Independent Television Service (ITVS), which co-produces and funds independent documentary storytelling, locates independence as key to expanding a cultural reflection of reality and lived experience:

> When you only commission stories [internally inside a media organization] and compare those to stories that are bubbling up from a supported ecology of artists and filmmakers deeply intertwined in communities and trying to understand culture—it really is a different strategy entirely than having an editor or commissioning editor decide there should be a topic covered. You see the difference in the work with an independent voice who has the freedom to creative control.. . . . You get a kind of truth that comes up with this kind of filmmaking.[49]

Similarly, Simon Kilmurry, who served as executive producer of the long-running independent documentary series on PBS, *POV*, before leading the International Documentary Association, positions editorial independence as a vital trait for documentarians revealing unseen truths:

> There's a venerable tradition and space within the documentary field around where the editorial control lies and who ultimately has that. One of the things that made me most proud to work for *POV* was accepting the independent editorial voice of filmmakers—my job was to protect them from people who might be afraid of what they are saying, or from the concerns raised by a powerful company or institution. That space is sacred.[50]

To be sure, editorial independence and freedom do not absolve makers of their ethical responsibilities or commitment to reflecting truth. Rather, independent creative makers may showcase truly unique perspectives, relative to narratives shaped entirely within the formal business of entertainment and journalism institutions.

Commitment to Truth and Ethics

In nonfiction storytelling that examines social challenges, a filmmaker's commitment to truth and ethics is crucial, and it co-exists alongside artistry in the creative process. Scholar Jonathan Kahana asserted documentary's "aesthetic of truth—of objectivity, authenticity, accuracy, spontaneity, exposure, and free speech."[51] Truth in documentary storytelling will always be a messy concept; indeed, even in the verité fly-on-the-wall approach—ostensibly observing life as it unspools—makers "still grapple with the question of what *kind* of truth cinema verité offers," as Patricia Aufderheide wrote, and may most comfortably articulate documentary's ability to "reveal" rather than standing by the idea that one objective truth is possible.[52]

A responsible, rigorous, ethical approach to reflecting truth is displayed in documentary practice and intent, even if the meaning of truth in creative nonfiction storytelling—an artistic rendering of life and events—will always remain imprecise and not fully resolved, not because creative nonfiction films are not truthful, but at least partially because our cultural understanding of media "truth" may be inseparably intertwined with journalistic conceptions of "objectivity" and a neutral, detached view. Creative nonfiction storytelling is not journalism as reflected by the model and norms of attempted objectivity, even if documentarians take seriously the integrity of their approach. And yet, in documentary, journalistic elements and process co-exist with creativity and artistic point of view; they are not mutually exclusive. Tabitha Jackson, director of the Sundance Film Festival (director of the Sundance Institute's Documentary Film Program at the time of this book's writing), contemplates documentary truth as an array of points of view that help shape a broader understanding of life and events:

> I find that to really understand something, we need the facts —thinking in terms of events in the news cycle and contemporary social issues rather than the human condition. What I need is to know the facts and for the passage of time and the different subjective truths for the truths to reveal themselves. . . . This speaks to the conversation about what is documentary's relationship to truth. There's not one answer, but there are many truths and that's why it is incumbent on us to be asking questions of presented truths, whose truths are they, and what are the implications of that? As we wrestle with the idea of truth, it's important particularly

in times such as these that we make a distinction between truths and facts. To me, facts are unassailable and exist over time. They are either facts or not facts. Truths are subjective, can change over time, have a relationship to meaning. And so, what we need or depend upon is the filmmakers who can direct their audiences to know what kind of film they are making—is this a fact or is it my subjective truth?[53]

The process of rendering truth in documentary is deeply contemplated by nonfiction storytellers, even if they don't regard "truth" as synonymous with journalistic norms of objectivity. In interviews with more than 50 contemporary documentarians working at the intersection of investigation and creative nonfiction storytelling, Patricia Aufderheide concluded that documentarians agreed strongly with—and adhered to—ethical standards and journalistic practices of fact-checking and research, and yet did not believe objectivity defined their work, nor did they want it to.[54] Artistic point of view, in other words, need not be oppositional to showcasing truth. In fact, documentarians see truth-telling as a key proposition for engaging audiences. Documentary director/producer Abigail Disney, president and founder of Fork Films, insists that the facts and fact-checking process in a social-issue film be "unassailable" in order for the film to resonate and be taken seriously by the audience.[55] Reflecting facts accurately also is a requirement for some modes of distribution in the media marketplace. At PBS, in the long-running *POV* series, for example, fact-checking is essential, as explained by Justine Nagan, executive director of the series' producing organization, American Documentary, Inc.: "Truth is important. Any statistic or number made on screen is fact-checked. We also look at who is the filmmaker, who funded it, what's the situation around the film, and then it goes through legal review as a final check [before distribution]."[56]

Documentary films express real life visually and often solely through the intimate, unnarrated portraits of humans and lived realities; this, too, requires a strong commitment to truth on the filmmaker's part. In Gordon Quinn's estimation, the filmmaker's transparency in the documentary process, and willingness to reveal that process, is key:

Because they [documentaries] do use the power of story, people look at verité filmmaking and they tend to believe it. . . . Most people watch *Hoop Dreams* and it seems true to them, not because of any technological kind of thing, but for the same reason that art rings true—it's the way the story is made and the way the story is told that makes people feel, yes, this has some integrity to it in terms of the sort of story that it is. . . . We're not journalists, and we are not fact-checking every word from our subjects' mouths. . . . but we are showing that in this context and in this situation, this person said this or acted in this way. And yet, we are concerned about a certain kind of integrity to the storytelling process and in what we're doing, and it's true in the editing, also.[57]

Why bring up such an obvious idea—that is, filmmakers' commitment to showcase life truthfully? If we look to documentary history, we find propa-gandist roots, even if well-intentioned. Truth, of course, is deeply intertwined with the intention and motivation and gaze of the filmmaker, inseparable from ethical responsibilities to documentary subjects.[58] Reflecting truth artistically is a pursuit, but the maker's intent and commitment to it is distinct from film-making approaches focused on propaganda or manipulation of the audience. For instance, in a review of Dinesh D'Souza's 2018 film, *Death of a Nation*, which was released in theaters, *Variety* critic Owen Gleiberman pointed out that "the facts don't matter," and, "It's tempting to call 'Death of a Nation' an outrage, but, of course, that's just what D'Souza wants. Scandalous untruth isn't simply his métier—it's his PR machine. . . . Dinesh D'Souza stretches the truth in a way that makes your head hurt (and your stomach turn)."[59] Indeed, we might call this a visual essay rather than a documentary. A commitment to showcasing truth, even with creative, artistic license—revealing lives as they are lived, incorporating legitimate facts, accurately reflecting subjects' lives as they are rendered on screen—is not only a basic tenet in documentary story-telling that aims to illuminate social problems, but an imperative for respon-sible practice.

Civic Motivation

Documentaries express the perspectives of their auteurs. For social-issue films, a civic, public interest motivation often sparks a maker's impulse, par-tially or predominantly, around a story—that is, the desire to share an injus-tice or unseen narrative or lens, fueled by the underlying belief in collective well-being or the public's right to know and perhaps even intervene. In 2018, in my *State of the Documentary Field* study of primarily US-based nonfiction filmmakers, facilitated in association with the International Documentary Association, we asked documentary professionals what compelled their work. Filmmakers said they were most motivated to make a positive impact on so-cial issues.[60] When asked to identify themselves as auteurs, almost 6 in 10 (58 percent) described themselves as artists who are issue advocates.[61]

A civic objective on the part of the filmmaker—reflecting a commit-ment to a shared sense of public good[62]—can manifest in a range of ways in which a creative nonfiction story can contribute to positive social progress, from raising awareness to offering a lens or narrative that may be largely invisible in the broader media landscape. Veteran documentary leader Cara Mertes—who directed *POV* and American Documentary, Inc., the Sundance Institute Documentary Film Program, and the Ford Foundation's JustFilms division before leading the foundation's international Moving Image Strategy program—reflects a broad cultural contribution that comes from a civic storytelling motivation, including "civic strengthening, trust-building, acknowledging difference while finding a common role and experience and language, and a way to discuss complicated issues like race, gender, disability."[63] Indeed, historical documentary narratives, like those produced by Firelight Media and documentary luminary Stanley Nelson, also can play this role in illuminating contemporary reality; as Firelight's president Marcia Smith sees it, the need for historical documentary narratives is profound, "given our lack of understanding in this country. One of the big things documentaries can do is put people's lived experience in some kind of historical context so they can understand."[64] Crucially, a filmmaker's civic motivation—which may include a desire to spark public dialogue or even mobilize publics around an issue—is not oppositional to artistic craft and product, as filmmaker Katie Galloway expresses:

> There is a line, or there has been, between filmmakers who say, "I'm not an activist, I'm not about that phase—I'm just doing my art and moving on," and then others who feel differently. I think it's kind of a false dichotomy in a lot of ways when you dig underneath. I am not afraid to say I'm not at all interested in people coming out of my films with their preconceived ideas reinforced and no movement in any way. . . . I am in discussion with people who are in the trenches, who are doing the work on a day-to-day level. I am trying to provide a tool—and sometimes a weapon—that is useful in the contemporary space on issues that I care about.[65]

For contemporary documentary filmmakers who interrogate social issues, contributing to public dialogue and progress is an impulse that helps propel their work, even while they are committed to artistic expression.

Entertainment Value

Creativity and entertainment value are vital for attracting and holding audience interest in contemporary nonfiction storytelling. Entertainment value is clearly reflected in a full range of documentaries—telling a real-life story in an entertaining way is not an imperative that belongs solely in the domain of social-issue documentaries. Entertainment value, which has increased dramatically in documentary art over its 100-plus-year existence—and certainly comes to life in the nexus of documentary storytelling and reality TV[66]—is a function of filmmakers' artistic sensibilities and creative freedoms. It's also a requirement for audiences, as John Corner wrote, given the "longstanding requirement for documentary to do some entertaining to gain and keep a popular audience."[67] Sheila Nevins, the 30-year past president of HBO Documentary Films who now leads MTV Documentary Films—widely credited for popularizing documentary as entertainment on premium cable—considered entertainment value even while she tackled HIV/AIDS, domestic violence, and poverty in her roster of award-winning HBO films: "I never thought of them as documentaries. I thought of them as theater. When I started, we called them docu-tainment. I am proud of making documentaries something HBO was proud of. They were independent films that became a priority for HBO because they were theatrical and they were cheap."[68]

Documentary's contemporary makers have steadily embraced creativity and entertainment value, illustrating nonfiction storytelling's "new playfulness"[69] that captures audiences and creatively interrogates even sobering social issues. Nonfiction stories that illuminate and spotlight and investigate social challenges embrace a full range of creative, narrative approaches, from intimate human portraits (*Bully*) to investigation (*The Invisible War*), to verité journeys into the lived experience of a troubling issue (*Heroin(e)*). Contemporary social-issue documentaries illuminate real life through the entertaining, artistic, often journalistic sensibilities of makers who are committed to sharing truths and contributing to the public good. They assemble disruptive narratives that connect with audiences in the marketplace and within communities.

About the Book

Story Movements: How Documentaries Empower People and Inspire Social Change reveals the rise, professional practices, and social influence of social-issue documentaries and makers in the post-millennial networked media era; it examines the role of documentary in democracy. Documentaries produced largely by independent makers spotlight the voices and perspectives of people and issues not often reflected in the mainstay of the media system, and they can capture the deeper human implications of complex social challenges. Within the contemporary public sphere—the cultural space where people debate and discuss social problems—nonfiction stories provide information and creative lenses into real life that can serve a monitorial function for wrongdoing and injustice but can also motivate, inform, and empower publics to engage in open dialogue and seek remedy for injustice.

At its core, this is a book about stories—in-depth examinations that reveal how filmmakers produce and view their work, and how documentaries play an influential role in helping publics contemplate reality. In these pages, I consider narrative persuasion, grassroots mobilization, the public diffusion of ideas and stories, civil society and public engagement, and the amplifying, symbiotic role of news media coverage. This is a book about culture—both broader culture and realities, and the micro cultures that envelop each social issue as a documentary story drops in. Culture, in this context, is essential as the civic public space where norms evolve, and where social problems can be raised and negotiated and reflected.[70] Communication shapes culture, and people consume and reconstitute culture; how we construct and understand reality and lived experience comes from this interplay.[71] In the big picture, it would be impossible to illuminate the influence of contemporary documentary without also positioning the context of a unique moment of upheaval—a simultaneous transformation of media, audience consumption patterns, and the role and practice of publics in social justice movements, large and small. Similarly, it would be futile—and uninteresting—to fully explicate the dynamics of story and community without locating each profiled social-issue documentary within its cultural context. Did *Walmart: The High Cost of Low Price* or *Blackfish* premiere in a cultural vacuum? Of course not, and this is key. Documentaries work within the zeitgeist of the social issues and realities they interrogate.

Themes recur throughout the book, and certain premises, assumptions, and imperatives undergird them. First, this volume does not dwell solely on the comprehensive history, nuts and bolts, and how-to technological lessons of documentary production, nor on rhetorical assessments of the documentary form. There are many beautiful existing works that delve much deeper into each of these topics. While the craft, professional practice, and motivations of documentary makers and leaders comprise the heart of the work, examining documentaries rhetorically through form alone would not sufficiently unpackage their cultural influence. The active roles of distribution, community engagement, and civil society are key.

Second, the backdrop of the transformative networked media age, which extends to expressions of activism and community engagement in public affairs and social problems, is a specific, meaningful context. Media platforms are expanding both public participation and the distribution of storytelling.

Scholar Henry Jenkins and his colleagues explained the value of this participatory culture in terms of "how new hybrid systems of media-content circulation can bring unprecedented power to the voices of individuals and groups without access to mainstream forms of distribution."[72] Documentary lives here, not only as fodder to entertain audiences. History tells us that earlier transformative media technology moments, like the adoption of 16 mm film and portable film gear and video from the 1960s to the 1980s, helped documentary makers and activists shape forms, practices, and approaches to community engagement. But technology did not evolve documentary storytelling or even lead it, even if it did—and does—provide opportunities for advancement and innovation. Junctures of social upheaval produce the underlying foundation—and indeed, the fuel. The post-millennial media age not only continues in that trajectory, but it may expand on it exponentially, given the global connectivity and participatory culture possibilities it supports. Given this premise, the book primarily focuses on trends, developments, and documentary films produced largely after the 2010s, although it begins—in Chapter 2—with historical highlights to reveal meaningful origins of these ideas.

Finally, this book takes the view that documentary plays a key role in democratic practice amid a consolidated entertainment and news media ecology by highlighting stories, people, and points of view we may not otherwise see (or see only infrequently) in dominant media reflections, and often, by changing the public conversation, and mobilizing the public in response. Documentary can interrogate power and provide a view of reality that can act as an alternative public sphere to critique the mainstream, but it can also infuse the mainstream public sphere and media narrative with counternarratives. Firelight Media's Sonya Childress expresses this idea succinctly: "Documentaries play a role in validating the lives of communities and people who don't see their lives reflected at all."[73]

In this context, social change is a journey partially enabled by documentaries that provide awareness of an issue, spark new public conversations, foster community solidarity, reveal stories from the lenses of traditionally marginalized people, provide a deeper intimate perspective of individuals or social issues often portrayed as statistics, or gradually contribute to shifting public opinion and social norms. All of these processes are vital to shaping matters of justice over time. The documentaries profiled here reveal a wide range along that spectrum of social change and public good.

As an imperative, the book expresses the perspectives of filmmakers and industry professionals directly. Through interviews with contemporary documentary directors, producers, and field leaders, this volume reflects both my scholarly inquiry and my perspective as a documentary producer. Notably, the ideas here, although grounded in academic foundations and theory, are shaped in large part by listening to filmmakers and studying their practices. My objective, then, is not only to present documentary professionals' work, but to allow their voices to define and re-define the art and practice from their own experience, alongside the work of dedicated scholars who have shaped our understanding of documentary and its societal role.

Documentary, of course, is a broad construct, and the art of nonfiction storytelling comprises many styles and approaches. I do not present a full articulation of documentary definitions, history, theory, or its many genres, nor is that my desire.[74] This book focuses on one specific approach to, and type of, contemporary documentary practice—social-issue documentaries produced with civic motivations and commitment to truth and artistry. Exact boundaries can be difficult to articulate, however. Within this context, this is not a book about a sub-genre of nonfiction creative expression that, unfortunately for many, may have come to connote contemporary documentary practice—that is, partisan essays that aim for ideological engagement or outcomes through seeming manipulation of both facts and audiences, as in Dinesh D'Souza's *Death of a Nation* or Steve Bannon's *Clinton Cash*, distributed widely through like-minded communities rather than major marketplace outlets, making record amounts of money along the way. To be sure, this sub-genre, if we want to reference these expressions in this way—ideologically motivated essays—may offer instructive insights about distribution, grassroots engagement, economics, and a particular style of ideological argumentation, but much has already been written about contemporary political essay- and argument-style films.[75] Much more remains to be interrogated, however. Such scrutiny is important and worthwhile even if these kinds of media products are not the focus of this book.

While it's true that various forms of community engagement and nonfiction storytelling about social issues could be construed as political in the broadest sense, given civic practice, there is a distinction between fact-based social-issue documentary storytelling that does not necessarily aim for disruption or manipulation along partisan, ideological political lines. For example, the profiled films in Chapter 7 (Shaping Laws: Documentaries and Policy Engagement) reveal bipartisan policy shifts that policymakers attribute to the documentaries' use of verifiable facts and core human narratives, not partisan-based argumentation. Further, in the kinds of documentary practice and output profiled in this book, I take the position that showcasing diverse perspectives and illuminating social justice challenges is not partisan by definition—and further, that the opposite position reflects the long-standing product of culture wars that have attempted to broadly reduce *any* deliberation about social-issue topics to partisan aims or ideological bias. As Patricia Aufderheide and I have expressed elsewhere on this topic:

> Accusations of liberal-left bias have been a feature in a larger conservative movement over decades to critique social inquiry under the rubric of partisan "political correctness." . . . As scholars have repeatedly demonstrated, journalism generally develops narratives that may cause discomfort and awareness of problems that may trigger concern for action, without exhibiting partisan bias (Scheufele, 1999). Indeed, the role of exposing issues has, from the origins of the nation, been seen as a core function of democratic life, in which ordinary citizens take political action based on knowledge. Research on the relationship of media and democracy demonstrates the vital link between a rich information environment and democratic participation (Baker, 2007; Barber, 1984; Keane, 1991). This relationship is not merely about an informed citizenry but about a rich media ecology; indeed, a narrow focus on political information and a highly motivated citizenry can function to exclude voices (Schudson, 1998).[76]

In this book, this position is central in thinking about documentaries that showcase the lived human experience and facts behind contemporary social issues, as we wrote: "Narratives are seen as rich social constructions participating in a reflexive, constantly active process of creating meaning, developing culture, and asserting agency."[77]

As a final undercurrent, this book takes an admittedly US-centric view. This reflects my primary lived experience and expertise as a documentary film producer, communication strategist, and scholar. However, I do consciously include examples and practices that are directly relevant and mirrored in a global context, reflected in similar expanding documentary communities around the world; several global organizations also are reflected here, such as the International Documentary Association and the UK's Doc Society. Comprehensively capturing the global phenomenon of socially engaged documentary storytelling and its role in the networked era requires a second book, generated by the concepts and ideas established here.

A Roadmap for Reading

Story Movements: How Documentaries Empower People and Inspire Social Change continues from this foundation in Chapter 2 (Evolving Documentaries and Social Change: Historical Highlights) with a highlighted, thematic cultural history of social-issue documentary. The contemporary moment evolves from social upheaval, technological and media advances, platforms of distribution, and form-changing storytellers who shaped the foundation of social change through documentary. The early documentary and activist pioneers profiled here also created mainstream and alternative distribution pathways to both the entertainment marketplace and grassroots communities.

Chapter 3 (Opening a New Lens: Documentary Functions as Civic Storytelling) presents the functions that social-issue documentaries play in the networked age—as counternarratives, monitors, creative interpreters, mobilizers, and centerpieces of efforts to strengthen civil society. Networked social justice activism is a backdrop. Chapter 4 (Activating Community: The Movement Builders) provides a journey into the vibrant contemporary landscape of social-issue documentaries within both organized and organically inspired public engagement efforts. The chapter introduces a professional ecology of organizations, activists, and collaborators working at the intersection of nonfiction storytelling and community engagement designed for positive social change.

Following from these foundational ideas, the heart of this volume is a series of in-depth case studies about contemporary documentaries that reveal complex social realities and challenges, each anchored by a core theme reflected in chapter titles: mobilizing, humanizing, shaping, interrogating. These stories unfold first in Chapter 5 (Mobilizing for Change: Inside the *Blackfish* Effect), which analyzes the social impact of the documentary *Blackfish* by examining contemporary layered distribution, narrative persuasion, the amplifying role of grassroots-engaged publics and organizations, the influence of emotion, and news media narrative. Chapters 6 through 8 anchor a set of documentary film stories within specific themes: Chapter 6 (Humanizing the Headlines: Documentary's Interpretive Framing) showcases documentaries that artistically reveal human complexity and interpret ideologically polarizing current affairs issues that may be covered with recognizable, often reductive, daily news patterns. Chapter 7 (Shaping Laws: Documentaries and Policy Engagement) delves into the documentaries that have helped to change laws. Chapter 8 (Interrogating Hidden Truths: Investigative Documentary) reveals how creative investigative documentaries are interrogating power under risky conditions, leveraging journalistic tools but embracing creative freedom that includes transparency about personal points of view. Finally, Chapter 9 (Imagining the Future: Why Documentary Matters) presents key themes to contemplate as the future of civic-motivated documentaries evolves: diversity and representation, the changing marketplace, career sustainability, and civic values. Each area requires active work in documentary communities as they continue to shape the landscape of this business and art form.

At its core, *Story Movements: How Documentaries Empower People and Inspire Social Change* positions contemporary social-issue documentaries as vibrant, active participants in the cultural cycle of reflecting reality—it illuminates the machinations of creative people and communities advocating for a more just world, activating creativity and stories as pathways to social justice.

The most radical thing in the world is the truth.

— Marc Weiss
Founder, *POV*[1]

2

Evolving Documentaries and Social Change

Historical Highlights

As an electic network of artists working in an era of social consciousness and movements for change, the documentary trailblazers of the 1960s and 1970s busily revolutionized their craft—building community, experimenting with accessible new production gear, and evolving the nonfiction storytelling form to open new portals into human struggle and triumph. Barbara Kopple was among them. Like others of her cohort, she was voracious—wanting to expose truth and confront dominant cultural narratives, working with like-minded collaborators along the way.

In 1973, after trailing a grassroots uprising of coal miners in Appalachia, Kopple—a then-fledgling filmmaker trained in the revolutionary observational documentary style that came of age in the 1960s—headed to Harlan County, Kentucky, the site of a simmering strike where angry workers and

Story Movements. Caty Borum Chattoo, Oxford University Press (2020) © Oxford University Press.
DOI: 10.1093/oso/9780190943417.001.0001

their families were fighting for health benefits and safe working conditions.[2] She and her crew stayed for more than a year, documenting the intimacy of the coal miners' daily lives and the violence that surrounded their struggle. Distilled from hundreds of hours of footage, Kopple's documentary premiered in 1976 at the New York Film Festival as *Harlan County, U.S.A.*[3] The film, as one review noted, "concentrates on the human story at the expense of the underlying economic changes"—with a point of view clearly sympathetic to the miners.[4] In a media interview, Kopple recounted, "I realized that nothing in the world was going to stop me from telling that story."[5]

In 1977, Barbara Kopple accepted the Best Documentary Feature Academy Award for *Harlan County, U.S.A.*, her directorial debut, widely noted as a legendary exemplar of independent social-issue documentary film.[6] It was a pathbreaking work that highlighted the form-expanding cinema verité approach, a filmmaker's civic motivations, and unequivocal evidence of artistry intertwined within an intimate interrogation of injustice. Notably, her early work brought together two traditions: "the theatrical (entertainment film) and the activist (politically engaged film)."[7] Through the cultural acclaim of her first major documentary, "Kopple became known as an artist as well as an activist,"[8] displaying a style and imprint that would inspire future filmmakers for years to come.

Barbara Kopple is among the pioneers who paved documentary's path to the future. Their stories bring to life rich moments of the past that birthed today's documentary practices and values, particularly independent storytelling. This chapter provides select historical highlights to reveal how shifting cultural backdrops nurtured fertile ground for documentary filmmakers, philanthropists, activists, and new organizations to shape the forms, marketplaces, and audiences for present-day creative social-issue documentary storytelling and the ecology of professionals who enable and produce them. The bedrock values and practices of contemporary social-issue documentary work did not emerge suddenly as a linear implication of the digital media revolution and its participatory possibilities. Instead, documentary processes and products evolved through individual organizations and people who laid the groundwork during the analog age, spurred by tumultuous demands for equity and a climate of social consciousness. This documentary tradition developed as both an alternative and a mainstream cultural force against the backdrop of an increasingly consolidated commercial entertainment and news system.

This chapter is not a comprehensive chronological historical accounting. Instead, it illuminates exemplary developments in the origin story of documentary storytelling and social influence through four key themes: enabling infrastructure developed out of movement culture and tension, civic motivation in documentary practice, representation of diverse voices and experiences, and shifting media platforms and technology that have aided documentary's marketplace expansion. As other chapters illustrate, these themes underlie present-day documentary praxis and public engagement—and they are central to the future.

Enabling Infrastructure Fueled by Movements and Dissent

Historically, consciousness-raising cultural climates have fostered documentary's enabling institutions. Opportunities for documentary story-tellers to finance and showcase their films have been supported by institutions and organizations that emerged largely as a consequence of advocacy and scrutiny and unrest. Documentary makers asserted their space, their share of voice and opportunities—acting in formative moments as organized, compelling coalitions, joined and abetted by supportive regulatory environments and philanthropy.

In the 1930s, news and entertainment media consolidation in the United States began a steady journey, charged by the economic need to appeal to mass audiences. The Communications Act of 1934, which created the Federal Communications Commission (FCC), set the stage to articulate the public interest obligations of broadcasters and establish basic regulation to ensure competition.[9] In the powerful Hollywood studio system of the time, the "Big Five" motion picture studios controlled film production, distribution, and exhibition in a network of vertical integration: Twentieth Century–Fox, Loew's-MGM, Paramount, RKO, and Warner Brothers (WB), although the system was eventually broken up in 1948.[10] Thus, systems of media dominance were established early.

Throughout the World War II years and into the 1950s, television became the dominant purveyor of cultural values and realities—a commercial business designed and financed to appeal to a broad cross-section of the American people. This mass audience was served with noncontroversial entertainment-oriented material, generally speaking.[11] At the same time, criticism of TV in the late 1950s led to increasing scrutiny about the banality of commercial entertainment and the scarcity of programming for public service aims. Cultural critics, opinion leaders and the FCC called for TV reform.[12] When FCC chairman Newton Minow famously decreed TV a "vast wasteland" in 1961 after decades of FCC regulation generally focused solely on technical matters rather than content, television executives paid attention.[13] The heads of the three networks met privately and soon reached an agreement with the FCC to expand public affairs documentary programming "as a symbol of public service programming."[14] Documentary's first major foray on television, then, came as a result of critical pressure and a supportive regulatory environment in a cultural moment of dissent.

And so it was that the 1960s became a heyday for investigative news documentaries produced inside the three broadcast networks—CBS, ABC, NBC—and funded through commercial advertisers. The networks' news divisions introduced new episodic investigative-style documentary series in the 1960s, including *CBS Reports, NBC White Paper,* and ABC's *Bell and Howell Close-Up!*[15] An estimated 90 percent of Americans watched at least one broadcast news documentary per month in the early part of the decade—including films like *Harvest of Shame* (1961), narrated by stalwart news star Edward R. Murrow, about the working conditions of poor migrant workers in the United States.[16] The film, which revealed inequality in America and castigated a Congress allegedly under the influence of the powerful agribusiness lobby, was met with criticism and controversy.[17] Internally produced broadcast documentaries had trouble with social justice material on a commercial system designed for mass advertisers. As scholar Michael Curtin wrote:

> Although pressure from government, corporate, and public opinion leaders spurred the evolution of the genre, it was difficult for news executives to sustain the programs within the context of a commercial entertainment medium. . . . But one of the fundamental problems with the programs was that they almost exclusively addressed themselves to a white, male, middle-class viewer and therefore tended to marginalize large segments of the audience, especially women and African Americans.[18]

Documentaries faded away from their prime-time viewing slots and the TV networks as the decade ended. When the CBS *60 Minutes* news magazine became profitable with shorter, entertainment-focused news segments in the late 1960s, and later, when the FCC rolled back public service requirements for broadcasters, longer-form investigative documentaries were dropped in favor of profitable, less controversial material.[19] The network news documentaries ended as their lackluster profit-generating ability became a thorn in the business of TV, as broadcast licensing requirements no longer required them,[20] and as breaking news became a profitable way for the networks to seemingly demonstrate their commitment to public service.[21]

Documentaries were left in a marginal place in the public sphere, positioned on the cultural outskirts. People had a hard time finding and watching them. In the 1950s and 1960s, audiences could view documentaries produced and distributed by National Educational Television (NET)—a PBS precursor financed by the Ford Foundation—which operated as an educational alternative to commercial TV of the time.[22] However, NET suffered from a "well-deserved reputation as dull, plodding, and pedantic."[23] Documentaries were thus relegated to the sidelines, not the mainstay of media culture where broad audiences could find them. The reality would change against an insistent social movement backdrop.

The Public Broadcasting Act of 1967 established the Corporation for Public Broadcasting (CPB), "a private, nonprofit corporation created by Congress" that serves as "the steward of the federal government's investment in public broadcasting and the largest single source of funding for public radio, television, and related online and mobile services"[24]—a significant development toward expanding public access to independent documentaries. A growing climate for media reform helped to birth public media, sparked in part by reports like the groundbreaking government publication issued by the National Advisory Commission on Civil Disorders chaired by Governor Otto Kerner Jr. of Illinois. The 1968 "Kerner Commission" report, the culmination of the Johnson administration's exploration of urban discord in America, warned of a growing racial divide and scathingly indicted the media for its failure to showcase diverse perspectives and reach a full cross-section of the population; it followed the 1967 Carnegie Commission on Educational Television report, which advocated for a robust public TV system.[25] The public media origin story, then, is located in movement culture and pressure for diverse media representation, alongside the commitment of philanthropy to social justice. As scholar Patricia Aufderheide asserted, "It [public media] came about partly because after World War II (which had proven the power of mass media to manipulate masses), major U.S. foundations such as Ford and Carnegie committed themselves to funding electronic media as a vehicle for greater social justice."[26]

The Public Broadcasting Service (PBS) came next, launched as "a private, nonprofit corporation, founded in 1969, whose members are America's public TV stations—noncommercial, educational licensees that operate nearly 350 PBS member stations and serve all 50 states, Puerto Rico, U.S. Virgin Islands, Guam and American Samoa."[27] Alongside the Kerner Commission report, "progressive filmmakers, cultural administrators, and grassroots advocacy groups influenced the practical applications of public television's programming mandate" during those fledgling years, wrote scholar Joshua Glick.[28] But public broadcasting, with a laudable but vague commitment to diversity and the public interest, immediately experienced institutional backlash. In

1970, after PBS aired *Banks and the Poor*, which aimed a trenchant investigative documentary eye on both the banks and Congress for discrimination against low-income consumers, the Corporation for Public Broadcasting attracted anger and outrage from the Nixon administration.[29] Still, despite the challenges for independent documentary filmmakers, public television seemed like a viable place for nonfiction storytelling given its underpinnings and mandate. Independent filmmakers focused there to expand the marketplace for documentaries.

Simultaneously, the community of independent, socially conscious documentary storytellers grew in the 1970s and 1980s, shaped in large part by leaders like Marc Weiss, who collaborated with like-minded thinkers and leaders to bring together the burgeoning independent nonfiction storytelling community in an unprecedented way. Weiss recalled that at a 1979 national convening, the US Conference for Alternative Cinema, also known as the "Bard conference" by its attendees,[30] "400 people showed up, and it was the first time all of these folks had been together in one place—filmmakers, activists, distributors, exhibitors," to discuss issues of funding, distribution, and connection to community engagement through documentary.[31] Fueled by participants' enthusiasm about the conference, Weiss and Jim Gaffney launched the Media Network in 1980, which acted as a support mechanism for independent documentarians but also as a curation platform to help communities leverage films for local civic engagement.[32] Independent storytelling networks continued to develop with the strength and leadership of the Association of Independent Video and Filmmakers (AIVF), and community media movement leaders like DeeDee Halleck, president of AIVF in the 1970s, who launched Paper Tiger Television in 1981 and Deep Dish TV in 1986, hubs for independent storytelling devoted to shaping and distributing perspectives and stories not readily found in mainstream entertainment and news.[33]

In 1982, as one example of a larger movement, Louis Massiah founded Scribe Media in Philadelphia, the long-standing organization that lifts up community-shaped documentary stories and trains new storytellers.[34] Scribe was necessary for the community, as Massiah recalls: "I realized Philadelphia did not have a media arts center. It did not have a place where people could have access to equipment, and most importantly, a place where people could share ideas and work together and collaborate. . . . But also, in the early 1980s and even late 1980s, unlike the proliferation of film schools and programs now, there weren't many places that were teaching film."[35] With similar motivation, media arts centers arose around the country, created by individuals and groups who were compelled to tell their own stories. These community-based organizations were funded in large part by the Ford Foundation and the MacArthur Foundation "as a means to democratize the access to the tools of media making," according to the MacArthur Foundation's Kathy Im, who leads the journalism and media program today.[36] The activating power of independent and community-motivated documentary storytellers thus coalesced and strengthened as local and national networks.

In 1988, after almost a decade of sustained organizing from the National Coalition of Independent Public Broadcasting Producers, the Association of Independent Video and Filmmakers, and their allies successfully pushed for what became the Independent Television Service (ITVS) with funding from the Corporation for Public Broadcasting,[37] designed to serve CPB's mission to support and ensure a diversity of voices in public TV, with a particular focus on marginalized communities of color and women.[38] The field-wide organizing led by independent filmmakers was purposeful, savvy, strategic, and unrelenting. Playing on an understanding of political context that included the increased power of diverse communities—and their constituent demands for Congress's attention—they brought together allied arts groups and delivered information to sympathetic journalists.[39] Shaped within a cultural climate marked by persistent urging from filmmakers and supportive philanthropies, ITVS—which serves as a vital source of nonfiction film funding—opened the door to documentary storytelling in an unprecedented fashion. In 1988, independent documentaries found a prime-time spot on PBS with the launch of the *POV* (Point of View) series, founded by Marc Weiss to reveal perspectives missing in the media marketplace, crafted by makers he deems "critical to the health of our democratic society,"[40] along with the documentaries launched on the *American Experience* series that same year, joining the investigative *FRONTLINE* strand that launched in 1983, and *American Masters* in 1986, and later, the *Independent Lens* series in 1999. Space for documentary storytelling on American television thus began to open, a reality owed in great measure to makers' community and action.

Infrastructure that enables documentary storytelling and its audience reach, then, did not arise as an organic artifact of a media marketplace that expanded over a century; instead, it was constructed as movement culture and pressure from the public, advocates, and independent filmmakers demanded it. Enduring documentary institutions and communities were shaped during a social movement climate that called for stories manufactured outside the business of media. To be sure, the full contemporary landscape for documentary storytelling does not reside solely in public media. The commercial entertainment marketplace widened for documentary storytelling as the form evolved and attracted new audiences, but the roots of this reality are located in the original enabling institutions that were urged into life by grassroots organizing and advocacy. Junctures of cultural tension have thus provided meaningful openings to propel documentary's expansion and opportunities. And, as professional communities, documentary makers comprise a powerful force, then as now, as future chapters also reveal.

Civic Motivation in Documentary Practice

The ideals of social progress have long inspired documentary practices, at least partially. But nascent social reform roots have morphed throughout documentary history; civic motivation is a broader articulation of this impulse to make change. Documentary makers express their civic inclinations by engaging communities directly, showcasing perspectives that are not often visible in entertainment and news, and shaping intimate stories with a drive toward positive societal impact. Embedded in this motivation, documentary makers and leaders have shaped a dual marketplace for their work—that is, the ability for audiences to experience nonfiction storytelling on mainstream media outlets, but also in community venues and gatherings where public dialogue happens in shared spaces.

Civic motivation has matured since the earliest documentary displays of vulnerable, marginalized people. During documentary's Great Depression years, a time period marked by poverty and tragedy, the documentary impulse for social reform was strong.[41] It also was a time, wrote media historian Erik Barnouw, in which radio, the dominant source of news and information for the country, maintained "a blackout on current problems."[42] The 1930s tradition was thus dominated by "social documentary," a form of institutional reform storytelling largely funded by the US government to support New Deal social mobilization policies and characterized as a media mechanism that "encourages social improvement."[43] With news-like voiceover narration and portraits of despair, films like those directed by Pare Lorentz, *The Plow That Broke the Plains* (1936) and *The River* (1938), were funded by US government agencies and aimed at shaping public opinion to support reformist government policies.[44] Explicit social reform goals with institutional points of view—a kind of benevolent "white propaganda, put forward from an overt source,"[45] as scholar William Stott wrote—epitomized those formative years.

The budding documentary tradition and its connection to social responsibility, however, has been the source of necessary introspection and critique, not only as prosocial propaganda[46] but also considering the potential pitfalls of a lens focused predominantly on social reform outcomes. The documentary approach of the time, despite well-meaning intentions, often portrayed on-screen communities and individuals as objects of pity without agency. This expository style of documentary narrative showed "relative indifference to the individuals and situations captured in order to shape proposals or perspectives on a general topic," wrote scholar Bill Nichols.[47] The early documentaries birthed alongside the form's original definitions were instructive, then, not only in shaping the fledgling craft—and advocating for social change in tumultuous times—but in elevating questions of representation, agency, point of view, and ethics taken up by documentarians and scholars in each generation to follow.

Government-funded films were not the sole domain of the earliest nonfiction storytelling. Independent documentary filmmaking infused with a social justice mission was alive and well in the formative years. The parallel documentary tradition of independent storytelling was embodied in groups like the Workers Film and Photo League (WFPL), which reacted against Hollywood and created an alternative perspective through its newsreel-style short films about life and injustice in the Great Depression, covering "demonstrations encampments, marches, and strikes—activities Hollywood either blacked out or covered with reactionary sentimentality," as documentary scholars Patricia R. Zimmermann and Helen De Michiel wrote.[48] The partial impulse of independent nonfiction storytellers, then as now, was driven by a desire to showcase a fuller spectrum of lived experiences than what was visible in the mainstay of the media system.

Later, throughout the 1960s and 1970s, social turmoil and demands for justice were meaningful backdrops for documentary's civic motivation. The cinema verité movement that took off in the early 1960s (from its evolution in the late 1950s) ushered in an enduring narrative style and helped to galvanize practices at the convergence of nonfiction storytelling and community engagement. Of all documentary moments and forms, the emergence of cinema verité—alternately referenced as "direct cinema," as coined by progenitor Albert Mayles,[49] or observational cinema but broadly referenced under the verité umbrella term[50]—remains arguably the most central to contemplating contemporary documentary. The new verité stories were enticingly voyeuristic instead of didactic. Unlike the expository voice-of-God social-reform documentaries of the 1930s, or the tight construction of the network-news documentaries of the 1950s and 1960s, verité attempted to showcase lived experience at length, with "ordinary people" as frequent on-screen subjects. Verité transformed documentary into nonfiction storytelling that reflected the nuances and complexities of daily life.

The desire to access and reveal human lives was well-suited to a time period steeped in impassioned activism. Many of the independent documentary storytellers of the time were shaped by, and reflective of, the 1960s and 1970s social movements climate. They were motivated to showcase narratives little seen in scripted entertainment or news coverage—and to tell these stories from the intimate perspectives of traditionally marginalized people and communities. For instance, in the mid-1960s, Kartemquin Films, one of the groundbreakers at the intersection of verité social-issue documentary and public engagement with current affairs, coalesced a burgeoning community of documentary filmmakers (Figure 2.1). Kartemquin's earliest films focused on labor struggles and later, efforts within the women's movement. Telling verité stories from the perspectives inside communities was key, according to Gordon Quinn, Kartemquin's co-founder and continuing artistic director.[51]

Simultaneously, verité makers developed the early roots and rich tradition of community-based grassroots social-issue documentary distribution— shaping documentary's dual marketplace. Newsreel, a documentary film collective formed in 1968 partially as a critical response to mainstream TV coverage of the 1967 antiwar protest and march at the Pentagon, espoused this social justice mission directly, establishing chapters in cities across the country.[52] Member filmmakers were charged with producing and distributing

Figure 2.1. Members of the Kartemquin Films collective, 1971: Vicki Cooper, Jerry Blumenthal, Betsy Martens, Gordon Quinn, Susan Delson, Teena Webb, Jenny Rohrer, Sharon Karp, Peter Kuttner. Not pictured: Alphonse Blumenthal, Greg Grieco, Judy Hoffman, Richard Schmiechen. Photo courtesy of Kartemquin Films.

documentaries that revealed perspectives missing from TV news coverage.[53] Marc Weiss recalled the impact: "When I first saw the Newsreel films, they hit me on a gut, visceral level. It was a glimpse into someone's reality that you would never have a chance to see otherwise. I could see how transformative that could be, turning upside down what you think you know about the person whose story is being told."[54] Associated with social movements and activist organizations—including the Students for a Democratic Society, the women's movement, and the Black Panthers—the collective was notable for producing documentary films about topics like racial injustice, but also for developing an alternative form of community distribution outside the mainstream TV system.[55] In this way, the Newsreel framework helped to establish a value for community engagement through grassroots distribution, a dominant norm in current social-issue documentary practice.

The dual distribution practice of civic-minded documentary—a way to reach into neighborhoods to stimulate public conversation—continued in the 1970s as a cadre of documentary filmmakers continued to create an alternative, community-based distribution system for nonfiction stories and sought ways to lift up marginalized realities to reach broader audiences. As an exemplar, throughout the 1970s,[56] Challenge for Change (CFC), a social activist documentary initiative from Canada's National Film Board, funded by the Canadian government, produced hundreds of films "predicated on the difficult-to-measure hypothesis that media can affect positive social change."[57] For CFC, the guiding principle was the collaboration between local communities—the subjects of the stories—and the filmmakers. CFC made films with its subjects and facilitated community screenings to open dialogue and shape collective perspectives about local problems and solutions.[58] Still, CFC was not without critique, as emphasizing social impact over entertainment production value perhaps limited its potential for broader audiences.

The essential formula and values of Challenge for Change—community-based participatory documentary storytelling with social change objectives—traveled back to the United States and left an indelible mark on the continued evolution of social-issue documentary practice, embodied in the work and legacy of filmmaker George Stoney. An American who served as CFC's guest executive producer for two years (1968–1970), Stoney is widely noted for his inaugural work as a founder of US-based community media—and "father of public access television."[59] After leaving CFC, he returned to the United States in 1970 to co-found the Alternative Media Center at New York University with documentarian Red Burns—early public access cable TV. Word spread, and the Alternative Media Center became a hub of participatory community-based independent documentary storytelling, known for publicly screening nonfiction stories, providing training services for emerging independent filmmakers, and lending technical support to distribute independent documentaries regionally and nationally across early cable systems.[60] According to the Ford Foundation's Cara Mertes, the community media movement was significant in solidifying "independent filmmakers as an independent entity in that larger ecosystem."[61] Organizations like Appalshop, which "uses place-based media, arts and education to document the life, celebrate the culture, and voice the concerns of Appalachia and rural America,"[62] exemplified the burgeoning network of media arts organizations shaping stories inside communities and fueling independent production, funded by the new National Endowment for the Arts, American Film Institute, the MacArthur Foundation, and smaller foundations.[63]

A community-focused, civic-minded approach to producing empowering nonfiction storytelling continued to evolve, inspired by verité roots. As one example, media scholar Kevin Howley referenced New York's Downtown Community Television (DCTV), a community media organization co-founded in 1972 by documentarians Jon Alpert and Keiko Tsuno, as "heirs to this rich tradition of participatory production" espoused by CFC.[64] DCTV's imprint in nonfiction, justice-oriented storytelling is evident in its ability to enact change for underserved communities in New York, and marked by its intimate storytelling style and training services for other independent makers around conscious representation and craft. The original DCTV philosophy encouraged filmmakers "to produce tapes by, for, and about their local communities whose cultures, problems, and perspectives were largely absent from mainstream television."[65]

Notably, DCTV honed its narrative technique by responding to local communities through grassroots screenings. In this iterative, audience-shaped fashion, DCTV's chief storytellers, Alpert and Tsuno, developed an intimate, action-based narrative documentary style that also attracted the attention of still-new PBS, along with broadcast network NBC, and later, premium cable giant HBO. Their style of socially conscious documentary storytelling gradually found a way to larger audiences in the mainstream TV marketplace, even while DCTV remained committed to community justice and a desire to spotlight stories missing from the widest swath of American TV and film culture. The organization's Emmy-award-winning work illustrated a duality in social-issue documentary process and product that remains today—an approach shaped with a civic-minded ethos but able to cross into a mainstream public and commercial entertainment marketplace to find a broad audience.

Throughout the ensuing decades—forged by the legacy, norms, trainings, and values established by documentary's civic pioneers—newer organizations and individuals absorbed early traditions and molded contemporary documentary practices. Indeed, these ideas are the underpinning of chapters 3 and 4, which focus on documentary's functions as civic storytelling and the movement builders who today engage the public alongside nonfiction stories. The civic motivations of documentary trailblazers remain embodied in conventions like documentary's dual distribution system in communities and the media marketplace, commitment to community, and the desire to spark public dialogue about entrenched social problems.

Representing Diverse Voices and Perspectives

Questions and struggles for representation have endured as documentary has matured and progressed—that is, who is telling whose stories? While many 1960s and 1970s verité and participatory filmmakers were dedicated to showcasing lives authentically, along with deep work within historically underserved communities, documentary storytelling was dominated by white male makers. But the climate of social consciousness and movement demands provided fertile ground for change. As scholar Joshua Glick wrote:

> As the 1960s progressed, other minorities and women drew inspiration from black liberation struggles. They shared some of the same criticisms of the limitations and inadequacies of the discourse of liberal integration as well as the desire for self-determination. Documentary media was essential to the black, brown, yellow, and women's movements. . . . With cinema being such a resource-intensive craft, many citizen groups, filmmakers, activists, and intellectuals fought for increased access to money, equipment, and training. Others went outside, and indeed positioned their work against, commercial or public systems of production.[66]

In documentary's formative years, filmmakers from traditionally marginalized racial, ethnic, and gender groups, acutely aware of the imbalance, took matters into their own hands—often supported by public broadcasting and philanthropic funding—as they developed collectives and organizations to train new filmmakers and tell their own stories, bolstered by a social movement climate. In so doing, their efforts indelibly shaped documentary forms, ethics, and infrastructure that continues to support diverse voices in nonfiction storytelling, even as parity and true pluralism remain as perennial pursuits and unfinished business.

For example, in 1971, the four New Day Films founders—Julia Reichert, Jim Klein, Amalie Rothschild, and Liane Brandon—created the self-distributing

collective "because the women's movement had arrived and a group of independent filmmakers couldn't find distribution for their feminist films,"[67] according to its origin story. While self-distributing their documentary *Growing
Up Female*, Reichert and Klein understood the value of reach in a movement
climate. " 'The whole idea of distribution,' explained Julia Reichert, 'was to
help the women's movement grow. Films could do that, they could get the
ideas out. We could watch the women's movement spread across the country
just by who was ordering our films. First it was Cambridge and Berkeley.
I remember the first showing in the deep South.' "[68] A trailblazer in alternative documentary distribution, New Day Films continues to welcome independent, socially focused nonfiction films and distribute them to educational
institutions and nonprofit organizations. Also responding to the lack of opportunities for women, Women Make Movies opened its doors in 1972 as a
video and film training facility for women storytellers, expanding to include
an exhibition and distribution service for films made by women, a service that
continues to this day.[69] An alternative distribution model led by women was
not incidental—it took shape as they responded to their broader media invisibility and created their own opportunities. According to Cara Mertes, "The
big documentary movement of women telling their own stories in the 1970s
was pivotal in the development of documentary work. Most of the documentary world today is populated by women across the different roles. That first
moment arrived in the 1970s as women took on documentaries as a form that
could help them."[70]

Similarly, multicultural organizations from the analog media days remain significant decades later, even as they are joined by newer efforts to
advance stories told for and about diverse communities and people. In 1977,
the Native American Public Broadcasting Consortium launched its national
program to cultivate, lift up, train, and help produce media stories created
by and about Native Americans,[71] later re-branding as Native American
Public Telecommunications (NAPT) in the 1990s and as Vision Maker
Media in 2013.[72] With a similar perspective, in 1979, the National Black
Programming Consortium, now known as Black Public Media, "began because there was a need to encourage the development of films and television programs about the black experience that involved creative risks and
addressed the needs of unserved and underserved audiences;" and Latino
Public Broadcasting launched from an earlier consortium with a similar
mission to represent and mentor Latinx storytellers and stories.[73] In the
summer of 1980, out of a conference hosted at the University of California at
Berkeley and primarily funded by the Corporation for Public Broadcasting,

the National Asian American Telecommunications Association (NAATA) launched, later re-named the Center for Asian American Media (CAAM), to represent Asian-American producers and stories.[74] It was followed by Pacific Islanders in Communication (PIC), which derived from the same conference but formally launched years later.[75] Recalled Stephen Gong, the current CAAM executive director who was present at the original 1980 meeting,

> We think about this [representation] so much in our work. The questions of who gets to tell these stories has been there from the beginning for all of us who represent marginalized communities. It is *the* number one and it's never been really fully reconciled. . . . When we say "who gets to speak?," we can't divorce that from who has the power and who gets to maintain it—whether it's Sundance or Tribeca or whomever, too.[76]

Training, mentorship, and network-strengthening opportunities for emerging documentarians was—and is—critical to leaders and organizations serving multicultural makers and stories. As award-winning documentarian Stanley Nelson says of film school in the 1970s: "We started a collective of black filmmakers from a number of different schools in New York City who were interested in documentary filmmaking. . . . I never felt like I was the only [black filmmaker], because at that time, besides film schools, there were other training programs, like at WNET, to try to get a diverse group of people into filmmaking. . . . There was this whole push into the industry."[77]

Other exemplar initiatives of the time were inspired by, and shaped within, the emergent film-based ethnic power movements centered in UCLA's Ethno-Communications program, which inspired collectives and organizations created by multicultural groups who understood the importance of shaping their own narratives (see Figure 2.2). Among them, Visual Communications, serving filmmakers and stories from Asian-American and Pacific Islander communities, launched in 1970,[78] founded by Robert Nakamura, Eddie Wong, Duane Kubo, and Alan Ohashi. Co-founder Nakamura, whose family was held in Japanese internment camps, "would later recall, 'we need to be visible,' to tell Asian American history from the perspective of Asian Americans, to present views from 'within,' " according to Joshua Glick.[79]

Black filmmakers in the Ethno-Communications program were similarly motivated—"vehemently opposed to Hollywood's long history of trafficking in black stereotypes for profit," as Glick wrote—and formed a core contingent

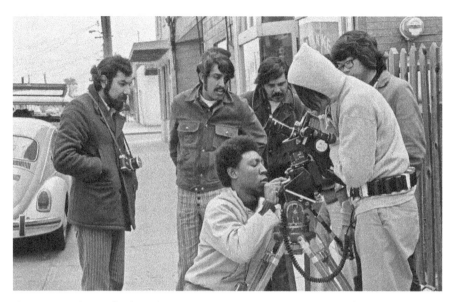

Figure 2.2. Filming the documentary *Sac River Delta* in 1971 as part of the UCLA EthnoCommunications program's Location Production class, with David Garcia (instructor), Willie Hernandez, Jose Luis Ruiz, Steve Tatsukawa, Eddie Wong (hooded), and Larry Clark. Photo by Robert Nakamura, courtesy of Visual Communications.

known as the "L.A. Rebellion,"[80] whose members would go on to make films and mentor other filmmakers, providing an indispensable network and ethos of empowerment and representation in documentary.

The seeds of initiatives and collectives that lifted up and created community among diverse storytellers bore fruit into the 1980s and beyond—not only in self-distributing, community-based spaces, but in the mainstream media market. In such generative soil, filmmakers like Stanley Nelson, for instance, reached large audiences with films that entertained while correcting inaccurate and missing narratives of the African-American experience. As Nelson recalled:

> When I first got into documentary filmmaking in the 1970s and 80s, I thought two things. I started in filmmaking in the Blaxploitation era and I thought there weren't really films being told about real black folks, but a lot of films like *Superfly* and *Shaft* and prostitutes and pimps. Then I thought there weren't documentaries told by African Americans about African Americans in general, about people of color, about themselves. I thought that was important for us to have the chance to tell our own stories from our point of view, and that's one of the reasons I got into making documentary films.[81]

His first documentary feature film, *Two Dollars and a Dream: The Story of Madame C.J. Walker*, about the African American entrepreneur and activist, aired on PBS as part of Black History Month in 1988,[82] later winning a CINE Golden Eagle Award and Best of the Decade award from the Black Filmmakers Foundation.[83] African American filmmaker Sam Pollard similarly found cultural acclaim in documentary in 1989 when he won an Emmy Award for an episode of the Peabody-Award-winning PBS series, *Eyes on the Prize II: America at the Racial Crossroads*,[84] and continued a successful fiction and nonfiction filmmaking career. Innovative filmmakers of color forged ahead with documentary work—including Ramona Diaz, Renee Tajima-Peña, Michael Chin, Orlando Bagwell, Sylvia Morales, and many others—despite working within a system that presented substantial barriers to multicultural filmmakers.[85]

As makers of color continued to push for media representation, in 1993, the Corporation for Public Broadcasting began funding the National Media Consortia (NMC)—in 2019 re-branded as the National Multicultural Alliance (NMCA)—a cohort of the original nonprofit organizations launched in the 1970s to lift up multicultural stories and makers (see Figure 2.3): Center for Asian American Media, Pacific Islanders in Communications,

Figure 2.3. National Multicultural Alliance (formerly National Minority Consortia) organization leaders speak on a panel at the International Documentary Association's 2018 Getting Real convening: Luis Ortiz, Stephen Gong, Leanne Ferrer, Leslie Fields-Cruz, and Shirley Sneve, moderated by filmmaker and professor Renee Tajima-Peña. Photo courtesy of the Academy of Motion Picture Arts and Sciences (AMPAS).

Vision Maker Media (under its original name, the Native American Public Broadcasting Consortium), and Black Public Media, later adding Latino Public Broadcasting.[86] Public media stations continue to distribute independent documentary films funded and co-produced by the consortia organizations, extending the visibility of diverse storytelling voices through community outreach and educational programs.[87] Documentaries and filmmakers supported by the multicultural consortia groups are not only seen in public media but also across commercial outlets, thus expanding the reach of diverse stories to broader audiences.

Training, mentorship, networks, and funding continues from many of the organizations and individuals who were compelled by liberation movements of the 1960s and 1970s—vanguards who pointedly interrogated inequity and demanded visibility. They undoubtedly influenced the present-day practice and business of documentary storytelling even as their pursuits remain as urgent as ever. Systemic, structural challenges endure. To be sure, gender, race, and ethnicity do not nearly comprise the full range of traditionally underrepresented voices, even as the trailblazing individuals and organizations profiled here provided models for efforts to follow. As Chapter 9 reveals in greater depth, new empowerment initiatives have surfaced in the networked era—similarly galvanized by vocal demands for equity and change—lifting up representation and the ethics of storytelling as a core value of documentary in democratic practice.

Technology Shifts and Expanding Media Platforms

As long as technology has innovated in the field, documentary makers have taken advantage of it in order to shape the stories they want to tell. But techno-determinism is not the core idea here. Platform and technology shifts have not *caused* the evolution in form or filmmaker motivations; documentary makers have always found a way, regardless of the tools at their disposal. Still, moments of transformation in media platforms and technology have meaningfully enabled story visions and the possibilities for audiences to see them. The marketplace for documentary storytelling expanded dramatically as technology and platforms shifted, and as the nonfiction form expanded creatively, attracting new and varied viewers.

In the early days of filmmaking, the expense and sheer size of film equipment locked out creative storytellers who lacked the budgets, training, and resources of institutions like motion picture studios or government agencies or TV networks. The 35 mm film gear of Hollywood movies was expensive, and the camera equipment required large, experienced teams to operate it. But change loomed on the horizon. Filmmakers wanted to film unvarnished life, and the backdrop of the post–World War II era changed the playing field for documentary storytellers and their technology. Although 16 mm film and cameras were available in the 1930s and 1940s, the technology wasn't widely used or available until the US Army used the gear in the war and brought cameras and projectors back to the United States to land in Army surplus stores.[88] In this way, as Patricia Aufderheide noted, "It is these economic and political forces, not the technology itself, that opened things up."[89]

The 16 mm film cameras—lighter, less bulky gear that allowed small, nimble crews to capture intimate human moments—contributed to the radical new cinema verité documentary chapter that inspired new voices and organizations.[90] Robert Drew, D. A. Pennebaker, David and Albert Maysles, and Richard Leacock were documentary progenitors who also innovated filmmaking technology by devising a way to record picture and audio simultaneously with the help of Jean Pierre-Beauviola, the French engineer and filmmaker.[91] Indeed, Robert Drew's 1960 observational documentary, *Primary*, is considered a game changer in the new storytelling revolution of the time.[92] In 1967, Sony introduced the DV-2400, the first Portapack video recording and camera gear, which recorded on half-inch tape and weighed only 20 pounds,[93] offering yet even more flexibility for documentarians interested in revealing intimate realities.

Without the narration or rigid construction of early documentaries, pathbreaking filmmakers like Frederick Wiseman unspooled the lives of the mentally ill in *Titicut Follies* (1967), a day in the lives of American high school students in *High School* (1968), and a portrait of a Kansas police department in *Law and Order* (1969), among other early films.[94] In the evolution of social-issue documentary practice, longtime documentary leader Cara Mertes singled out Wiseman for his part in expanding the TV marketplace to include the new nonfiction style: "The emergence of Frederick Wiseman was really important to this work—he started in 1968, and by 1971, he had a ten-year grant from the Ford Foundation to make a film a year."[95] His films would go on to shape documentary marketplace demand and audience interest on PBS, year after year through the 1970s,[96] and later, commercial documentary outlets like HBO would pick up the observational style of Wiseman, Drew, the Maysles brothers, Pennebaker, and Barbara Kopple.

Emanating amid the storytelling possibilities of the verité movement, the video format of the 1970s presented yet another accessible mechanism for production, providing documentary makers with a new way to capture intimate human stories and to facilitate community civic dialogue.[97] Participatory, community-based nonfiction storytelling and collaboration found deep roots in this moment. Kartemquin's Gordon Quinn pointed to the technology shift not as a means to itself but as a broader connection to intimate storytelling:

> We made the leap right to video in those early days. It was parallel and we were doing both—video and 16 mm—but video was important, because it was designed to be used by people and show it in their living rooms or a meeting or something. . . . The whole story of verité and the Maysles and Leacock and Pennebaker—the camera that could fit on your shoulder, the crystal-controlled sound so there was no wire distance between the audio person and the camera operator— that was incredibly important to us in those early years . . . . But what's more important is what we were trying to do and why did we need this technology and how was it evolving. . . . It's a dialectical relationship—technology makes things possible, but what you are trying to do and who you're trying to reach is central.[98]

Documentarians thus embraced the democratizing potential of the new gear as they endeavored to reveal stories of social justice and struggle missing elsewhere in media reflections. Boundary-pushing storytellers and new documentary approaches helped expand the marketplace as the decades progressed and new distribution outlets appeared. Documentaries of the 1980s moved away from a dominant verité approach, adding to the nonfiction mix form-bending performative, entertaining narrative styles. The era germinated, among other approaches, a reflexive documentary storytelling style exemplified by films such as Errol Morris's classic, *A Thin Blue Line* (1988);[99] a "performative" documentary mode,[100] illustrated in Marlon Riggs's *Tongues Untied* (1989), the pathbreaking film that examined the experience of gay black men in America from a firsthand perspective;[101] and "participatory" mode, as in Michael Moore's *Roger & Me* (1989), an entertaining and poignant portrait of the filmmaker's hometown of Flint, Michigan, as the long-standing General Motors plant closed its doors and left town.[102] In so doing, documentary storytellers found new ways to narratively mix political complexities with social and personal experiences, increasing the creative entertainment value and enticing media business decision makers to see nonfiction storytelling as a viable form of entertainment for broader audiences.

As the 1980s blurred into the 1990s, the cable television business—the emerging player in the panorama of commercial entertainment and news—began to gradually compete with the once-dominant entertainment and news fortresses of the broadcast "network era."[103] Steadily, as new cable TV networks set up shop and audiences expanded, the marketplace for documentaries opened in a new way, beginning the steady climb toward the digital era's explosion in social-issue documentary storytelling and its multi-layered marketplace.

While not the sole player, premium cable powerhouse Home Box Office (HBO) can be credited as an early adopter that expanded the commercial marketplace for risk-taking documentary and attracted new audiences through series like *America Undercover*,[104] which premiered in 1983 and won dozens of Peabody and Emmy Awards for films showcasing topics like abortion, racial profiling, sex, and the death penalty. and more.[105] The 30-year past president of HBO Documentary Films, Sheila Nevins, inspired by the intimate style of the Maysles brothers and Wiseman, envisioned HBO documentaries as a hybrid of reality and drama, finding the entertainment value in the unexpected twists and turns of everyday people, as she reflects: "Ordinary people are the most extraordinary. . . .I think the way people survive the turmoil of life is extremely interesting. How do they do it? How do you live with a child who is going to die? How do you bury a child? How do you survive being beaten by a husband and not telling anybody? I don't know how people do it, but I'm fascinated by how they survive. People are forever interesting."[106] Nevins's visionary lens helped shape a commercial audience's understanding of documentary as a form that could be as entertaining as it was thought provoking.

In this newly competitive media environment—with emerging cable networks breathing life into the old investigative documentary form[107]—the 1980s and 1990s marched toward the new century. Beyond television, theatrical distributors of scripted feature films—including Warner Brothers, Fine Line, Fox Searchlight, and Miramax—exhibited documentaries in the same time period,[108] expanding the reach of nonfiction storytelling beyond the art-house theater crowd and paving the path for changes to follow. Several feature documentaries made millions in the theatrical box office, including *Imagine: John Lennon* (Warner Brothers, 1988); Michael Moore's first film, *Roger & Me*, distributed by Warner Brothers in 1989; *Madonna: Truth or Dare* (Miramax, 1991); and *Paris Is Burning* (Miramax, 1991).[109] The Sundance Film Festival, a major launchpad for independent documentaries, held its first festival under the Sundance name in 1985 and heavily supported documentaries starting in the early 1990s; and the International Documentary Festival Amsterdam (IDFA), the largest documentary festival in the world, launched in 1987.[110]

A prologue to today's multi-platform media marketplace for social-issue documentary storytelling is embodied in a basketball story: In 1994, William Gates and Arthur Agee, two African American teenagers living in Chicago, exploded onto the big screen in *Hoop Dreams* (see Figure 2.4), Kartemquin Films' three-hour documentary about life and sports aspirations, directed and produced by Steve James and produced by Frederick Marx and Peter

Figure 2.4. Steve James, Peter Gilbert, and Fred Marx film Kartemquin Films' 1994 hit documentary *Hoop Dreams.* Photo courtesy of Kartemquin Films.

Gilbert.[111] After winning the Best Documentary award at the 1994 Sundance Film Festival, the documentary Roger Ebert called "the best film of the 1990s" achieved financial success, contributed to shifting the rules for the Best Documentary Feature Academy Award category after the film was excluded from consideration,[112] and expanded audience enthusiasm for socially conscious documentary storytelling as the early rumblings of the digital age continued. Kartemquin's Quinn noted the invigoration generated by the film:

> By the time we get to the 1990s, we were all thinking about how to reach beyond the choir. . . . *Hoop Dreams* was a magnificent example of that—a film that's almost three hours long, no famous people, enormously successful, and many people watched *Hoop Dreams* who would never watch a film about a social problem. They would never watch a film about a—quote—inner-city family. But they watched *Hoop Dreams* because it was about sports, it was about coming of age, and it was really about family. That greatly influenced the films that came after it for us and brought us back to those verité roots.[113]

Hoop Dreams was notable not only for reaching broad new audiences but also for its theatrical box office success. The film made almost $12 million in global box office—nearly $8 million domestically and $4 million around the world.[114]

At the time, it was the highest-grossing theatrical documentary of all time.[115] But *Hoop Dreams* was momentous for another pivotal reason, signaling a technology shift that would help to open the field for social-issue documentary storytelling as the new millennium approached: It was filmed on video, which made the story financially possible given its five-year production span, but it was transferred to film to allow a theatrical release.[116] A quarter-century after its premiere, *Time* magazine noted the movie's decisive contribution to documentary:

> The film ushered in a new wave in which documentarians, buoyed by newly inter-ested financiers and the opportunity to screen in national theaters, imbued diffi-cult topics with personal warmth, rigorous patience and narrative force. In many ways it is the forebear to the documentary boom happening right now, in which works like *Leaving Neverland*, *Minding the Gap* and *Surviving R. Kelly* are driving na-tional conversations about justice, abuse and equality.[117]

The digital era of documentary storytelling began slowly at first, picking up steam in the early 2000s. Between 1996 and 2002, about 15 documentaries were released in US theaters each year, a number that tripled in 2003, reaching 50 in 2004.[118] The juggernaut documentaries of the early 2000s were unques-tionably political in content and intent, from *Farenheit 9/11* (2004), directed by Michael Moore and produced by Jim Czarnecki and Kathleen Glynn, Moore's signature essay-style expose of the US invasion of Iraq, which re-mains the highest-grossing documentary of all time at $119 million;[119] to Robert Greenwald's *Outfoxed* (2004), also known for early internet-based distribution; to the 2006 Academy-Award-winning film about Al Gore's quest for climate change awareness, *An Inconvenient Truth*, directed by Davis Guggenheim and produced by Laurie David, Lawrence Bender, and Scott Z. Burns, which grossed $24 million at the box office.[120] The widespread cul-tural awareness of these films contributed to the dynamism of the documen-tary digital era and audience enthusiasm. In this early millennial moment, documentary bifurcated—in one direction, toward the blockbuster partisan-essay documentaries, and in another, toward intimate human portraits or entertaining explorations of life and injustice, often in tandem with public en-gagement around social challenges. This book focuses on the latter.

In the early 2000s, documentary impulses were at least partially fueled by the culture of unrest marked by a post-9/11 environment and the controver-sial Iraq War. They were also simultaneously enabled by the new hardware and software of filmmaking, as well as a dramatic expansion in media platforms. About three decades after its Portapack contributed to the verité movement of the 1960s, in 2004, Sony launched its first consumer-grade digital video camera that conformed to a high-definition 1080i standard.[121] Digital video (DV), in use and standardized since 1998,[122] advanced to mini-DV tapes, and finally, to cameras that would record to memory cards and hard drives in 2006.[123] The hardware of documentary filmmaking was thus more accessible than ever before, adding to the revolutionary new access to film editing proffered a few years earlier. In 2002, Apple won a Primetime Emmy Engineering Award for the impact of Final Cut Pro, the first professional-grade home-computer-based editing system; in a statement, then-CEO Steve Jobs said, "Final Cut Pro has democratized professional video editing by bringing the capabilities of a $50,000 editing bay to everyone for under $1,000."[124]

At the same time, the storytelling marketplace beyond the traditional theater—that is, the convergence of the internet and TV—was rapidly changing as new media platforms emerged. In 2005, for the first time, audiences could view TV outside of the linear schedules of the network era.[125] YouTube, a curious novelty for amateur storytellers armed with new cameras and computer-based editing equipment, launched in 2005, allowing users to create and upload their own videos.[126] Netflix, the early leader among the streaming-entertainment innovators—which had quietly launched as a mail-order DVD business in 1997[127]—asserted its full identity, leveraging the revolutionary convergence of home computers and TV.[128] After more than a decade of increasing consumer affection for customized-entertainment services through the mail, Netflix continued to disrupt the entertainment industry by offering internet-streaming entertainment in 2010, its first original scripted programming in 2012, and its first bona fide original scripted hit a year later, *House of Cards*.[129]

In 2013, Netflix acquired its first independent documentary feature film, the Sundance-Film-Festival-award-winning examination of the 2011 Egyptian revolution, *The Square*, and streamed it one year later,[130] thus opening the door to a huge new investment in documentary storytelling. Fast forward several years later: "People who have never watched a documentary in their life are watching them on Netflix," said Netflix chief content officer Ted Sarandos in 2015 at the UBS 42nd Annual Global Media and Communications Conference.[131] His interest in documentaries was backed by a commitment to invest billions of dollars in original content—with a specific affection for social-issue documentaries.[132] In 2017, Ava DuVernay's urgent racial injustice manifesto, *13th*, a Netflix documentary, was nominated for an Academy Award. In 2018, two independent social-issue documentaries distributed on Netflix, *Strong Island* and *Heroin(e)*, vied for Oscars.[133] Between YouTube and Netflix and a host of online outlets, a ripe environment opened up for social-issue documentary storytellers to distribute their work beyond the legacy media gatekeepers, in a new streaming entertainment marketplace.

Given the marketplace expansion, audiences—communities, individuals, civil society—can access the stories on both legacy TV networks and digital-native platforms in an era of new competition for viewers. Since the early 2000s, public television and cable networks have expanded their documentary offerings. In 2002, PBS announced a major expansion of *Independent Lens*, its independent documentary film series launched in 1999, from 10 episodes a year to 29 films per season, broadcast in a primetime slot.[134] World Channnel, distributed by American Public Television, launched in 2006. Between 2012 and 2013, documentary programming strands and units—showcasing independently produced films as well as internally produced content—opened up with legacy media brands, both online and on air: *Time* magazine announced Red Border Films focused on short- and long-form documentaries; CNN premiered CNN Films, a documentary series that launched with the global gender equity film, *Girl Rising*; and *the New York Times* continued to feature Op-Docs, short-form documentaries focused on topical issues.[135]

Firmly ensconced in the streaming, social-media era, audiences can find and watch documentaries on digital-native platforms like YouTube, Vimeo, Netflix, Amazon Prime, Apple, and Hulu alongside legacy HBO, PBS, CNN, Showtime, Starz, Discovery, and National Geographic and an increasing number of networks. The expansion across both streaming platforms and legacy outlets has advanced the ability of a documentary to pave the way for social change. On this point, documentary scholars Ezra Winton and Jason Garrison have addressed the unique—often overlooked—challenges of distribution, particularly when considering documentary stories that offer counternarratives to dominant media narratives.[136] Without adequate distribution, independent documentaries are limited in their ability to spark public dialogue. Increasingly layered distribution strategies enabled by expanded media platforms—that may, for the same film, include theaters, festivals, TV, digital streaming, and grassroots community screenings—means a contemporary documentary can enjoy a much fuller, more dynamic, longer relationship with multiple audiences, in physical and virtual public spaces that include community center meeting halls and Capitol Hill.

Today, the role of social-issue documentary remains unique in the landscape of contemporary news and entertainment—an essential mechanism by which to transmit often unseen perspectives about pressing social challenges or corrective historical narratives. Despite new audience access, corporate consolidation in the media business continues at a dizzying scale and pace. In the digital era, with the data-collection power and algorithmic business models of the streaming networks—and news aggregators, content producers and distributors like Facebook and YouTube—the lines blur yet again as competition for cultural dominance in news and entertainment picks up while consolidation continues unabated, paved by the path of the Comcast-NBC Universal merger in 2011,[137] and AT&T's acquisition of Time Warner in 2018.[138] The underlying power of the internet, too, is increasingly consolidated, as the Internet Society reported in 2019: "A small number of large companies influence the nature of an open, collaborative and interoperable Internet."[139]

As scholar Ben Bagdikian warned in 2004, "The media conglomerates are not the only industry whose owners have become monopolistic in the American economy. But media products are unique in one vital respect. They do not manufacture nuts and bolts: they manufacture a social and political world. New technology has expanded the commercial mass media's unprecedented power over the knowledge and values of the country."[140] Within the context of documentary and its historical evolution as a mechanism to foster civil dialogue—one that can distribute counternarratives and open a door to a fuller expression of lived realities—monitoring the backdrop of internet control, governance and consolidation is critical. Further, an artistic community that seeks to access audiences and revenue in the digital age cannot afford to ignore the regulatory climate that can open or further shutter a broad, rich, diversity of stories and viewpoints.

And thus, we emerge from history into the now, a moment in which documentary technology, audiences, and the marketplace have changed and expanded. Public engagement practices with social problems have transformed in a climate characterized by renewed calls for social justice, empowered by the networked media era.[141] In an attention economy,[142] the ability to cut through the clutter and authentically reveal unseen stories and lives is a domain of documentary storytelling that aims to illuminate social realities and invite the public's scrutiny. Many of documentary's pathbreaking organizations and enablers of the time are still deeply engaged, bridging the evolution and passing values on to new makers and organizations. Historically, tumultuous demands for equity and justice expanded opportunities for documentary storytellers and the societal impact of their work.

The history and cultural context of social-issue nonfiction storytelling practice is thus a textured set of stories that spotlights documentary's unique positioning as a mediated purveyor of reality and societal values. Documentary traditions have been incontrovertibly fashioned by two positions—both the mainstream commercial and public entertainment marketplace and also by independent, alternative traditions that began and operated within communities and movements for equity. Documentaries are art and business, call to action and entertainment, ripe for sparking civic participation and democratic practice in the networked media era.

What's always been true about nonfiction storytelling is that the ground truth comes up. Big moves that happen in culture are not a top-down thing. . . . Culture is something deep and important. There's no way to switch a light switch and tell people what to do. Culture is made with everyone participating.

— Sally Jo Fifer
President and CEO,
Independent Television Service[1]

3

Opening a New Lens

Documentary Functions as Civic Storytelling

In September 1955, America's virulent racism revealed itself through a photo of the lifeless, brutalized face of a murdered 14-year-old African American boy, Emmett Till. Tortured and lynched by two white men in Mississippi in August 1955, his killing sparked renewed momentum for the civil rights movement when *Jet* magazine published photographer David Jackson's image of the boy's face, unrecognizable due to the violence of his death, as Mamie Till Bradley looked down at her child's body.[2] In the final arguments of the murder trial, defense attorney Sidney Carlton reminded the jury—all white men—that if they did not acquit, "Your ancestors will turn over in their grave, and I'm sure every last Anglo-Saxon one of you has the courage to free these men."[3] The men were released less than two hours later, following a jury deliberation; according to one juror, "We wouldn't have taken so long if we hadn't stopped to drink pop."[4] In Money, Mississippi, life marched on.

Story Movements. Caty Borum Chattoo, Oxford University Press (2020) © Oxford University Press.
DOI: 10.1093/oso/9780190943417.001.0001

In 2003, almost a half-century later, documentarian Stanley Nelson and his Firelight Media production team sat quietly in the dark after screening their new film, *The Murder of Emmett Till*, at the Schomburg Center for Research in Black Culture in Harlem, New York City. The film, which aired on PBS and later won a Peabody Award (see Figure 3.1),[5] painstakingly reconstructs and revisits the incident through interviews with Emmett's family and friends, archival footage and photos, and testimony from witnesses at the scene of the murder and the trial.[6] The credits rolled and the lights came up, and the audience response was immediate, as Firelight Media's president Marcia Smith, also the film's writer, recalls:

> We were shocked by the audience reaction. We weren't shocked that they loved the film, but that their reaction was to be outraged that we had interviewed people in the film who were witnesses to different pieces of the Emmett Till story who had never been called to testify in court. People were amazed by that because these were people that we uncovered, essentially, through the production process.[7]

It was a new moment and a profound one—both for Firelight Media and the long-ago shelved, forsaken procedural details of Emmett Till's murder

Figure 3.1. Documentary director Stanley Nelson receives a Peabody Award for *The Murder of Emmett Till* at the 63rd annual Peabody Awards (May 2004), with writer Marcia Smith and editor Lewis Erskine. Photo by Anders Krusberg, courtesy of the Peabody Awards, University of Georgia.

and the trial. Sparked by the public's response at the first showing, the Firelight team launched a community engagement campaign to petition the US Department of Justice to reopen the murder case based on new testimony and witnesses in the documentary. As Smith recounts, "We printed up postcards and had people fill them out at screenings, put them on chairs at screenings, and we would collect them and mail them to the Justice Department. And in fact, about a year later, the Justice Department did re-open the case."[8] After beginning a new investigation in 2004, federal prosecutors exhumed the body of Emmett Till in 2005, the first step toward finally performing the autopsy that didn't happen a half-century earlier.[9]

Although the government was ultimately unable to pursue new prosecution, the film represented a milestone marker for the team. For Firelight Media, the outcry of community audiences spurred their recognition about the power to mobilize people in the digital era, fueled by viewers' responses to an emotional, factual, artistically rendered narrative. As director Stanley Nelson recalled, "We realized that these films could do something very different than just be something that goes up on screen. There are things that can surround films, like calls to action that became really important to us in general. . . . [T]here's something we can do here with the energy that these films move people."[10] The campaign launched Firelight's documentary-centered contemporary public engagement operation practices that "rely heavily on long-standing partnerships with national civil rights organizations—like the NAACP, Color of Change, Advancement Project, Center for Constitutional Rights—to reach into local communities while shifting the conversation on a national level," as articulated by Firelight's director of partnerships and engagement Sonya Childress.[11] Firelight Media's work in nonfiction storytelling and community engagement exemplifies the civic role of documentary in the evolving digital media age.

This chapter argues that documentaries play an active part in democratic practice through their functions as civic storytelling—that is, social-issue documentaries act as counternarratives, monitors, mobilizers, and artistic interpreters that can reveal the depth of a social issue through a creative, often long-term, view of social problems and human triumphs, strengthening civil society through collaboration and partnerships. Nonfiction films are often intentionally leveraged to spark public dialogue and participation even as they capture attention as works of art. Documentary functions as civic storytelling do not arise in a cultural vacuum, of course, but instead emanate within a transformative media environment alongside evolving practices—and challenges—for contemporary activism. Communication mechanisms abound but threats to free speech and free expression originate from governments and corporate entities alike.

Contemporary Social Action: Characteristics and Practices

Amid revolutionary protests in the Middle East and the tumultuous Occupy Wall Street economic uprising in the United States and around the world,[12] by the time that *Time* magazine honored "The Protestor" with the 2011 *Person of the Year* superlative,[13] the possibilities and realities of civic practice empowered by digital media platforms were rapidly coming into focus. The primary social media networks that would become the grassroots megaphones and organizing mechanisms for new public engagement, Facebook and Twitter, were several years into their maturation after launching a few years before, in 2004 and 2006, respectively. People adopted the new free participatory forms of online communication quickly. In 2008, just 21 percent of US adults reported using at least one social media network, a proportion that doubled three years later to 50 percent in 2011,[14] *Time*'s year of "The Protestor." By 2018, almost three-quarters (68 percent) of American adults 18 and older reported using Facebook and 24 percent said the same of Twitter,[15] dramatic increases over a decade. In 2018, Facebook reported 2.23 billion active global monthly users, and Twitter reported 335 million monthly users around the world.[16] YouTube, a repository of eyewitness raw videos and professionally produced stories alike, is now well trafficked. In 2018, 73 percent of all US adults reported using YouTube.[17]

The pro-democracy Arab Spring of the early 2010s was notable as a social-media-era movement progenitor, among other reasons, for the activism infrastructure afforded by Facebook, which, according to media scholar Zeynep Tufecki "was a boon to activists—it meant that things spread easily."[18] Twitter also featured prominently, although Tufecki cautioned against an overly simplified interpretation of techno-determinism dominated by ruminations about "whether social media themselves caused these movements,"[19] and the reductionist notion that "after Twitter and Facebook were created, they somehow caused revolutions to happen."[20] Instead, she articulated a richer focus on the complex interaction between human actors, technology, and media in networked protest: "Technology influences and structures possible outcomes of human action, but it does so in complex ways and never as a single, omnipotent actor—neither is it weak, nor totally subject to human desires."[21] The pathbreaking activism practices of the Arab Spring uprisings were both virtual and physical, hallmarks of new social movements.[22] They created practices evident in the Occupy Wall Street uprisings, and a few years later within movements like Black Lives Matter and #MeToo.

Black Lives Matter (BLM) emerged first in July 2013, launched in a Facebook post and a Twitter hashtag—#BlackLivesMatter—in response to the acquittal of George Zimmerman, who killed an unarmed African American boy, 17-year-old Trayvon Martin.[23] The hashtag and vocal public response sparked the viral voice of a burgeoning movement founded by three African American women—Alicia Garza, Patrisse Cullors, and Opal Tometi—and the beginning of its formal organizing and policy work directed at police brutality and other forms of racially motivated injustice and discrimination directed toward African Americans.[24] Emphasizing the agenda-setting power of Black Lives Matter on Twitter, the social media actions of the movement—according to scholars Deen Freelon, Charlton McIlwain, and Meredith Clark—predicted "mainstream news coverage of police brutality, which in turn is the strongest driver of attention to the issue from political elites."[25] The fervent social media activity was transformative. The communication practices of the movement's leaders and grassroots participants fueled public interrogation and sparked news coverage that amplified racial justice messages.

More than a decade after Tarana Burke founded a public effort, "Me Too," to direct attention and resources to women of color, particularly African American women, who have experienced sexual violence,[26] women all over the United States and the world quickly added their stories and voices to a #MeToo Twitter hashtag in late 2017, sparked in response to sexual harassment and assault allegations against the Hollywood producer Harvey Weinstein.[27] Rapidly, the movement and rallying cry shaped news conversations. As women shared their stories, harassers and abusers faced public and private reckoning.[28] *Time* magazine marked the occasion, as it did in 2011, by declaring the women who came forward with sexual harassment and assault stories—"The Silence Breakers"—as the 2017 Person of the Year.[29]

Contemporary social-justice movement practices reveal a clear renegotiation of message and media gatekeepers, and the ability for ordinary people—as aggregated voices—to shape news and public agendas by sharing stories and perspectives that are often systematically excluded from dominant cultural narratives. The rules and possibilities for public engagement have changed. Networked social movements are distinct from analog-age activism in meaningful ways, according to media scholar Manuel Castells.[30] They are leaderless,[31] even if leaders and organizational structures emerge over time. Calls for justice can originate and gain traction without the infrastructure and message filters—or megaphones—of large, established organizations.[32] This open-access activism extends the possibility for a range of new players to participate, even those who don't typically describe themselves as agitators.

In related fashion, networked movements live in a created "space of autonomy," a hybrid public arena that includes cyberspace and urban space, or both digital and physical.[33] The activism is "multimodal,"[34] presenting offline, physical opportunities for gathering and dissent, along with online organizing—creating a kind of togetherness that empowers a group that comes together with shared visions for changing a status quo. Public and media discourse is crucial. Tufecki, writing about the "attention economy," noted that groups and individuals with social justice demands are able to shape a media agenda, with attention as a requirement and commodity of networked activism.[35] While digital-era tools have not *caused* new public demands to address injustice, they have empowered new participants and opportunities for individuals and communities to amplify narratives that expose wrongdoing and call for remedy. Injustice is visible through the networked era's tools—user-generated video platforms, social media, digital recording and editing equipment for documentarians, and others.

And yet, the paradox: the infrastructure of the internet is precarious for free speech and independent voices, including documentary makers, civil society, and activists. Companies that provide digital platforms for creative expression and civic engagement are not guided by altruistic or public interest missions. Threats to freedom flourish in the internet age, warned scholar Laura DeNardis:

> From a global perspective, real-world freedom, whether expressive or economic liberty, does not always match the promise of Internet freedom. Governments have shut down the Internet. The business models fueling the digital economy have become utterly dependent on the invasive collection of personal data. Concerted, targeted actions of troll armies have silenced voices. Oppressive systems of filtering and blocking have enacted highly efficient censorship. Content freedom is on the decline.[36]

In the era of "the Internet in everything,"[37] risks abound for artists and publics speaking truth to power. While Manuel Castells asserted in 2012 that social media channels "are spaces of autonomy, largely beyond the control of governments and corporations that had monopolized the channels of communication as the foundation of their power, throughout history,"[38] they are, in fact, commercial enterprises optimized for profit, not social justice, even if their participatory qualities have aided in the latter. Internet infrastructure is increasingly consolidated within a handful of companies.[39] Government and corporate surveillance is powerfully enabled by individuals' use of social media and dependence on internet-based properties in modern life.[40] Complexities will continue alongside the technological evolution, requiring storytellers and activists to remain vigilant.

Regardless, voices of the people continue to find a way—whether or not an unfettered true *public* space exists. If *Time* magazine's *Person of the Year* commemorations—"The Protestor" in 2011, and "The Silence Breakers" in 2017—are any indication, an active civic culture fueled by grassroots voices is alive and well. Positioned within this context, the underlying backdrop—a networked age—and the role of social-issue documentaries is the steady hum of this book, and where we turn next.

Civic Culture and Public Engagement in A Networked Era

Social change—a shift in the status quo, an expansion of justice—is a process and an outcome of individuals and groups who come together as a collective. It requires the active participation of individual people and civil society organizations that work collaboratively to raise public awareness, shift cultural and media narratives, and demand remedy to social problems. Entertainment media storytelling is central within this interplay, as a mirror to reflect what's wrong and a portal to imagine what could be, to spark public conversation, and to shape social norms as a cultural purveyor of both information and entertainment that, as media scholar Jeffrey Jones wrote, "humanizes, simplifies, and embodies complex issues, concepts, and ideas."[41]

Social change requires open public space for stories and dialogue and critique. Formal activist movements need this freedom to express, but so, too, do smaller acts of communities coming together to uphold values, strengthen solidarity, demand change, and advocate for public good—the underpinnings of democratic practice. This is the domain of civic life and the public sphere, the cultural space in which members of publics—individuals and organizations—reveal, discuss, and negotiate social challenges together, thus shaping public opinion and advancing social progress.[42] Despite the ideal scenario of an open public sphere, a specter looms large in a polarized, divisive climate: the deterioration of a "communication commons—a public space characterized by diversity, tolerance, reason, and facts."[43] The imperative, then, is to develop shared values and solidarity as people work together to shape their world.

Civic values and public participation lie at the heart of democracy. "Civic," according to scholar Peter Dahlgren, supplies a wider frame to position the value of citizen engagement in public life than "political" because "civic" centers a shared societal value system motivated by a sense of the public good and the well-being of others, "a kind of 'service.' "[44] As he wrote: "The civic resonates with the notion of public, in the sense of being visible, relevant for, and in some way accessible to many people, that is, situated outside the private, intimate domain. 'Civic' then carries the implication of engagement in public life—a cornerstone of democracy."[45] Formal political activity—like voting behavior—is not the sole focus of public participation in a civic context.

Key to the idea of civic practice is the power of people who come together as publics. In philosopher John Dewey's classic conception, as reflected by Peter Dahlgren, "publics"—the individual people who "engage in talk with one another," thus shaping public opinion and negotiating social challenges and realities[46]—are not simply consumers of material goods or passive members of their communities, but active civic participants in community life. Individual people thus help to shape and reconstitute their worlds together as they "vote, participate in the social life of the community and communicate, expressing opinion and discussing issues of the day, and so communications ('shared experience') provide the basis of democratic revival."[47] Notably, contemporary civic practice does not require membership in formal organizations and institutions of citizenship—like labor unions, associations, and the like. As people publicly talk, critique, and push for change, they are engaging. Publics are not, then, audiences who merely absorb information and entertainment; publics "often actively direct attention onto messages they value."[48]

In parallel, civil society organizations—nonprofit organizations like community groups and issue advocacy groups, referenced interchangeably in this book as NGOs (nongovernmental organizations)—act on behalf of civic and public interests,[49] amplifying or sometimes organizing individual voices toward the public good. They comprise a form of "publics." However, in a networked participatory culture that opens space for individual voices, NGOs are not the central or sole core organizing centerpieces of small and large efforts for social change. Scholars Lance Bennett and Amanda Segerberg position NGOs in digital social movements as participants alongside individuals who publicly share their stories to assert identity and motivate social change. Facilitated by this synergistic model—the "logic of connective action"—individual people have new abilities to shape public and media discourse around public issues alongside NGOs as they together shape "digitally enabled action networks."[50] These networks don't require permanence to be powerful; they may be temporary, joined loosely in solidarity in support of, or in opposition to, an idea or perceived injustice.

The active engagement of publics in civic life is transformed in the continued evolution of what media scholars Henry Jenkins, Sam Ford, and Joshua Green characterize as the participatory culture of the digital media age. Media narratives have moved from a "distribution" model to a "contribution" model, a hybrid mechanism by which people have new access to share stories and messages with one another.[51] In a networked era that fosters public participation, individuals can more readily and publicly share content and information, a scenario that has also allowed previously marginalized groups and people the opportunity to assert their lived experiences and perspectives. Spreading particular stories and content thus "determines what gets valued."[52] The networked culture allows the potential and actual ability for a multiplicity of people to claim a share of voice.

Against this backdrop, culture—the narratives and values transmitted through art and creativity and media—is a force for enforcing and reinforcing the status quo, and for disrupting it.[53] Media play a dominant role in raising and negotiating social challenges not only by attracting attention but also by providing information and shaping public opinion.[54] Human lives are observed through media stories, which are not just vehicles to carry information, of course, but emotional, imaginative constellations of characters and narratives. Our social identities and relationships with one another are thus shaped by media representations.[55] In considering the powerful role of narrative and media in reflecting social problems, scholar Stephen Duncombe wrote that stories are a mechanism for encouraging public engagement and for seeing cultural realities: "The truth does not reveal itself by virtue of being the truth: it must be told, and we need to learn how to tell the truth more effectively. It must have stories woven around it, works of art made about it."[56] Art, including documentary, can thus act as a form of cultural resistance, asserting unseen realities, or a form of civic imagination, painting a portrait about how a state of affairs *could* be.[57]

In contemplating the role of media narratives to shape cultural understanding and call for social change, two tiers are relevant—*representation*, whose stories are told and whose are not; and *interaction*, the ways in which audiences engage with one another[58] and with media, including digital-age platforms.[59] Both tiers are central to positioning the role of documentary and the community engagement that happens in tandem. Social-issue documentaries represent human lives in ways that are distinct—intimate and emotional, often featuring little-seen voices and perspectives—from the mainstream business of entertainment and daily news. This is not to claim, naively, that media narratives offer uniformly positive, empowering portrayals; indeed, the opposite is true when we consider the range of ways in which traditionally marginalized individuals and groups have—and continue to be—rendered invisible or reduced to harmful stereotypes. Instead, disruptive media narratives, as in those carried by social-issue documentaries, may cut through precisely because they are unexpected. Interaction, too, is often fostered intentionally for social-issue documentary storytelling in a way that is distinct from other forms of scripted entertainment or journalism. Interaction with social-issue documentary narratives manifests in live grassroots and community screenings, not just living-room or theatrical entertainment experiences, and in participatory online spaces.

Contemporary social-issue documentaries are positioned squarely within the dynamic participatory culture that continues to evolve. In an age that offers grassroots access to the public stage, social-issue documentaries function as civic storytelling—a form of cultural discourse that illuminates ignored realities, provides social critique and source of civic imagination,[60] and often compels public participation. This conceptualization of contemporary social-issue documentaries as civic storytelling positions the interplay among publics, civil society, media narratives, and the tools and conventions of contemporary activism. Documentary storytelling, in this context, is not a form of media content to passively consume but a nucleus of civic practice that empowers public engagement.

Functions of Social-Issue Documentaries as Civic Storytelling

How do documentaries benefit democratic practice? What societal benefits do documentaries provide when they reflect and transmit intimate human stories infused with emotional, artistic, and narrative depth? Functions and forms of documentary, as scholar John Corner noted, are fluid and "historically contingent," but by examining documentary practices (how the film is crafted), form (how it sounds and looks), and functions (its value and use for audiences, as well as its intended impact), we can see "documentary identity" in a particular moment.[61] Situating documentary storytelling in its cultural context is key to understanding its functions.

This cultural moment is characterized by participatory possibilities and a niche-oriented media environment. While dominant sources of news and entertainment continue to capture attention though sheer market domination and robust marketing budgets, contemporary publics are "challenging more established media for the right to interpret public discourse."[62] There are simply more stories, and more narrative perspectives, for audiences to actively access and consider. In the contemporary public sphere, social-issue documentaries serve five distinct, but often overlapping, functions as civic storytelling: They transmit *counternarratives* to reveal perspectives that are invisible or infrequent elsewhere in media or news portrayals; serve in a *monitorial* role to spotlight issues of importance; act as *artistic interpreters* to probe, reveal, and analyze the depth of a story or issue; *organize and mobilize* public engagement with social challenges; and *strengthen civil society* to foster ongoing progress. For creative nonfiction storytelling that illuminates and interrogates social challenges, these functions are not mutually exclusive, nor does each documentary facilitate all of them. And yet, elements of at least one civic function can be found in many contemporary social-issue documentary stories—and the motivations of their makers.

Transmitting Counternarratives

Dominant or "master narratives," a system of stories and values transmitted and repeated through entertainment and news media, "play a large role in how we perceive the world around us"[63]—and thus, create a shared understanding about social realities and people, whether they are accurate or not. Through a composite portrait of people and problems echoed consistently in media portrayals, a grand narrative emerges, signaling heroes and villains, realities and uncontested "truths," which together shape an entrenched cultural depiction of a state of affairs.

In an ideal and authentic scenario, media stories would seamlessly reflect the many voices and struggles that comprise the human experience—the full complexity of lived reality. In the absence of this diversity, media counternarratives help expand public understanding. Stemming from critical race theory, "counterstorytelling" is "a method of telling the stories of people whose experiences are often not told (i.e., those on the margins of society) . . . storytelling and counter-storytelling these experiences can help strengthen traditions of social, political, and cultural survival and resistance."[64] This underlying concept is expanded here to include a broader view of traditionally marginalized perspectives, groups, and individuals—including but not limited to race and ethnicity. Documentaries about social issues can act as counternarratives that provide alternative, new, or little-seen perspectives about people and their experiences beyond dominant media reflections. In so doing, documentaries provide a perspective through which to agitate or correct a dominant—or missing—narrative and perspective about the human experience, thus helping to build a more equitable, accurate cultural portrait. Documentary reflection is powerful as a source of counternarrative and corrective narrative, as expressed by Loira Limbal, director of Firelight Media's documentary fellowship program for makers of color:

> Documentary film is important for groups of color who have not seen their full humanity portrayed in significant ways over the years—we need to see our real lives for ourselves because it impacts what we believe our worth is and what is possible for us. But also other folks need to see because they are still the ones who still make the decisions that impact our lives, and dictate and control our lives in important ways. I am particularly interested in how we tell those everyday stories that are not the superlatives, not just the extremes. The only time a person of color is worthy of having their story told on screen does not have to be when they are some superhero or when they are in their most acute moment of crisis—our regular, everyday humanity. There is a real opportunity there for all of our imaginations to be shifted about who people are, or who they can be, or who they should be.[65]

Consider the 2017 documentary, *Whose Streets?*, directed and produced by Sabaah Folayan and Damon Davis, and produced by Jennifer MacArthur and Flannery Miller. Following a steady stream of news coverage about protests in Ferguson, Missouri, documentarians identified a glaringly missing voice in the prevailing public narrative about the 2014 police shooting of Michael Brown, an unarmed African American teenager. Ferguson community members were largely voiceless in the composite news portrait, other than their appearances as disjointed soundbites within the cacophony of breaking-news frames. *Whose Streets?*, which premiered at the 2017 Sundance Film Festival and on PBS in 2018,[66] provides a viewpoint that challenges the one constructed by repetitive images of violence and riot-gear-clad police on cable and broadcast TV news. The film, according to one review, "privileges the point-of-view of predominantly working class and poor African-Americans in a suburb of St. Louis . . . a straightforward attempt to redress an imbalance of storytelling power—to see and hear people who felt misrepresented or ignored at the time."[67] The resulting narrative is the story of families and parents experiencing fear, pain, grief, and resolve—a stark, human contrast to the dehumanizing dominant news portrait of violence.

Similarly, *When I Walk* (directed and produced by Jason DaSilva, produced by Alice Cook and Leigh DaSilva), which premiered at the 2013 Sundance Film Festival and on PBS in 2014, shares an experience of physical disability from the on-screen perspective of the filmmaker, DaSilva, as he works through his recent multiple sclerosis diagnosis.. Along with the film, he launched a parallel social action initiative, the web-based AXS Map, which provides information about various forms of mobility infrastructure in public places.[68] By providing a counternarrative—in this case, a story crafted through the perspective of an individual living with a disability, not readily seen in dominant media narratives—he provides an empowering first-person creative lens and a contribution to structural social change.

Failing to question or counter dominant cultural narratives perpetuates injustice by ignoring voices that have traditionally not enjoyed as much—or any—access to shaping or transmitting stories of their lived realities to audiences. In this way, counternarratives in documentary storytelling are crucial to democratic practice by expanding collective understanding, not only at one point and within one story, but building and accumulating over time, incrementally shifting grand societal narratives about people and their lived realities and histories.

Monitoring

Documentary as monitor is inspired by the idea of media's societal surveillance function,[69] a concept that is traditionally presented as a function of journalists who warn the public about issues that should cause concern.[70] Social-issue documentaries play a monitorial role as civic storytelling—they often serve in a watchdog capacity, alerting the public to social issues and realities, including nascent or ignored topics on the horizon. Evolved from the journalistic fourth estate concept—acting as a necessary check on institutional power[71]—social-issue documentaries function in a similar sense, albeit with a more intimate, creative narrative style. In their unique monitorial function, social-issue documentaries transmit an emotional, artistic portrait even as they act as instructional harbingers of looming social issues. They are art and entertainment as much as information.

Investigative-style social-issue documentaries readily serve this monitorial function. As exemplars, consider Josh Fox's film *Gasland* (produced by Trish Adlesic and Molly Gandour), one of the first film-based examinations of fracking, which fueled an increase in community mobilization about the practice;[72] *The Invisible War*, directed by Kirby Dick and produced by Amy Ziering, which broke open to a civilian audience the widespread problem of sexual assault in the US military;[73] or their film *The Bleeding Edge*, an exposé of invasive medical device implants.[74] In 2006, the premiere of the Academy

Award–winning documentary, *An Inconvenient Truth*, was a watershed moment for climate change awareness. The film functioned as monitor and warning call about looming global danger, albeit through a creative, intimate narrative style that shaped a story around former US vice president Al Gore's PowerPoint presentation about climate destruction. Veteran documentary maker and Participant Media chief impact officer Holly Gordon reflects, "I often think about what a phenomenon *An Inconvenient Truth* was. It was a documentary film that broke all the rules of what was engaging content . . . and then it turns out that he drops a bomb of understanding around the world."[75] In *Science* magazine, Representative Rush Holt (D-NY) wrote in 2007 about the film's role in spurring wider public recognition of climate science:

> Gore can be given as much credit as anyone for these developments. The film earned over $24 million at the box office, the book has been a best seller (760,000 copies are in print), and 1.5 million DVDs have been sold. Students are being shown the film in school, and municipalities are scheduling viewings in public spaces. Word of mouth and this year's Academy Award for Best Documentary Feature have also fueled *An Inconvenient Truth*'s success.[76]

Sally Fifer, president of the Independent Television Service (ITVS) describes the monitorial function of social-issue documentaries, which, in her words, "really act like a canary in a coal mine for the big issues coming up," owing at least partially to their community-shaped independent nature: "[Through independent documentary submissions to ITVS] we tend to hear what's in the zeitgeist sometimes years before it's known more broadly in the culture. These independent filmmakers are there on the pulse, and these issues come from the ground up."[77] In 2012, ITVS launched *Women and Girls Lead Global*, an initiative with USAID (US Aid for International Development) and the Ford Foundation that curates international documentaries about the lived experiences of and inequities facing women around the world.[78] The initiative was a direct response to openly listening to independent documentary filmmakers serving in a monitorial role, ears to the ground within communities. According to Fifer, through the stories of independent documentary storytellers, ITVS foresaw a collective urgency to address gender inequity years before many other institutions explicitly focused spotlights and resources in that direction. As the Ford Foundation's Cara Mertes reflects: "Documentaries are the ways we alert ourselves to the dangers that surround us. There's a rise in documentaries because the issues are so profound, and the dangers are so profound."[79]

Through their intimate access and artistic sensibilities, documentarians are able to act as monitors by casting a vigilant eye on the horizon and warning the public, and sometimes directing them to learn more or get involved. They do so creatively, thus capturing public attention and often setting a media agenda for public scrutiny to follow.

Artistically Interpreting

Social-issue documentaries convey stories with depth and intimate detail and nuance that can surpass daily news framing of topics—or, in the case of events revisited years later, a deeper dissection of meaning with the hindsight of a retrospective creative view. By artistically interpreting and providing deeper analysis of a social issue, topic, or event, creative documentaries can help to contribute a public narrative that moves beyond incident-based framing and into the domain of visceral human experience. This function of social-issue documentary storytelling is inspired by a reflection of journalism's "interpretive function"—that is, " 'investigate government claims,' 'discuss national policy,' 'discuss international policy,' and 'provide analysis of complex problems.' "[80] And yet, it's not precisely the same idea here. In social-issue documentaries, an artistic rendering and analysis of an issue comes to life and adds new context by sharing the subtleties of individuals' lived experiences, or by interpreting an event years later, or by leveraging a creative style that provides a new way of seeing, or by telling a story from a transparent, identifiable point of view rather than an assumed place of "objectivity." As Brenda Coughlin, director of engagement and impact at the Sundance Institute Documentary Film Program, asserts: "The films I really love are the ones that add context to context to context. That role of [documentaries] has become increasingly important. . . . It's the age of visual mediation that we're really in. That's part of documentary's role in the public sphere."[81] An emotional connection is key to this artistic interpretation of social issues and news, in the eyes of Participant Media's Holly Gordon:

> In a documentary, if you don't build emotion between the audience and the characters in your film—whatever that emotion may be, like outrage, fear, surprise, empathy, love, hate—then your film is probably going go to fall flat. It will feel expository and emotionally inept. Journalism and documentaries do work together, but they perform different functions for the audience. One is to understand the facts, the other is to understand the humanity behind the facts.[82]

For example, years after the tragedy of the Sandy Hook Elementary School shooting in 2012, a documentary film released in 2016, *Newtown*, directed and produced by Kym Snyder and produced by Maria Cuomo Cole, provides a lens not only into the events of the day, but also deftly unpackages the on-going trauma, grief, and resilience of the families and community over the following months and years—a deeper, more intimate contemplation than breaking news images and incident-based daily reporting.

As another illustration, *Minding the Gap*, directed by Bing Liu and produced by Diane Quon, is not an instructional recitation about domestic violence and its legacy, nor simply a film about boys and skateboarding; as *The New Yorker*'s Richard Brody wrote about the Academy Award–nominated film: "Those images of skating, however, are merely the background and context for the film, and the diverting thrill that they offer is crucial to the film's substance. That substance—domestic trauma, systemic racism, and economic dislocation—is also the very stuff of society, and the near-at-hand intimacy gives rise to a film of vast scope and political depth."[83] Yance Ford's *Strong Island*, produced by Joslyn Barnes—the Academy Award–nominated 2017 film about the death of Ford's brother in a racially motivated killing—exemplifies documentary's creative interpretation function. His personal point of view and creative vision come together in a film that is equal parts true-crime investigation and personal exploration into his family's grief and trauma, using family photographs as an artistic motif. As a *Variety* review noted: "Ford's intent as a filmmaker isn't just to expose and protest the injustice of his brother's murder. It's to say: Behold what was lost. A life. A human being. A complex soul. A family's equilibrium. *Feel what was lost.*"[84]

Tabitha Jackson, director of the Sundance Film Festival and former director of the Sundance Institute Documentary Film Program, talks about documentary's ability to "make meaning," not just transmit information:

> The kinds of nonfiction filmmaking work and documentary I'm engaged with tends to be feature-length. In terms of meaning-making that comes from documentary, [it's about] the passage of time—the time it takes to make work, the time it takes to watch work, and the meaning that is made from the events and protagonists the work is expressing. . . . There's a part of me that thinks journalism is there to say what happened, and documentary is there to say, "what does it mean?"[85]

Firelight Media's Marcia Smith locates this function within the backdrop of the consolidated media business: "When we have a news industry that is as fragmented and commercialized as it is, documentaries play a really important role, because we don't get deep dives into issues that are affecting big swaths of the population through the news and entertainment where the money goes."[86] As ITVS' Sally Fifer sees it, when social-issue documentaries dig into the human, community-based implications of a social challenge, they "bring out the complexity of a situation that can help it to be reframed. . . . It's about a deeper comprehension you can only get when a storyteller spends a long time with the subjects and they really peel back, and the story really gets told in a deeper way."[87] For social-issue documentaries, this function is an artistic interpretation as much as an informationally driven one; an immersive lens is the crux of the idea. Through a creative perspective that allows a deeper, creative examination of a topic, documentaries can analyze and reinterpret and interrogate versions of reality that benefit from another angle or a more expansive outlook.

Organizing and Mobilizing

Social-issue documentaries provide a story-based mechanism to organize and mobilize publics around ideas and issues, inviting them to discuss and seek remedy for social problems—whether that participation happens online or in person. While journalism, too, includes a mobilizing function,[88] documentaries are distinct in sparking public dialogue and engagement due in part to their layered distribution models and practices. Social-issue documentaries are transmitted through a dual marketplace—distributed through commercial and public media networks as well as community-based screenings, which bring intimate nonfiction stories into public spaces for purposeful interactions with audiences.

Through grassroots screenings, including those hosted and supported by civil society organizations, social-issue documentaries facilitate communal gatherings that inspire an emotional collective experience and a space for public dialogue. In this way, documentaries build "alternative public spheres," groups of publics who come together and become vocal, active participants who engage in the issues they experience on screen.[89] Indeed, the mere existence of a nonfiction film can often serve as the reason to bring together community members to consider a social challenge in the first place. With a movie, there's something to do and see, not simply a problem to deliberate. Documentary-sparked mobilization happens in online spaces as well as physical ones; social media channels act as curators and megaphones to mobilize and convey public dissent or community solidarity.

Several notable films exemplify social-issue documentaries' public mobilizing function, and the examples abound throughout the book. For instance,

Bag It, directed and produced by Suzan Beraza and produced by Michelle Hill, a comedic documentary that warns about the environmental impact of continued plastic bag pollution, toured communities working on legislative efforts to ban plastic-bags.[90] As a digital mobilizer, a clear example is found in *Surviving R. Kelly*, Lifetime's 2019 documentary series about long-standing allegations of sexual abuse of young girls at the hands of singer R. Kelly, which sparked the #MuteRKelly public outcry for change. The series was executive-produced by dream hampton, Tamra Simmons, Jesse Daniels, and Joel Karsberg, and produced by Allison Brandin. Mere weeks after the series' premiere, RCA Records dropped Kelly from the label[91] and prosecutors in Georgia and Illinois pointed to new legal investigations.[92]

For Abigail Disney and Fork Films, the grassroots screenings that mobilize audiences are more meaningful than the entertainment marketplace—at least as far as community engagement is concerned: "There are films that get launched in theaters, but way more than 10,000 people saw our film [*The Armor of Light*] in a church basement than in a theater. As a change-maker and a person who wants to organize, I so prefer the church basement for the screening. You're all in the film together, and the lights come up and you want to talk. All of what's meaningful happens in those conversations."[93] Firelight Media's Sonya Childress sees the mobilizing function as key to reaching the audiences they care about: "We have to meet our communities where they are—whether that happens in a church basement or a community center or a classroom."[94]

Physical and digital mobilizing is an outcome, but a disruptive story is the key. By mobilizing audiences—either bringing them together in screenings and community events to discuss issues and realities, or by inspiring action online or physically or both—documentaries meaningfully encourage public dialogue, a cornerstone of democratic practice. As communities and publics come together, the possibility for new understanding—and solidarity—emerges.

Strengthening Civil Society

Social progress is difficult to achieve without the collaborative efforts of civil society, the organizations that advocate for social progress, "nurturing a collection of positive social norms that foster stability . . . promoting collective action for the common good" as "people power writ large."[95] Documentaries that interrogate social problems and inequities are enriched by civil society networks—issue advocates, community coalitions—already working deeply on the ground, challenging and pushing the issues forward on a daily basis.

In return, nongovernmental organizations (NGOs) can be newly empowered when they work with documentaries as collaborators, partners, grassroots organizers, and message amplifiers.

Documentary collaborations with nonprofit organizations and supportive commercial brands come together in various forms, from broad coalitions to individual partnerships, sometimes developing stand-alone initiatives of their own right that continue well past the original film's life cycle in the marketplace. For instance, in 2004, while filmmaker Libby Spears was directing *Playground*, the 2009 documentary about sex trafficking in the United States (profiled in Chapter 7), she founded the nonprofit organization Nest, which continues to create media products and other resources to advocate an end to sexual violence against children.[96] The 2013 documentary *Girl Rising* became a nonprofit organization that champions girls' equity on a global scale through media campaigns and community partnerships.[97] Filmmaker Jen Brea—inspired by making *Unrest*, her 2017 documentary film about her personal experience with a neglected health condition, myalgic encephalomyelitis (ME), known as chronic fatigue syndrome—built launched a new advocacy nonprofit organization, #MEAction, which mobilizes patients and their families "to make ME visible and fight for health equality."[98] In a different approach, the nonprofit advocacy organization Just Vision, which "increases the power and reach of Palestinians and Israelis working to end the occupation and build a future of freedom, dignity and equality for all," produces award-winning documentary films that air on TV and stream online, but also leverages them as centerpieces of ongoing grassroots community engagement and peace-building work.[99]

As a model that shapes documentary and civil society alliances on a broad scale across issues, the UK-based Doc Society's global Good Pitch program (see Figure 3.2) convenes social-issue filmmakers, funders, activists, and NGOs at events hosted around the world, bringing them together to ignite grassroots social justice efforts with documentary storytelling at the fore.[100] Financially supported by a network of philanthropies, Good Pitch invites selected documentary storytellers to showcase their work and "pitch" assembled aligned civil society actors—nonprofit organizations and community groups, issue advocates, government agencies, philanthropists—to create community engagement and financing partnerships to expand their films' potential as change agents. As Doc Society's co-founder Beadie Finzi explains: "Good Pitch was this idea that we could bring together documentary filmmakers with all kinds of agents from across civil society—foundations, NGOs, campaigners, philanthropists, policymakers, brands, media—to gather them around the leading social and environmental issues of the day

Figure 3.2. Documentary filmmakers, NGOs and philanthropies gather at Doc Society's Good Pitch convening held in Miami, Florida, in 2017. Photo by Lauren Colchamiro, courtesy of Doc Society.

with the idea that together, we could forge coalitions and campaigns that were good for all of those partners, good for the filmmakers, and good for society."[101] Alongside Good Pitch, Doc Society launched its Impact Labs, four-day immersive public engagement strategy workshops for curated social-issue documentary film teams, and the Impact Field Guide, an online resource guide that helps makers and strategists interested in engaging communities with documentary film.[102]

Beyond Good Pitch, other documentary-centered organizations have developed initiatives and models to foster organizational partnerships. Firelight Media trains social justice organizers working inside movement organizations to leverage documentaries in their public engagement work, with a specific focus on professionals of color—a program launched in 2017.[103] In 2019, the documentary nonprofit organization Working Films launched a new initiative, Putting Films to Work, which trains Georgia-based nonprofit organizations to leverage documentary storytelling for community engagement and advocacy.[104] For Working Films' co-director Molly Murphy, the value resides not only in the documentary training aspect of the work, but in bringing community-based organizations together: "We will be training the organizations about how to use documentaries to advance their goals and fulfill their missions. . . . The work is also about strengthening the capacity of these organizations to work together. Having opportunities for them to come together and share experiences and learnings will be an important element."[105] Synergy is key.

For a nonprofit organization, the experience of working collaboratively with a documentary film and its team can be transformative when values align. John Valverde, CEO of YouthBuild, for example, shifted his organizational approach after partnering with a documentary film that reflected his group's mission to support low-income young people in the United States between the ages of 16 and 24. He had not considered storytelling as valuable to his nonprofit's core operations until he met documentary filmmaker Katie Galloway in 2017 at a Good Pitch event in Miami.[106] Galloway was there to showcase her documentary in production, *The Pushouts*, produced with Dawn Valadez, Daniella Brower, and Sharon Tiller, which profiles the journey of Dr. Victor Rios, a celebrated sociology professor and book author who built a new life after dropping out of school and joining a gang. The documentary chronicles Rios's teen life into his current work to lift up a group of similar young people—" 'pushouts' trying to stay enrolled, learn and graduate against the odds."[107] Galloway wanted to reframe the narrative about young people who, as she explains, "never had a first chance."[108] It was the first time Valverde witnessed this angle projected in an emotional media story—that is, a redemptive narrative about the resilience and strength of vulnerable young people pushing back against structural barriers, rather than stories of individual tragedy or moral failings. It provided the hope he wanted to use to push for change.

Invited to the same Good Pitch gathering, veteran documentary filmmaker Rick Perez, former director of the Sundance Institute's Stories of Change initiative with the Skoll Foundation, offered a funding opportunity for Valverde and Galloway to work together on their shared missions. In Perez's work, partnerships between documentaries and like-minded organizations reflect natural areas of synergy:

> Movements aren't made of one person. Change really does happen in an ecosystem. Storytellers are among the artists and creatives who speak to us in ways that are unexpected, inform in a way that is emotional—they speak the language of emotion. That's its own power. That is a different language and a different tool than the actual execution of changemaking.[109]

Through their collaboration, YouthBuild launched a program to screen *The Pushouts* around the country for individual chapters and the young people themselves, along with stakeholders and other decision makers able to provide future opportunities for them (see Figure 3.3). Notably, he wrote his new strategic plan and vision for the organization at the same time. As the organization moves forward, its strategic imperatives now reflect Valverde's experience watching audiences respond to stories of hope and resilience on screen—a reframing away from familiar media tropes of trauma and pain.[110]

For Katie Galloway, YouthBuild is a vital mechanism to continue her film's influence beyond its 2019 PBS broadcast, to inspire under-resourced young people and critically examine the underlying systems that disadvantage and dismiss them, as she reflects: "[The film] raises the issues and makes people feel, and then we can step into that space and grow and strengthen the organization. We can do things that maybe weren't possible before because it [the film] opens up dialogue and it makes people think differently, and it activates and engages a bunch of people who would not ever pay any attention to a five-minute puff-piece [video]."[111] The connection between intimate, human nonfiction

Figure 3.3. *The Pushouts* panel at the 2019 Television Critics Association Summer Press Tour, with director, producer, and writer Katie Galloway; film subject Dr. Victor Rios; film subject Martin Flores; producer and co-director Dawn Valadez; and co-founder and chairman of Latino Public Broadcasting Edward James Olmos. Photo by Rahoul Ghose, courtesy of PBS.

storytelling and organizations working on structural change is a synergistic power—the sum greater than the parts—that can build lasting legacies.

When documentary storytellers and civil society groups find mutually beneficial value in their efforts to remedy social justice challenges, their collaborations can be transformative—propelling influence beyond one film and into the future. Organizational coalitions coalesce around individual films, but they often continue with future stories and new opportunities to come together, thus strengthening the infrastructure and organizing power of a wide network of civil society groups over time.

Through their emotional, artistic, entertaining, informative, investigative characteristics, social-issue documentaries can thus open the door to interrogate dominant cultural narratives and invite new or little-seen perspectives. By convening individuals and communities in physical and online spaces to watch nonfiction films, makers and activists supercharge the power of story to compel public interest and spark new conversations. Against the backdrop of contemporary civic practices and platforms, the process is enabled by organizations and individuals working in a public campaign function. Unpackaging the roles these movement builders play, and how they work, is where we travel next.

Documentary stories are like fuel and a torch to light the way. They are what communities need to motivate themselves and educate themselves—documentaries can help to inspire and mobilize the base of membership, community-based or social justice organizations.

—**Sonya Childress**
Director of Partnerships & Engagement,
Firelight Media[1]

4

Activating Community

The Movement Builders

Lee Hirsch intimately understood the story he wanted to tell, and he knew why it mattered. Years before he and his producing team began crafting their award-winning documentary film, *Bully*, he was a target of peer abuse him- self.[2] To Hirsch, the idea of so-called harmless bullying was so deeply in- grained in US youth and school culture—broadly regarded as a time-honored rite of passage endured by generation after generation—that it was generally rendered invisible. But things changed in the social media era.

A fresh public spotlight on bullying started in late 2010, when Tyler Clementi, a Rutgers University freshman, died by suicide after being victim- ized by cyberbullying.[3] As news of his death reverberated, radio host Dan Savage produced the initial short-form video that sparked a public cam- paign, *It Gets Better*, created to empower lesbian, gay, bisexual, transgender, and queer (LGBTQ+) young people.[4] Individuals and organizations added to the viral spotlight with their own statements of *It Gets Better* solidarity via

Story Movements. Caty Borum Chattoo, Oxford University Press (2020) © Oxford University Press.
DOI: 10.1093/oso/9780190943417.001.0001

YouTube, spreading the short-form videos on social media and creating the beginnings of a virtual movement of support.[5]

As tragedy and the viral power of the social media age opened a new door for public awareness and dialogue about bullying, director Lee Hirsch, along with co-writer and co-producer Cynthia Lowen and executive producer Cindy Waitt, were already producing a documentary to help shape a new cultural norm—moving from passive bystanders to active upstanders willing to intervene and report bullying behavior. Their movie, *Bully*, which illuminates "the pained and often endangered lives of bullied kids, revealing a problem that transcends geographic, racial, ethnic and economic borders,"[6] according to the film synopsis, opened at the 2011 Tribeca Film Festival, launched a theatrical release in more than 200 cities,[7] and premiered in 2014 on the PBS *Independent Lens* series[8] within a moment of heightened public attention about bullying and suicide in the United States, among LGBTQ+ youth but also more broadly.

Hirsch knew, of course, that bullying was not unfamiliar as a concept. But he speculated that a casual "kids will be kids" dismissal was the general cultural frame—rather a perspective about a violent threat with catastrophic results—because the public, and the adults who interacted on a daily basis with children and teens in school, couldn't quite feel the depths of the devastation facing victims and their families. He set out to do what statistics could not—to reveal the individual stories of three teens' daily experiences with peer violence and intimidation. It was a narrative, emotional way to interrogate and shake up the collectively dulled senses of a cultural status quo that seemed, to Hirsch, far too accepting of bullying culture:

> The insight this film unlocked was this idea that we had a really obvious human rights problem—millions of young people experiencing abuse daily—and yet, we had very little societal agreement about the scope or the legitimacy of the problem. We wanted to do a film that really showed what kids are going through and what the stakes are, and how violent and terrifying it could be, that we would be able to move people into a different place. It would be undeniable. The film was designed to really kick people in the ass in a lot of ways. The complexities of thinking about how to build a movement and what that would look like came later.[9]

Hirsch and his producing team spent time researching the core issues and identifying the primary civil society organizations and individuals already working on social change strategies around bullying. They pinpointed what they perceived to be a major gap in public engagement—the intimate human stories—along with an opportunity to create a connected network of adults who intervene in the daily lives of young people. Hirsch recalls, "There was a lot of research-driven work that was out there—there were definitely efforts happening nationally, but there was nothing that had galvanized people."[10]

Bully evolved into a full-fledged outreach and community engagement campaign powered by a comprehensive list of civil society partners—the beginnings of a coalition-based effort with an intimate, emotional documentary story as the centerpiece mobilizing element. By the time *Bully* premiered at the Tribeca Film Festival in 2011, the producing team had secured the endorsement of 25 influential groups listed as partners in the film's credits.[11] The film quickly and steadily became more than just something to watch.

The social action campaign for *Bully* launched as The BULLY Project, "a national movement to stop bullying that is transforming kids' lives and changing a culture of bullying into one centered in compassion and action."[12] At its launch, *Bully* worked with Donors Choose, a program that connected teachers and students with opportunities to create field trips to see the film.[13] During the post-production phase, Hirsch invited feedback from Facing History and Ourselves, the education nonprofit that provides anti-bias curriculum and trainings for schools and teachers,[14] which in turn developed a *Bully* curriculum and facilitated online workshops with more than 2,500 teachers across the country to teach them how to talk about the film and the issue.[15] The program developed into screenings and discussions nationwide.

Well after its moment in the entertainment marketplace, the impact of *Bully* and The BULLY Project is far-reaching. More than a million students, parents, educators, and others in the United States have seen the film through the project's 10 Million Kids Campaign or have participated in the *Bully* curriculum program that includes 50 different resources for educators.[16] In 2014, The BULLY Project joined with the US Conference of Mayors to launch a localized anti-bullying initiative across the country, the Mayors Campaign to End Bullying.[17] Across all 50 states, more than 200 mayors facilitated community events to "to educate, inform and inspire lasting bullying prevention efforts" in an effort to create safer environments for young people.[18]

The human intimacy of the documentary and the concerted efforts of The BULLY Project's collaborations with issue advocacy groups, educators, and public officials, Hirsch believes, paved the path to bypass bureaucratic gridlock and create a fresh network to directly influence the lives of a new generation of digital-native young people, as he reflects: "Previously, bullying had been really divisive. A lot of people had drawn a line in the sand as something they couldn't support, and I think we were able to knock that wall down and move different communities. . . . Now, if I meet people in their late teens or early 20s, they have usually seen *Bully*. It's pretty extraordinary."[19] Years after its film festival and TV premieres, contemplating the influence of *Bully* is incomplete without including the advocacy organizations, teachers, school systems, and expert groups that coalesced around the documentary. Supportive partnering nonprofit organizations, foundations, and influential leaders enabled The BULLY Project to function as a contained movement, even as the film provided a vital narrative rallying point for action.

Bully and The BULLY Project embody the collaborative efforts of documentary storytellers, strategists, and civil society organizations who come together to shape and facilitate social change initiatives around evocative nonfiction films. The grassroots power of the digital era has merged with the civic, community engagement documentary motivations established in the analog age. In the United States and around the world, companies, nongovernmental organizations (NGO), and philanthropic organizations are coalescing professional communities of practice around the capacity of documentary to open public dialogue and mobilize publics—that is, identifiable professional networks comprising "groups of people who share a concern or a passion for something they do and learn how to do it better as they interact regularly."[20] The resulting nexus of nonfiction storytellers, civil society, and social impact practitioners is an evolving professional ecosystem with social justice as the motivation. While the work unquestionably derives from social-issue documentary impulses established in earlier decades, the primary organizations and initiatives emerged or evolved since the 2000s—the same time frame that birthed participatory media platforms and fueled new modes of public participation in social challenges. This is story-centered civic engagement in the networked culture.

This chapter introduces the professional ecologies, motivations, and practices of story-based movement builders in the midst of the contemporary media age—the individuals and organizations who empower and mobilize publics to come together in pursuit of dialogue and change, inspired by the emotional narrative lens of documentaries that illuminate social issues and provide eyewitness portals into injustice. They are the foot soldiers in the networked, participatory civic culture, contributing stories that shape collective understanding of reality and sense of collective public good.

As this chapter reveals, while activating publics is a legacy practice in social-issue documentary, shaped from the pioneering efforts and dual marketplace established in earlier junctures, the participatory media era has witnessed a surge in community engagement organizations and initiatives with nonfiction storytelling at the fore. At the center of this ecology are documentary filmmakers themselves—directors and producers who create evocative, artistic stories and bring them to the public eye. Beyond critical acclaim and news coverage, the social impact of their stories is enabled by two central groups of professionals in the documentary field: the enabling *civic connectors and enabling institutions* who supply resources and community-building convenings, and the *community and impact engagement strategists* who work alongside filmmakers to transform their work into engines of community empowerment and social progress. Together, these are the documentary story-centered movement builders. As they work together, the ecology of documentary makers and organizations continue to shape a dynamic community of practice, learning from one another and evolving story-based public engagement best practices, ideas, and ethics.

The Civic Connectors and Enabling Institutions

As individuals and groups, the civic connectors and enabling institutions in the social-issue documentary ecosystem serve in a leadership and convener role. They provide the financial resources and infrastructure necessary to produce and showcase social-issue documentaries, but they also champion opportunities for filmmakers and change-makers to engage communities. The precise operating models within this group are not uniform—some produce and distribute their own films, some finance documentaries or nonprofit organizations that work with social equity missions, others provide spaces for developing public engagement strategies or convening documentary makers and communities. Regardless of business models, the documentary civic connectors and enabling institutions have shaped a constellation of story-centered, civically motivated social justice organizations and people—a national and international community of practice. They supply the essential foundation and support for this realm of socially engaged documentary work.

As the core of the civic connectors group, leading global philanthropies expand support for documentary storytelling by financing films and cultivating a network of nonprofit organizations that spark public engagement around nonfiction stories. Announced in 2011 from the Sundance Film Festival, the Ford Foundation launched its JustFilms program with an initial five-year, $50 million commitment that continues to support independent social-issue nonfiction storytelling at the epicenter of film and social change. As JustFilms' director Cara Mertes noted in a 2015 blog post, "Ford has been at the center of the growth of this field since the late 1960s: JustFilms can trace its DNA back to the early days of public television, the media arts center movement, community media and public access, and the American independent film movement that continues to grow today."[21] Since its launch, JustFilms has supported hundreds of independent documentary films that "explore urgent social justice issues and seek to challenge inequality in all its forms";[22] and in recent years it has cultivated a growing system of documentary storytellers and civic engagement organizations in the United States and around the world, acting as a leading voice and champion of independent storytelling, creative expression, and social influence. To build a stronger national and global landscape of documentary-centered civic storytelling organizations, Ford and JustFilms funded the first international network of social-issue documentary resources with $23 million over five years, connecting stalwart leading US-based documentary organizations like the Independent Television Service (ITVS), Sundance Institute, Tribeca Institute, and Firelight Media with leading international groups like the UK-based Doc Society and International Documentary Festival Amsterdam (IDFA), and also expanding resources for documentary-based organizations in the Global South, including Ambulante, InDocs, DocuBox, APAN/Brazil, Arab Fund for Art and Culture, and DocEdge.[23] To Mertes, the need is global and urgent: "The notion of free expression and the ability to galvanize the public around new ideas through nonfiction storytelling is vital. The strength of a nonfiction community is directly related to the strength of the democracy itself."[24]

Similarly, the MacArthur Foundation—which, along with the Ford Foundation, supported the community media arts centers movement of the 1970s and '80s—is a vital enabling institution for documentary storytelling that interrogates social issues. The MacArthur Foundation's long-standing commitment to independent documentary storytelling continues with an eye firmly trained on supporting stories that come from community, and thus may be neglected within mainstream entertainment networks—or not resourced by commercial financing. Kathy Im, who directs MacArthur's Journalism and Media Program, reflects:

> We believe that documentaries, journalism, media-based activism, and entertainment media work together to help audiences fully examine and understand the human impacts of public policy. . . . We feel a great responsibility to support an enabling infrastructure for nonfiction storytellers who can share their insightful visions with the public, and thus portray a more complete and contextual picture of society.[25]

MacArthur's senior program officer for documentaries, Lauren Pabst, roots independent documentary as central to democracy: "When the artists and journalists assembling these narratives come from communities that are both most affected by an issue and have been historically underrepresented among professional media makers, and they have access to holistic support in the creation of their work, what emerges are documentaries with the weight and leverage to be influential. These documentaries are unapologetic about their point of view, rooted in context, and armed with evidence captured by the camera."[26] Other global philanthropies like Omidyar Networks have contributed to the expanding organizational landscape of nonfiction storytelling and social change as they recognize the need for authentic narratives in social justice efforts. In his 2019 announcement of a new storytelling fund facilitated by the Sundance Institute, the leader of Omidyar's Luminate group positioned narrative as key to social change efforts: "We believe that when thematic storytelling is used strategically to articulate pressing public issues and movement-building campaigns it can be a tremendously powerful tool for change."[27] Similarly, the billion-dollar Skoll Foundation joined creative forces and financial resources with the Sundance Institute in 2008 to create the Stories of Change initiative, which funds and shapes documentary films that pair with community leaders working to solve social problems around the world.[28] Documentarian Rick Perez, who directed the program inside the Sundance Institute, describes the initiative as a shared vision between storytellers and social change agents:

> Some people are great activists, some people are great strategists, some are great organizers, some people are great artists. It's impossible to expect an artist to have all those sills and be able to execute them. How do we imagine networks where people are connecting and discovering their shared vision and shared dreams, mutual inspiration, coming together to imagine a better future and planning together to work toward a better future? We can't expect artists to be superheroes and one film to change a particular issue. But we can expect lots of people, and lots of films, working together in shared mission and communion.[29]

Smaller-scale funders like the Fledgling Fund financially support public engagement campaigns that often accompany documentaries,[30] including, for example, its funding and strategy support work for *Bully*. Created in 2005 in response to the potential for nonfiction storytelling to "educate, engage and mobilize us around entrenched and complex social issues that affect the most vulnerable,"[31] the Fledgling Fund facilitates annual convenings for its filmmaker grantees, immersing them in trainings and fostering lasting relationships to help shape strategic impact campaigns around their stories. Through Fledgling's year-long impact engagement lab residencies, social-issue documentary film teams become grassroots mobilizers and develop connections with like-minded storytellers. As executive director Sheila Leddy explains:

The objective is to build the capacity of the filmmakers, but also to build community among the participants. What ends up happening beyond the curriculum is that you end up building a community of filmmakers who are supporting one another, often out in the world at the same time. Even though their films might not be on the same topic, they might be thinking about festivals and impact and distribution and communication, how to build the strategy and hone their campaigns to use their resources really wisely.[32]

Film production, distribution, and investment companies also reside in the network of social-issue documentary conveners and funders. In 2004, Ebay's billionaire co-founder, Jeff Skoll, created Participant Media, a film company with a "double bottom line"—committed to measurable positive social impact alongside profit.[33] To date, as an exemplar financial investor in socially engaged documentary storytelling, Participant has funded, produced, and distributed dozens of influential movies, with a list that includes the Academy Award–winning films *An Inconvenient Truth*, *The Cove*, and *CitizenFour*; the Academy Award–nominated *Food, Inc.*, and *Countdown to Zero*; and more than 50 additional titles in the nonfiction category. The company's documentary expertise is led by chief content officer Diane Weyermann, whose professional origins are notably rooted in human rights and philanthropy. In 1996, she founded the original Open Society Institute documentary film fund, which became the field-leader Sundance Documentary Film Program in 2002; Wyermann, who directed the Sundance program until 2005, launched many of the organization's long-standing programs for nonfiction storytellers.[34] Her philosophy, as expressed in a media interview, centers on the integrity of artistic practice:

We do have a specific mission, which is social change, social impact, some way of engaging an audience around the stories. That is the aim of the company, and that's really why it was established by Jeff Skoll 15 years ago. . . . To me, the way to be effective is to actually make great films, and have great stories, and great characters. I think that has the best chance of having some greater kind of impact rather than going at it the other way around, which is you're issue driven, you're impact driven—that immediately puts you into this category of, "I think I know what that kind of film is," and that's not how we approach the stories we tell.[35]

Alongside the company's expert curation and financial investment in documentary film, Participant's chief impact officer, Holly Gordon, emphasizes community partnerships to foster positive social progress:

"How do we take every opportunity we have with this extraordinary content that—because of the commitment of a distributor—will receive millions of dollars of support from just an awareness-building perspective, and transition that to create the most change we possibly can with that piece of content? Normally, that happens with partners. How can we build robust, deeply and mutually rewarding partnerships and collaborations with the organizations and individuals that have devoted their lives to making change on the issues that our films touch on? Participant never acts alone."[36]

In the late 1990s, another tech billionaire, Microsoft co-founder Paul G. Allen, founded Clear Blue Sky Productions, which later rebranded as Vulcan Productions,[37] a film company co-founded by Allen's sister, Jody Allen, that aims to intentionally create social change through its films distributed theatrically, on TV, and online. The company's Peabody and Emmy Award–winning documentaries, including the Netflix film *Chasing Coral*, have tackled pandemics, mental health, economic inequality, climate change, and more.[38] Both Participant Media and Vulcan Productions maintain active social-impact divisions that endeavor to drive public engagement with their documentary stories.

Impact Partners, a documentary financing company, invests in nonfiction films that "participate in social or civic dialogue,"[39] according to executive director and co-founder Dan Cogan. The company launched in 2007 in response to a hopeful cultural moment, and yet, a declining sense of confidence in the formal electoral political system as a mechanism for change—in Cogan's words, fueled by a perspective about "the value of documentaries to raise awareness to inspire social change and mobilize community around issues people care about," working within a network of philanthropy and distributors to ensure the widest possible audience for critical films. And documentary production companies like Kartemquin Films and Chicken & Egg Pictures, which produce intimate social-issue documentary films act as mentors, training grounds, and supporters for new and diverse storytellers.

Beyond organizations devoted to nonfiction storytelling, physical space for professional community building is central to the rise of civic practice empowered by documentary—and to continued development of the nonfiction field in general. Film festivals and large-scale documentary gatherings play a foundational organizing, field-building, and training function for an ever-growing network of philanthropies, filmmakers, and grassroots engagement strategists working at the intersection of nonfiction storytelling and social change. Although film festivals have evolved since the 1980s to become increasingly active players in the film industry—not just a place for exhibition—the increasingly central convening and training role has moved in tandem with the evolution of the digital age, and "since [the] mid-2000s festivals have moved increasingly into various segments of training and funding of all stages of film production and distribution,"[40] wrote scholar Skadi Loist.

For instance, the Sundance Film Festival, long an important hub for independent storytellers, provides a gathering place for documentary teams, social justice organizations, and professional development, with workshops and self-organized convenings by filmmakers and teams devoted to activism engaged by stories. The International Documentary Festival Amsterdam (IDFA), the world's largest nonfiction film festival, has been the backdrop for several gatherings of documentary-centered community engagement practitioners—the Global Impact Producers Assembly facilitated by Doc Society—congregating more than 100 like-minded professionals spanning the globe.[41]

AFI DOCS, the documentary film festival directed by the American Film Institute (AFI), invites documentary film teams to Washington, DC, to participate in its AFI DOCS Impact Lab, an immersive training program that helps develop documentary-based civic engagement campaigns, including policy efforts on the federal and local levels.[42] In 2014, the International Documentary Association (IDA), the leading global membership organization for nonfiction storytelling professionals, premiered its inaugural Getting Real conference. Just four years later in 2018, the biennial gathering convened more than 1,000 documentary filmmakers and organizations from 20 countries around the world to build community with panels, workshops, and discussions designed to shape and position documentary storytelling and civic practice, alongside other topics.[43] In Europe, the Moving Docs collaborative brings together filmmakers, distributors, and civil society from 20 countries in the European Union, who connect their shared interests in artistic production, social justice, and audience engagement.[44]

Within the past two decades, the leaders and organizations highlighted here—and others—have thus seized the possibility for empowering social justice with the help of intimate nonfiction storytelling, and they have created the infrastructure for a contemporary field that builds on the legacy established in the analog media days. Because they are close to the people and storytellers working on the ground in communities around the world, the leaders of these institutional enablers are also knowledge centers, subject-matter experts, thought-leaders, and connectors—central players who collaborate to develop local and international professional communities. They work alongside, and help to empower, the community and impact engagement strategists who leverage documentary films to engage publics in meaningful ways—to raise awareness, shift public understanding of people and problems, and build community strength and civic power.

The Community and Impact Engagement Strategists

With tactical skillsets that include strategic communication, grassroots organizing, and digital strategy, entrepreneurs from the worlds of public media, film production, communication, and political organizing have coalesced to create contemporary public engagement practices centered around documentaries. These are the community and impact engagement strategists of the documentary field—the professionals who leverage nonfiction stories to promote public dialogue and fuel positive change. Within the networked era, a new label emerged in 2012 to codify this kind of work: the "impact producer."[45] The "impact producer" moniker, building an intentional network and community of practice, was established first from a series of global convenings that began that year, facilitated by the UK-based nonprofit organization Doc Society, founded in 2005 as BRITDOC by three veterans of the UK's Channel Four—Jess Search, Beadi Finzi, and Maxyne Franklin.

Working alongside nonfiction filmmakers, impact producers design and implement intentional audience-engagement strategies customized to the social issues and impact objectives of the films—strategies that can range from legislative advocacy to in-school screenings. According to Jennifer MacArthur, a pioneering impact producer, the job requires a research-based understanding of a social issue and its potential levers for change, as well as an acute prowess in film distribution and marketing, as she wrote for *POV*'s blog: "The job of an impact producer is one part sociologist, one part behavioral psychologist, one part historian, one part activist, one part publicist, one part fundraiser, one part program evaluator."[46] With global convenings and networking opportunities—including Getting Real hosted by the International Documentary Association, the Global Impact Producers Assembly hosted by Doc Society, and other film-festival gatherings—and a growing library of case studies and resources, the job and function of impact producers is evolving as a global community of practice. The network of documentary engagement strategists continues to expand.

Intentional civic practice and participation fueled by documentary stories is a legacy activity established in the analog age, even as the contemporary central groups and leaders are products of the post-millennial years. Documentary-centered community and engagement strategists, whether or not they reference themselves with the precise "impact producer" label, are positioned in the social-change professional ecosystem in several ways. First, they operate as stand-alone nonprofit organizations or for-profit consulting groups, like Working Films, Active Voice, Picture Motion, Peace Is Loud, and

Film Sprout, which work on individual documentaries or larger film-based initiatives. Engagement strategists operate also as specialized teams that emerged from larger organizations, like Firelight Media's Partnerships and Engagement team, ITVS's Engagement and Impact division, and POV Engage, which foster community engagement and screenings with independent public broadcasting documentaries, or Participant Media and Vulcan Productions' in-house social impact departments. And many documentary-focused engagement professionals are also solo practitioners for hire by film teams.

The foundation of this work can be traced to screening documentary films for the audiences and organizations likely to be most affected by them—the individuals and communities featured on screen. As legacies of participatory community-based storytelling, groups like Active Voice and Working Films (along with groups like New Day Films) are among the progenitors whose principles and foundations continue to reverberate in public engagement strategies for documentaries. In 1993, as executive producer of the PBS independent documentary series POV, Ellen Schneider held what is now known widely in the documentary field as a "braintrust screening," bringing together eight leading HIV organizations to watch the Sundance award–winning documentary *Silverlake Life: The View from Here*.[47] Groundbreaking at the time, the film depicts the love and devotion of a gay couple and their daily experiences living with AIDS. Schneider knew HIV-focused groups would be able to leverage a powerful public-awareness and community-building moment from the film's PBS broadcast:

> That was the first time I went to leaders and said let's do this together. The response was fantastic. Even though the film was so challenging and complicated and personal, and there was no data in it, there was no call to action, it really inspired a lot of creativity and resourcefulness on the part of these national organizations. That's when I realized this really deserved a strategy—not just encouragement, not just random invitations to do something interesting. The power of this work had so much potential, and it could be so powerful and effective in the hands of people who are dealing with these issues every day. This felt like the beginning of what public television and individual artists could bring together for everyone.[48]

Expanding the learnings into other documentary initiatives—including Kartemquin Films' *The New Americans*, a seven-hour series focused on immigrant and refugee experiences, and the *Television Race Initiative* about race relations—Schneider developed a documentary public engagement framework in the late 1990s that positions community screenings at the authentic heart of the work. She launched her consultancy as Active Voice in 2000, working with independent documentaries to develop public engagement strategies and grassroots screenings, noting the need for deep listening within communities: "We wanted those films to be the entry point for a much deeper conversation for what democracy can be like when people can learn, advocate, and are responsible for each other."[49] The legacy of community and brain trust screenings, along with strategic NGO partnerships, continues in today's engagement work across the network of strategists, in public media and well beyond.

Similarly, Working Films' contemporary public engagement work began with a documentary film—*The Uprising of 34*, a 1995 documentary directed by George Stoney and produced by his protégé, filmmaker Judith Helfand. The film tells the story of North Carolina textile workers on strike in 1934, an exposé of unions and power and stigma so sensitive that the participants had never shared their stories until they relayed them on screen more than 50 years later.[50] Stoney and Helfand screened the film-in-progress to the community and the on-screen subjects, leveraging their responses and ideas to shape a nationwide public engagement strategy to raise conversations about labor and power in similar places.[51] The model of bringing the film to communities, with discussion materials to deepen conversations, led to the launch of Working Films in 1999 by co-founders Judith Helfand and the late film festival director Robert West. As Helfand recalled about the organization's genesis: "We were filmmakers who understood movement building and how to link films to movements."[52]

Evolving and reinventing through the present day, Working Films today (see Figure 4.1) is one of the leading nonprofit groups that engages with organizational partners and communities to implement social change strategy, leveraging documentaries "to advance social justice and environmental protection."[53] Molly Murphy, Working Films' co-director, positions the mobilizing function of documentaries as a long-term mechanism to strengthen community power and civic efficacy:

> Documentaries are unique in being able to bring people and organizations together who might otherwise be in silos. You can't do it around a lecture. . . . It's about cultivating community in a lot of ways, including grassroots groups forming among the audience, or a coalition forming because organizations have come together for the first time.[54]

Working Films' core strategy is to curate documentaries on a single topical theme and then develop partnerships with neighborhoods and organizations to spark public involvement in community problems, according

Figure 4.1. Working Films and its local partners participate in a 2017 community engagement event and screening of the documentary *Democracy for Sale*, with Gene Nichol, Tracy Deyton, Zach Galifianakis, director Lucian Read, and Tracy Edwards, in North Wilkesboro, North Carolina. Photo by Jimmy Davidson, courtesy of Appalachian Voices.

to Murphy: "We are not just resourcing individual organizations, but our focus on partnerships and building groups together who might not otherwise work together is key."[55] For example, in 2015, Working Films led a campaign to raise awareness and spark public involvement in fracking and toxic water contamination in North Carolina, curating a collection of short documentary films under a campaign brand, "Fracking Stories," and convening social justice and environmental groups to rally North Carolinians to get involved in the state regulatory process.[56] Working Films has expanded to become a financial supporter of social-justice documentaries, training resource for new nonfiction filmmakers, social-change strategy consultant for individual films, and community mobilizer engaged in local challenges.

The roster of documentary-centered impact and community engagement strategists also includes consulting firms like Picture Motion and Film Sprout, both established within the streaming, social-media era as groups available for hire by documentary film teams and media organizations.[57] Between them, the two agencies, which merged in 2019, have developed and implemented grassroots and public engagement campaigns for hundreds of award-winning social-issue documentary films, including *Roll Red Roll, The Hunting Ground, Trapped, The Invisible War, Vessel, Audrie & Daisy, Sonic Sea, Whose Streets?, Unrest, 13th, An Inconvenient Sequel, Food Chains, American Promise*, and more. Film Sprout's president, Caitlin Boyle, views documentary films, because they are "communal and immersive," as grassroots organizing work that can bring together diverse constituencies:

> We see the ways in which that gathering force that films have put the pressure on and lentsome urgency to things that might otherwise feel overwhelming for people. . . . A film we worked on in 2014 was called *Vessel*, and many of the groups that hosted that film were state-based abortion groups, so they collect money to help women who can't afford abortion to pay for them. They raised so much money to help support those women . . . That concrete civic and social activity that's really individualized happens very powerfully. You can count it and you can see it in real time. It happens right away, and it's quantifiable. More broadly, there's probably something else happening that's more ambient and hard to quantify, which is a more informed public, coalition building, cross-sector collaboration..[58]

As a nonprofit consultancy, the documentary engagement group Peace Is Loud launched organically from Fork Films' documentary, *Pray the Devil Back to Hell*, a 2008 film directed by Gini Reticker and produced by Abigail Disney that illuminates the role of women's leadership in conflict resolution and peace-building. Evolving from the global community engagement work of Fork Films' first documentary, Peace Is Loud is now a stand-alone organization that works with documentary production teams to design and implement community organizing and engagement campaigns with nonprofit stories at the center. As one recent example, the team worked with director Kirby Dick's 2018 independent documentary, *The Bleeding Edge*, which sparked an online outcry about invasive medical devices and safety regulation; one week before the film's release on Netflix, a major medical device manufacturer pulled a product from the marketplace after scathing media attention.[59] According to executive director Jamie Dobie, Peace Is Loud's public engagement campaigns are designed to further ongoing efforts for change: "When we take on a film, we take it on within a movement."[60] Based on the organization's guiding principles, positioning documentaries within movements already in play—and leveraging films' emotional resonance, monitorial function, and convening power—lends story-based tools that may be missing within existing efforts for justice.

To invite audiences into civic dialogue, documentary-centered community engagement also takes place within production organizations and public media. For these operations—such as Firelight Media, POV Engage, and the ITVS Engagement and Impact team—each documentary film produced, funded, or distributed by their parent organizations is designed for an active life both in the entertainment marketplace and at the community level. Sparking public dialogue and mobilizing audiences for active involvement is part of each film, facilitated through in-house engagement teams.

As one exemplar, years after its community screenings with *The Murder of Emmett Till*, Firelight Media's work has evolved to include grassroots engagement campaigns centered around Stanley Nelson's documentaries about the African American experience, a learning and mentoring mechanism for documentary filmmakers of color through its Firelight Documentary Lab, and an incubation lab for impact producers through the Firelight Impact Producer Fellowship.[61] Notably, Firelight's Impact Producera Fellowship, a mentorship and training program for impact producers of color (see Figure 4.2), takes a unique perspective: Its cohorts, according to Sonya Childress, who directs Firelight's Impact Producers Fellowship and community engagement programs, "represent three groups—traditional documentary producers

Figure 4.2. Firelight Media Documentary Lab and Impact Producer Lab fellows, staff, and mentors at the 2018 fellowship convening. Photo by Chandler Cadet, courtesy of Firelight Media.

looking to gain impact-producing skills, cultural strategists or impact producers looking to strengthen their skills set and raise their visibility in the
field, and full-time staff at social justice organizations looking to integrate
nonfiction film into their organizing or narrative shift work."[62] In addition
to bolstering social-change skills for filmmaker teams, by training professionals who already work full-time inside social justice or communication
organizations—such as the NAACP Legal and Educational Defense Fund,
for example—the skillsets of documentary-centered engagement strategists
migrate into professional environments beyond film, thus increasing the network dramatically. Childress describes Firelight's composite training and
mentorships as instrumental to creating "an ecosystem of storytellers, producers and impact producers who are committed to telling stories about diverse
communities, and reaching and engaging communities of color."[63] Further,
she states:

> We see our work [at Firelight] as doing three things: we produce films about under-
> represented communities or moments in American history and we center the ex-
> periences of people of color—primarily African Americans—we build up the voices
> of documentary filmmakers of color so that we can encourage more stories about
> these experiences and build the careers of these diverse filmmakers, but we also
> serve audiences of color. . . . It falls into our mission to bring these diverse stories
> about communities of color *to* communities of color. We know narratives about
> people of color directly impact their lived experiences. If we don't interrupt nega-
> tive narratives, narrow narratives, it has a direct impact on communities of color—
> how they are seen, how policies are created for them or about them[64]

With grassroots campaigns around PBS-broadcast documentary films like
The Black Panthers: Vanguard of a Revolution, Freedom Riders, and *Freedom
Summer*, Firelight's engagement work, embedded deeply in grassroots
screenings and partnerships, serves as a vital connection between history and
contemporary movements for justice and equity. As Childress explains:

> We use historical documentaries to put contemporary issues into historical con-
> text, and usually to connect contemporary organizing with its historical precedent.
> We like to place contemporary organizing on a continuum and use our films to
> show there has been a long history of resistance and agency around these same
> issues, by communities of color. Our films are often used as blueprints for contem-
> porary organizers, and young organizers in particular, many of who are learning
> about civil rights through our films in many cases. Because they showed successful
> organizing strategies, our films are often used as a blueprint for activism.[65]

In the sum of the parts, the efforts are deeply connected—Firelight's films and community engagement campaigns, and its training and mentorship programs for documentary filmmakers and impact producers of color—as a steady mechanism to empower communities and storytellers who have been historically marginalized and harmed by dominant cultural and media narratives. In so doing, they are asserting full cultural citizenship, fueled by stories.

A final category of documentary-centered public engagement is found within public media, where engaging diverse communities through storytelling is a core mission. As the legacy of public media's long-standing mandate and commitment to foster civic dialogue, the internal POV Engage and ITVS Engagement and Impact teams work to ensure that independently produced PBS documentaries reach deep into neighborhoods, cities, and towns, both urban and rural. Throughout the TV seasons for both the *Independent Lens* and *POV* documentary series, which together distribute about 50 total films each year, the in-house engagement teams work with hundreds of local partners across the country to facilitate free grassroots screenings—more than 1,000 per year—in public spaces that include libraries, churches, jails, community centers, and schools. Justine Nagan, executive director of American Documentary, Inc., the nonprofit organization that produces the *POV* series, positions intimate, human-centered nonfiction narratives as civic connectors:

> I think meaningful dialogue [in response to watching a documentary] can happen online and it can also happen in person. . . . Any opportunity we have right now to connect with people that's not divisive is meaningful. As our news is getting more and more fed to us and narrowed and we are more siloed, and it's served up by algorithm, having a documentary, particularly in public spaces, means you can have an unexpected connection with another human or neighbor or citizen. Those moments aren't common anymore.[66]

The community engagement efforts that originate within public media are not leveraged for political social activism, but the practice is shaped from public media's role in showcasing a diversity of lives and perspectives—designed to spark meaningful public conversation.[67] In so doing, through independent nonfiction stories told from community perspectives, audiences experience complex, nuanced ways of looking at their world and discussing it with the people around them.

Community and engagement strategists customize their efforts for each documentary, but most employ a mix of strategic communication and grassroots organizing work, bringing films directly into local spaces—from schools to policymaker offices to libraries and beyond—and engaging with aligned partnership organizations. Unlike traditional film promotion, the objective is not only media coverage and visibility, but a deeper penetration into the cultural conversation and engagement with people who are impacted by the issue illuminated by a film—or those in a position to help. The objectives can vary—from strengthening movement-based groups on a national level or motivating local dialogue and civic participation—but at the core, documentary engagement strategists create community around nonfiction stories. They work to increase the public visibility of social issues and lived realities through documentary films, cultivating media attention and grassroots engagement through social media and digital platforms, and in physical spaces. In so doing, they strengthen coalitions and communities over time as they empower organizations with the ability to position nonfiction stories at the heart of social-change efforts.

Critical Reflections

In a variety of professional environments, the landscape of civic connectors and engagement strategists who merge community with documentary storytelling continues to expand. They have formed a professional field, forging global and local connections, sharing best practices and new ideas. In this way, the work unfolds with each new player and story.

Critical reflections remain important to interrogate, both in the present day and over time. On the one hand, while the values of public interest motivation and justice are embedded within the missions of civic connectors and enablers—such as foundations and production groups—it is also a professional network that wields enormous power as a collective of gatekeepers and decision makers. Maintaining an awareness of this power, and continuing to listen to makers and organizers from the ground up, is crucial to ensuring that the network remains open, flexible, and expansive. Art and creativity must remain central rather than supporting didactic activism dressed up like a documentary.

Similarly, maintaining the ethics and rigor of public engagement practices is vitally important. Professionals who endeavor to mobilize communities around documentary films must remain responsible for, and accountable to, the people with whom they collaborate. As many impact producers and organizational leaders reflect, engaging communities thoughtfully and responsibly—that is, collaborating in such a way that affords decision-making power to local and partnering organizations around film screenings and public discussions—is not the same function as marketing, which serves to attract eyeballs or sell tickets. Groups like Working Films and others, along-side many documentary filmmakers, have taken a leadership position against what they call "extractive" storytelling and public engagement work, which seeks to exploit narratives and community solidarity to serve film projects; instead, Working Films advocates for and participates in field discussions around "accountable" practices.[68] Conscious team-building with organiza-tions, articulating shared values, and finding mutually beneficial ways to lev-erage documentaries with civil society groups and communities are essential practices and norms, honed in convenings and trainings.

Civic engagement work around "impact" also suffers when the work is de-signed in ways that are surface-level, naïve or purely transactional, focused on quick and simple "metrics of impact" like views and shares—or envisioning change in complex social challenges as quick opportunities to simply sign a pledge, for example. In 2012, the short-form advocacy documentary *Kony 2012*, which went viral, was the recipient of scathing criticism from the public and human rights activists, not only about its facts and framing,[69] but for its reductionist approach to imploring the public to foster social change in Ugandan human rights by spreading the word or purchasing an "action kit" that included merchandise.[70] As this chapter's opening *Bully* story illustrates, youth bullying was not "solved" even if the imprint of the documentary's ex-pansive, long-standing public engagement work is meaningful and ongoing. Engagement strategists who work in a thoughtful, customized fashion must be skilled in the deeply human enterprise of building effective collaborations with organizations who bring different areas of expertise and talent to the coa-lition table. As scholar Bill Nichols asserted, "Even great, powerful social issue documentaries do not alter dominant ideologies or bolster alternative ones in a direct, measurable, lockstep way—although they may well contribute to changing how we see and understand an issue."[71] Indeed, while social prog-ress is a journey, and often a long, complicated one, documentaries can play a valuable role in mobilizing communities to think about, or perhaps even involve themselves in, complex human quandaries through this approach to ongoing, meaningful cultural work.

The vibrancy of social-issue documentary storytellers, civil society, and grassroots organizers working together is a living, breathing, morphing prac-tice and network of passionately engaged professionals who embrace the motivating potential of intimate true stories that invite us into the human experience. Fostering public engagement and even intentional social change is not, however, the goal or desire of every documentary maker who creates a story about how lives are lived; indeed, the intent of this chapter is not to propose that this is, or should be, the case. Above all, documentary films should do what they do best—paint portraits and weave tales that are rich, creative, artistic expressions of reality, entertaining and engaging audiences. But for those who *do* endeavor to expand social justice through nonfiction storytelling, a global network of like-minded thinkers and doers is alive and available in unprecedented fashion.

Documentary and public engagement practices also unfold within a constellation of tremendous challenges and constraints, as has historically been true of artistic or journalistic efforts to expand equity through activating the will of the people. The obstacles are myriad: Threats and dangers to documentarians are real—physical and legal. Free expression in the United States and many corners of the world is often a threat to governments and corporate bodies; shutting down the voices of artists and people is an ongoing pursuit by individuals and institutions with power. These are perennial quandaries to be debated and processed by the leaders and new voices who will evolve the art and practice. Despite the challenges, if history is any indicator, the possibilities for social progress in the digital, networked century will undoubtedly continue to be irresistible to those who endeavor to spark public conversation and fuel change through documentaries.

For sure, we had the facts on our side. Everything we were saying was
air-tight, without a doubt. . . . Clearly, if an 80-minute documentary
can cause that much rage from a multi-billion-dollar, 50-year industry,
we were something to be taken seriously. Clearly, we had poked the
dragon.

— **Gabriela Cowperthwaite**
Director, *Blackfish*[1]

5

Mobilizing for Change

Inside the *Blackfish* Effect

In January 2013, in a packed theater on a Saturday night, *Blackfish* premiered at the Sundance Film Festival.[2] Against the heart-thumping backdrop
of a dramatic musical score, with images of orcas bearing the sagging fins
characteristic of captivity,[3] the independent documentary tells the story of
Tilikum, a 12,000-pound orca living in a tank at SeaWorld, the billion-dollar
aquatic theme park and zoological organization. Through director Gabriela
Cowperthwaite's lens, an emotional portrait emerges: Tilikum, captive for
decades, had "killed several people while in captivity," according to the film's
synopsis.[4] Unspooling the tale of Tilikum's life, *Blackfish* personifies him as
a star character, complete with the tragic back story of his capture and sepa-
ration from his family. Quips a reporter in a clip from the film: "If you were
in a bathtub for 25 years, don't you think you get a little irritated, aggravated,
maybe a little psychotic?"[5]

Story Movements. Caty Borum Chattoo, Oxford University Press (2020) © Oxford University Press.
DOI: 10.1093/oso/9780190943417.001.0001

In a 2013 interview, Cowperthwaite, who produced the film with Manuel Oteyza, described her motivation to make the documentary: As a mother who had taken her children to SeaWorld, she found herself confused about the park and its public narrative. Was there more to discover? As she put it in a press interview, "Why would America's lovable Shamu turn against us? How could our entire collective childhood memories of this delightful water park be so morbidly wrong?"[6] Digging deeper, her perspective changed from curiosity to a firm belief in Tilikum's sorrowful story:

> Two years after I wrote the treatment in 2010 we finished "Blackfish." I can say that my crew and I are all profoundly changed by the experience. I know that killer whales are not suitable for captivity. I am dedicated to spreading the word. The early deaths, the grieving, the boredom, the daily fighting and the attacks—what we learned over two years is impossible to shake. Once you see it, you can't unsee it. My hope is that we take the "Blackfish" momentum and use it to help evolve us out of animals for entertainment. These silly marine park tricks are of no social, educational or conservational value. We advocate, instead, for captive killer whales to be retired into sea sanctuaries where they can live out the rest of their lives in a dignified, sustainable manner.[7]

While Cowperthwaite consistently advocated against closing SeaWorld's doors given the company's financial resources to help marine animals in other ways, her perspective about releasing orcas and ending their labor as performers was clear (Figure 5.1). Her film is unequivocal in its editorial stance: Tilikum should not have been captured in the first place, and, as she notes, "I was hoping they [Seaworld] would be forced to understand that there's a better version of educating the world about animals that involves sanctuaries. . . . So I was truly trying to bring everybody onto the same team."[8]

From the earliest reviews, the media narrative around *Blackfish* was generally consistent. Two days after the Sundance premiere, the *Hollywood Reporter* called the film "emotionally devastating" and "a shattering reality," noting: "For anyone who has ever questioned the humaneness of keeping wild animals in captivity and training them to perform tricks for food, this will be trenchant, often harrowing stuff. Perhaps even more so for those who have never considered the issue."[9] Similar stories followed as *Blackfish* departed the film industry cocoon of the Sundance Film Festival and opened in theaters across the country in the summer of 2013, on CNN in October, and on Netflix in December of that year. Steadily, signs of the film's impact appeared on the cultural scene. High-profile musical performers cancelled shows at SeaWorld, publicly citing the issues raised by *Blackfish*.[10] A California state lawmaker proposed unprecedented new legislation to ban state aquatic

Figure 5.1. Cinematographer Chris Towey and director Gabriela Cowperthwaite filming *Blackfish*. Photo courtesy of Gabriela Cowperthwaite.

parks from featuring orcas.[11] By 2014, SeaWorld's stock price plummeted[12] and public attendance declined.[13] In the same year, Southwest Airlines and Virgin America, two of the park's major corporate sponsors, ended their long-standing relationships with the company.[14] In 2015, net second-quarter income had dropped by 84 percent.[15]

Finally, in March 2016, the coup de grâce landed. SeaWorld made a stunning announcement: After more than 30 years and millions of dollars in revenue, its captive orca shows would come to an end.[16] In an interview after the SeaWorld statement, Cowperthwaite responded to the news:

> Breeding of orcas is at the epicenter of their entire culture and more importantly, their business model. And they chose to do away with it. So I believe this is a total game changer. . . . I hope this is the first announcement of many. And that this is a portal of entry into future conversations. But for now, I think it's important to acknowledge this pivotal shift they've made. The idea that we just got closer to caring about the same things, speaking the same language, is pretty massive progress.[17]

Over a three-year span of time, from the 2013 Sundance Film Festival premiere to TV and streaming debuts to the 2016 SeaWorld announcement, the cacophonous public battle—that is, unrelenting social media chatter, organized and organic activism from animal rights groups and the public, a consistently negative media portrait of the public relations skirmish, and reports of company trouble—came to be known as an environmental justice movement and final outcome labeled "the *Blackfish* Effect."[18]

This chapter considers a single question, leveraging the story of *Blackfish* as extended analysis: What factors explain the *Blackfish* Effect, and what can the story reveal about the role of documentaries in social change? Positioning *Blackfish* within the context of contemporary networked activism offers a lens to consider how a nonfiction story can capture attention and fuel grassroots public engagement. As this chapter illuminates, social change is aided by documentary storytelling through several elements: narrative persuasion and the role of emotion, amplified community from online and offline activism, cultivated media narrative, strategic layered distribution, and a call to action embedded in the storytelling. While this schema is not the only way to contemplate social change with documentary storytelling at the fore, and it doesn't mean to imply only one way to compel public participation, it's offered here as a strategic model. Analysis of *Blackfish* as a cultural phenomenon illuminates a central concept: The emotional lens of an investigative nonfiction story, combined with planned and organic public engagement and activism, sparked news coverage and shaped a consistent media narrative through every distribution stop in the film's life cycle.

Narrative Persuasion and the Role of Emotion

From the first moment audiences meet Tilikum on screen, the emotional resonance of his life tale is unmistakable. To open his story, *Blackfish* reveals Tilikum's capture at sea in the early 1980s, rendered visually and recalled by on-screen subjects as a violent tragedy. The process of separating the young orcas from their families was "just like kidnapping a little kid away from his mother" in the eyes of John Crowe, the hired fisherman who captured Tilikum, who recalls crying as he did his work that day.[19] On screen, Crowe says, "The worst thing that I've ever done is hunt that whale."[20] Following Tilikum's abduction, the film interprets a portrait of his life in captivity—reflecting on a small tank not suitable for such a huge creature. Through the lens of *Blackfish*, Tilikum is envisioned as a pitiable victim with almost human-like characteristics and feelings and mental health challenges—a character doomed to claustrophobically swim laps in a pool for years on end.

The emotional influence of storytelling is on clear display in *Blackfish*, and the impact of the narrative is a dominant centerpiece of the documentary's inciting power. Stories are distinct from other mechanisms of communication; generally speaking, they have a beginning, middle, and end, and they speak to audiences through emotions and the experiences of characters, rather than through a non-narratively orchestrated collection of facts and information. As sociologist Francesca Polletta asserted: "All stories have characters and a point of view or points of view from which the events in the story are experienced. Characters need not be human or even living. But we expect to experience the moral of the story through characters' fates."[21] Narratives influence audiences through their emotional experiences with characters and plots and situations. Stories are thus capable of "providing a deeper understanding than logical explanations or non-narrative accounts."[22]

Why and how are people so influenced by narratives? Narrative persuasion is a well-developed body of research with insights about how stories impact audiences. According to the theory of narrative transportation, when audiences are deeply immersed in a story, they can be absorbed into the story world, even forgetting their surroundings.[23] Through this immersion, viewers' cognitive defenses to persuasive messages are down,[24] which in turn can shift knowledge, attitudes, and even behaviors.[25] But audiences also are influenced by narratives as they identify with a story's characters.[26] As they experience stories, transported into story worlds and connecting empathetically with the on-screen characters, audiences can thus be temporarily transformed and impacted, even moved to take some kind of action. Existing documentary research, including my own, bears this out: Documentary storytelling can be persuasive in part because of narrative transportation and a powerful emotional response from the audience,[27] and also due to the power of a documentary's perceived realism as a true story.[28] The entertainment value of a story also matters when it comes to engaging audiences.[29] In other words, stories are not synonymous with mere transfer of information.

Through the testimonials and perspectives shared by audiences on social media channels, along with news stories' consistent references to the emotion and sadness of Tilikum's story, it's safe to say that *Blackfish* evoked emotion. This is meaningful, in addition to the persuasive characteristics of stories. Affect and empathy comprise an emotional response that is an evidence-based driver of motivated action, according to psychologist Paul Slovic.[30] Further, *Blackfish* focused on a specific named orca as the key character, a deliberate narrative choice made by the filmmaker.[31] The director did not rely on statistics about the scale of animals and orcas in captivity to tell the story, even though she worked with scientists to craft it[32]—a meaningful decision that aided in the film's ability to spark compassion and action. Instead, as Cowperthwaite reflects:

I feel the visuals [on screen] speak so strongly. . . .A bunch of facts and percentages about how many animals die in captivity can have an effect on *some* people, but I do believe that a story is more persuasive and can hit a bigger audience. . . . The moment you see yourself, you find your place in that story—you find your footing.[33]

Research shows that human apathy is a more likely outcome when large numbers and statistics are used to present a scenario of suffering or tragedy. But the opposite occurs with a story focused on an identified individual—compassion and a desire to take some kind of action increases when people experience an individual story.[34] Although research in the area of emotion and compassionate decision making focuses primarily on human victims of suffering, according to Slovic, "When it comes to eliciting compassion, the identified individual victim, with a face and a name, has no peer. . . . But the face need not even be human to motivate powerful intervention."[35]

Storytelling's persuasive characteristics—that is, the ability to spark emotional response through an entertaining composition—along with the framing centered around the tale of an individual character, help to illustrate how and why *Blackfish* evoked such a vocal public and media response, at least from the perspective of the documentary's narrative style itself. Stories move us deeply, and narratives behave differently from constellations of facts and numbers that reveal the scope and scale of a social problem. *Blackfish* was a devastatingly emotional story that focused on a lead subject, Tilikum, who was brought to life almost as a human character, sparking public fury amplified by news media narratives and a vocal group of activists.

Amplified Community: Online and Offline Grassroots Activism

"Collective action is different from individual action, both harder to get going, and once going, harder to stop," wrote Clay Shirky in *Here Comes Everybody: The Power of Organizing Without Organizations*.[36] The statement succinctly describes the groundswell of public pressure inspired by *Blackfish*. Almost from the first moment after its festival premiere, picking up viral steam over the next few years, *Blackfish* inspired the kind of grassroots activism characterized by scholar Manuel Castells as "multimodal"—taking place both online and offline.[37] Media coverage and individual audience members consistently echoed the themes of the film with tweets and Facebook posts—increasingly calling for boycotts of SeaWorld. Hashtags sprang up as megaphones for public criticism in response to the film, from "#DontGoToSeaworld" and "#ThanksButNoTanks" to simply "#Blackfish."[38]

It was not an entirely organic public outcry, nor did director Gabriela Cowperthwaite orchestrate the activism herself, as she notes: "While I was making the film, I didn't engage any animal activists. I did not reach out to them at all, by design, not because they don't have the most valuable things to say on the subject—they actually do—but for the film to be coming from my filmmaker voice, it needed to come from someone who went to SeaWorld and took her kids there."[39] Instead, responding to the documentary as an unprecedented opportunity to engage a broader public using the networked tools of the digital age, leading vocal animal-rights groups shaped and bolstered the targeted mobilization against SeaWorld. In this way, established activist organizations aligned with the public, forming diverse "digitally enabled action networks"—combined forces of civil society organizations and individuals—that exemplify the connective action characteristic of digital activism.[40] Indeed, an existing community of advocates had been campaigning against animal captivity for years. With its inspired swell of media coverage and public outcry, *Blackfish* provided a unique opportunity to position their demands in a broader mainstream. Members of the public and animal-rights organizations created a renewed grassroots movement that revealed itself through physical protests and raised voices in social media. They became an amplified community, united in support of Tilikum's story, calling for change from SeaWorld (see Figure 5.2).

Figure 5.2. Protestors line SeaWorld Drive in San Diego, California, in 2014. Photo by Lindsay Bullis for the *San Diego Reader*, courtesy of Lindsay Bullis.

Contributing its voice to the cause, the Oceanic Preservation Society (OPS), the environmental advocacy organization elevated by the 2009 Academy Award–winning documentary *The Cove*—which scathingly indicted dolphin slaughter in Japan—distributed a supportive online open letter and joined with the filmmakers in a public response to SeaWorld's attack ad against the film.[41] Promoted and shared across social media, OPS called the SeaWorld open letter ad "ludicrous," writing, "No amount of advertising will counter the Blackfish effect."[42] Similarly, the Humane Society of the United States, which had previously raised public awareness about captive orcas—including danger to human trainers—encouraged its followers and constituents to see the film.[43]

But among the various groups that publicly endorsed the film, PETA (People for the Ethical Treatment of Animals) was the dominant player behind the grassroots power of the *Blackfish* movement; the intersection between the film and the organization's activism amplified the ongoing impact dramatically. Expanding its own efforts to target SeaWorld as far back as 1998,[44] PETA launched an aggressive campaign, SeaWorldofHurt.com, to respond to the organic cultural opportunity that opened with the *Blackfish* premiere. PETA's dedicated campaign combined physical protest and digital social action centered around six elements: a campaign website, litigation, direct action (petitions and protests), social media promotion and marketing, corporate pressure (encouraging corporate partner boycotts), and media attention.[45] During the live broadcast of the documentary on CNN in October 2013, the PETA social media team live-tweeted with the hashtags #Blackfish and #BlackfishOnCNN, adding to CNN's own tweets and those of the viewing public; the tweets created a trending topic about *Blackfish* in the United States.[46] After the film's television debut, donations to PETA—formerly on the decline—spiked, enabling the group to finance continued media stunts well after the film's premiere. In 2015, PETA reported a budget of $4.5 million after a deficit of more than $250,000 just two years prior, as well as a 30 percent increase in donations.[47]

With the new public spotlight aimed well beyond the passionate animal welfare community, PETA leveraged the momentum of the film at every possible moment in its marketplace distribution and media cycle. Among its actions during the three *Blackfish* Effect years from 2013 to 2016, PETA organized anti-SeaWorld actions at the 2014 Rose Bowl Parade—covered by major media outlets, including CNN, *Blackfish*'s broadcaster—and financed an ad campaign about orca breeding, an angle covered in the film.[48] PETA's campaign portal, SeaWorldofHurt.com, continued the pressure and momentum, and the public followed—from about 30 visitors per day before the

Blackfish broadcast premiere to more than 1 million in 2015.[49] In the end, wrote scholar Ashli Stokes, "all of PETA's direct-action strategies deployed in the wake of *Blackfish*'s release help capture audience attention and spread the anti-SeaWorld message, making it difficult for the company to use its defensive posture surrounding the orca issue successfully."[50]

Adding to the well-orchestrated, vocal NGO activism that helped coalesce public outrage, celebrities' tweets and support for the film echoed the activist messages and engaged their own fans and followers.[51] Many directly instructed their fans to boycott SeaWorld. For instance, comedian Russell Brand tweeted in 2013: "Do watch 'Black Fish.' Don't go to SeaWorld, a stain upon humanity posing as entertainment. #liftedfromanearlyreviewofmine," and singer Ariana Grande posted: "I highly recommend all of my fans watch #Blackfish and never go to @Seaworld again. Used to love that place. Beyond heartbroken #FreeTilly."[52]

In short, the film wasn't released into a cultural vacuum. It fell into a prime spot with social-change infrastructure ready to leverage a strategic distribution strategy and well-produced documentary story. With audiences fired up and ready to act, professional animal rights groups captured the momentum and provided publics with ways to take action, raise their voices, and directly pressure SeaWorld. Along the way, PETA led the way in successfully generating new media coverage with each protest action and trending hashtag. The multiplying, amplifying factor of celebrity endorsements and public outrage helped the story to reach outside the animal welfare community. It stretched well beyond the choir. The outcry became impossible to ignore or dismiss as niche activism.

Cultivated Media Narrative

As a film selected to premiere at the competitive, prestigious Sundance Film Festival, *Blackfish* was almost guaranteed to receive at least a modicum of attention from news outlets. But media coverage over the course of the three core "*Blackfish* Effect" years was distinct; it evolved steadily away from traditional film reviews and much deeper into the drama-filled story of the ensuing activism and SeaWorld's response, which generated enticing angles with new news value. Media scrutiny was trained on *Blackfish* from its earliest festival premiere and picked up over time as the documentary moved through different distribution phases—but attention intensified as SeaWorld took a defensive public stance.

The film's profile increased as SeaWorld and the filmmakers engaged in a prolonged public relations battle, adding to the media coverage already garnered by PETA's activism and additional visibility from the Oceanic Preservation Society and its devoted followers. News media outlets played a classic media agenda-setting function[53] through their ongoing coverage of *Blackfish* and protests swirling around it, conferring value to the public importance of the film and establishing its cultural significance. Given the news agenda's ability to shape public opinion,[54] the media attention contributed to the public outcry about *Blackfish*. In cyclical fashion, the news stories also reported on the activism that erupted around *Blackfish*, not only the battles between the documentary filmmakers and SeaWorld—or the film itself.

Beyond the sheer volume of media coverage, ranging from opinion-leading news outlets like the *New York Times* and the *Washington Post* to media trade publications, the cultivated media narratives about *Blackfish* first emphasized the emotion of the film's storytelling, and later, as the film captured public consciousness, they advanced a theme of a billion-dollar company publicly attacking a small independent film. As Cowperthwaite recalls, "We didn't have the ability to mobilize as fast as they [Seaworld] did, and we didn't have the money to take out an ad. All we had was trusting that the media would listen to us and turn this into a story. . . . Media saw a little of the David and Goliath baked into that, and so we got our day in court."[55] News coverage focused on the story of the film itself—that is, the emotional narrative of Tilikum—and then the battle with SeaWorld. Neither helped SeaWorld, and both amplified the documentary. Media framing works by emphasizing particularly salient angles—or "frames"—of a public narrative,[56] acting as "a central organizing idea or story line that provides meaning to an unfolding strip of events. . . . The frame suggests what the controversy is about, the essence of the issue."[57] In this case, the media narrative about the documentary evolved into a consistent negative frame for SeaWorld, which echoed in new stories sparked by each fresh report of a cancelled performance act or declining stock price or departing corporate sponsor. The media frames in the *Blackfish* saga were clear and repetitive: This documentary is important, it's emotionally compelling, and it's hurting SeaWorld.

The cultivated media narrative that helped fuel "the *Blackfish* Effect" began in earnest—and sparked a consistent media angle about SeaWorld's fight with the film—in the summer of 2013 as *Blackfish* moved toward its theatrical around the country. With its stark subject line—"a dishonest movie"—SeaWorld's hired public relations firm emailed reporters a treatise with eight key assertions that revealed, according to SeaWorld, the movie's falsehoods: "Although 'Blackfish' is by most accounts a powerful, emotionally-moving piece of advocacy, it is also shamefully dishonest, deliberately misleading, and scientifically inaccurate."[58] The resulting media stories from the likes of the *New York Times,* the *Washington Post, Businessweek*, and media trades like IndieWire, instead of crafting simple reviews of the film, included the public attack from the company, as well as full rebuttals from the filmmakers.[59] The tactic backfired for SeaWorld. In his story for the *New York Times*, reporter Michael Cieply wrote:

> In an unusual pre-emptive strike on the documentary "Blackfish," set for release on Friday in New York and Los Angeles by Magnolia Pictures, SeaWorld Entertainment startled the film world last weekend by sending a detailed critique of the movie to about 50 critics who were presumably about to review it. It was among the first steps in an aggressive public pushback against the film, which makes the case, sometimes with disturbing film, that orca whales in captivity suffer physical and mental distress because of confinement.[60]

Filmmaker Cowperthwaite responded to the SeaWorld attack and published a point-by-point rebuttal on the film's website: " 'For 40 years, they were the message,' she said, referring to SeaWorld. 'I think it's O.K. to let an 80-minute movie' have its moment."[61] The president of *Blackfish*'s distribution company, Magnolia Pictures, praised SeaWorld's emailed attack as helpful publicity for the film: "From a marketing standpoint, this is turning into the gift that keeps on giving. . . . Frankly, I've never seen anything like it."[62] The *Washington Post*, reporting on the film and SeaWorld's PR strategy, illustrated the cultivated media narrative:

> Without getting into the details of the back-and-forth, it's safe to say that SeaWorld comes across as a mite defensive. After all, McDonald's didn't even issue a press release after Morgan Spurlock's "Super Size Me" came out. Sometimes it's best not to call attention to the people who are pointing fingers at you. . . . It's hard to imagine anyone coming out of this movie and not swearing off the next vacation trip to Orlando, San Antonio or San Diego.[63]

Well after the summer theatrical premiere, SeaWorld's PR tactics continued— timed with each phase of the film's distribution, with the next stop at CNN's premiere. In October 2013, after declining an on-camera interview, SeaWorld sent a statement to CNN, calling the film "inaccurate and misleading."[64] CNN published the interview online in the days leading up to the TV broadcast. Simultaneously, the network's news segments aired debates about captive orcas. In December 2013, as the film prepared to stream on Netflix, SeaWorld again targeted the film, this time with an open letter advertisement titled "SeaWorld: The Truth Is in Our Parks and People."[65] Published as paid ads in national publications and in metropolitan newspapers where SeaWorld parks operate—including Orlando, San Diego, and San Antonio—the tactic likely generated more publicity for the Netflix premiere and deepened the cultivated media narrative about the film's emotional impact as media outlets covered the advertising. For example, one story noted: "SeaWorld, of course, calls the movie 'inaccurate' and has responded with a newspaper advertising campaign and an open letter. Unfortunately, SeaWorld's response seems hollow—it hasn't offered a direct refutation to many of the points raised in the film, nor is its letter nearly as emotionally compelling as the footage it seeks to rebuke."[66] Finally, in the early part of 2014, SeaWorld launched a web campaign, "The Truth About Blackfish," calling the documentary "propaganda."[67] Each time SeaWorld released a statement to the public or media, the filmmakers responded with statements of their own, which were tweeted and promoted by activists and the public. News stories published and aired it all.

When all was said and done, although Cowperthwaite offered detailed rebuttals to counter SeaWorld's various point-by-point public statements, her consistent message was straightforward and difficult to dispute—and it was the simple missive that echoed in the words and stories of public dissenters, activists, and news stories: "Killer whales are 100 percent not suitable to captivity."[68] Alongside consistent media narratives about the documentary's wrought emotional impact, the public relations war assuredly supplied an ongoing mechanism to keep the controversy in the news cycle. The cultivated media narratives repeated a steady drumbeat about orcas in captivity, thus amplifying public interest in the film and the expanding, viral activism that surrounded it.

Strategic Layered Distribution

"Dissent may be the engine of change, but without distribution it doesn't get very far at all," wrote scholars Ezra Winton and Jason Garrison on the topic of documentaries that engage social issues.[69] Public engagement with social-issue documentaries can take place more readily when the films can be seen by a wide—and often targeted and niche—constellation of audiences. Strategic, layered distribution across platforms over a period of time is essential for social change fueled by documentaries—and yet, this component is often critically unexamined, even if filmmakers recognize this point. Indeed, as Winton and Garrison stated: "There are many dirty little secrets swishing around the film industry, but the least-glamorous and most academically overlooked one happens to involve the very foundational measure of success the whole structure rests upon. Ask any independent filmmaker, they'll tell you 'it's the distribution, stupid.'"[70]

A key characteristic of independent documentary storytelling is its oft-used dual-distribution approach—both grassroots distribution and marketplace entertainment and news distribution. Distribution opportunities have exploded in the streaming media age. While documentaries about social issues may have had trouble reaching audiences even in the not-distant past,[71] the challenge is mitigated a bit in the era of YouTube, streaming networks, and ever-increasing competitive cable networks. As relayed in a 2017 *Documentary* magazine editorial, "The marketplace is transforming actively and, at times, convulsively, and it is expected to continue to do so for the foreseeable future as technology offers up new modes of content delivery. . . . [T]he rate of change to the global distribution landscape is nothing short of dramatic."[72] For independent documentary filmmakers, a hybrid distribution strategy expands beyond the traditional layering of festival premiere, theatrical screenings, and TV premiere[73]– along with parallel grassroots community screenings—to now include the likes of Netflix, Amazon, iTunes, Apple TV, Hulu, YouTube, and more. Documentaries can now leverage every possible distribution mechanism, positively exploiting new audience enthusiasm for the form—an evolution owed in part to the strong, decades-long nonfiction storytelling commitment from legacy players like PBS and HBO, resulting in a moment in which, as one trade reporter pointed out, "Documentary as a whole isn't just booming. It's bursting all over the media landscape."[74]

Beyond helping to satisfy the financial needs for documentarians who license and sell their films, distribution provides the essential infrastructure for public engagement. Strategic, layered distribution for a social-issue documentary film matters for social change as publicity and vocal viewers trigger news media moments and opportunities for new audiences to engage at different phases in a film's life cycle. Each distribution tier for *Blackfish* stoked public and media interest—and each precise display outlet, from the Sundance Film Festival to theatrical screenings to a CNN premiere to Netflix streaming, was meaningful.

The *Blackfish* foray into the entertainment marketplace began in January 2013 with an optimal debut at the elite Sundance Film Festival, which has become synonymous with documentary filmmaking of the highest caliber. Although it's hardly the only route to audiences and success, Sundance is a signifier of value that directly relates to a documentary's distribution potential. This function extends beyond the Sundance Film Festival to others like the Tribeca Film Festival, Full Frame Film Festival, True/False Film Festival, Telluride Film Festival, SXSW, AFI DOCS, International Documentary

Festival Amsterdam (IDFA), Toronto Film Festival, and others. High-level film festival premieres or screenings confer irrefutable cultural value to documentaries, and they are "critical to distribution contracts and television broadcast slots,"[75] wrote scholar Patricia Aufderheide. Patrick Connolly, vice president of programming at AMC Networks, Sundance TV Global, notably stated that his network licenses documentaries with "film festival pedigree."[76] In other words, distribution deals take place at festivals not only because they build industry and audience buzz but also because elite film festivals serve as cultural validators of competitive documentaries.

Following the Sundance Film Festival premiere, the filmmakers licensed the US rights for *Blackfish* to Magnolia Pictures and CNN Films for theatrical and TV distribution.[77] Like a well-publicized festival premiere, theatrical releases for documentaries help to expand public interest and engagement. As veteran documentary distribution pros Susan Margolin and Jon Reiss wrote in *Documentary* magazine, "There still is no substitute for a theatrical release in terms of creating awareness and value in the marketplace."[78] Opening a documentary film in theaters also is invaluable because of the publicity effect: "Critics, who provide the essential publicity for these works, are more likely to review a theatrical film than a television program," wrote Aufderheide.[79]

For a high-profile movie, or even a smaller one magnified by chatter on social media, theatrical openings generate media stories in communities around the country. In the summer of 2013, when *Blackfish* opened in theaters in Los Angeles and New York, followed by other communities around the country, media outlets published stories—but they also covered the growing movement around the film, along with SeaWorld's attempts to change the public narrative. Theatrical distribution introduced the film to new audiences. Cultural interest in Tilikum's story—and a way to get involved—deepened.

The summer months of 2013 led up to the TV premiere on CNN in October. For *Blackfish*, a premiere as part of CNN Films, the documentary unit of the network, equated to a broad-appeal distribution strategy that exposed the film to a mass audience. At the time, CNN attracted a relatively even-handed ideological audience composition—equal parts conservative, moderate, and liberal.[80] In a media interview, Courtney Sexton, CNN Films' vice president, remarked that the network makes nonfiction film programming decisions based on broad audience appeal: "We have to go into something believing that there is an audience that will come to it, and not just your typical arthouse, New York–L.A. audience. . . . We really are looking to find projects that will resonate in middle America because that's where our brand is, in our channels in homes across the country."[81] CNN Films continued to position *Blackfish* in the cultural mainstream, likely increasing the potential for the activism and public engagement to expand beyond a niche-focused animal-rights audience.

CNN Films' distribution also fired up a synergistic publicity and news media machine across the channel. Not only did CNN use its platform to air news stories about orcas in captivity,[82] but the network also published an interview with a SeaWorld spokesperson the week of the premiere.[83] CNN was rewarded for its marketing strategy with a dramatic ratings victory on the October 23, 2013, premiere date; according to the *New York Times*, "The channel swept the ratings among every group under 55 years old. That meant not only the group that is most often sold to news advertisers, viewers ages 25 to 54, but also the younger age groups used for sales in entertainment programming."[84] Twitter noted more than 68,000 individual tweets about *Blackfish* the night it aired on CNN, reaching 7 million people, amplified by celebrities, activist groups, and news programs.[85] The network continued to keep the story on the agenda for months after the premiere, illustrating multiple sides of the captive-orcas issue,[86] including at least one story that criticized the film's lack of focus on marine conservation in aquatic parks.[87]

As the final move in a multifaceted distribution strategy primed for visibility and public engagement, *Blackfish* was released on Netflix in December 2013. With Netflix's exploding popularity and growth—reaching upward of 44 million subscribers by the time *Blackfish* joined its viewing menu, up from 23 million just two years before[88]—the film was able to engage yet another audience, and a potentially vast one. The final distribution layer enabled *Blackfish* to leverage the considerable buzz already generated by media coverage throughout every distribution phase, amplified by the grassroots promotion of the Netflix viewing opportunity from PETA's SeaWorldofHurt campaign.[89] The case of *Blackfish* potently illustrates the interplay between media attention, audience awareness, and engagement—amplified by activist narratives and actions—afforded in part by strategic, layered distribution. Together, the cultural exchange fueled the potential for social change by keeping a relentless eye on the controversies and debates that bubbled up around the film and SeaWorld's denouncement of it.

Public Call to Action Embedded in the Story

Blackfish did not simply raise awareness about captive orcas. The documentary incited the public to take some form of action—like calling for SeaWorld boycotts, live-tweeting during the CNN broadcast, engaging in physical protest—even though the filmmakers themselves did not explicitly call for it. While some social-issue documentary films are centered within intentional campaigns that encourage public action, often in partnership with civil society organizations, *Blackfish* serves as a reminder that public engagement can take place organically, or, in this case, when it's orchestrated and encouraged by savvy NGOs well-versed in rallying voices. An emotional, well-told mediated story can agitate or inspire the public to act.

This is a well-established idea that originates, at least in part, from Entertainment-Education, a model of entertainment storytelling for social change developed in the late 1960s and early 1970s, continuing today on a global scale.[90] Notably, the original practical and theoretical model for Entertainment-Education took shape from a TV telenovela that organically sparked the public to write letters and take action in response to a moving, empowering storyline.[91] The Entertainment-Education approach to social change through mediated entertainment stories often includes an epilogue that offers a way for viewers to take some kind of action.[92] In parallel, offering a "call to action" is a key component in other forms of social-change and behavior-change communication.[93] The strategic idea is to capitalize on viewers' support immediately after they have been moved by a story.

Social-issue documentary practice has evolved this notion in a practical way for filmmakers who endeavor to cultivate social impact through their stories. According to Diana Barrett and Sheila Leddy, leaders of the Fledgling Fund, a philanthropic organization that supports social-change initiatives centered around documentaries, the organic viewer response to the nonfiction story is matched by an intentional campaign, if it exists.[94] The call-to-action efforts have a better chance of success when the action is clear—and when it is conveyed by the film's story itself, not only the marketing materials around it.[95] In stories with institutional or complex solutions, articulating a meaningful, effective call to action can be challenging, but offering concrete individual ways to get involved in the documentary's core social issue—even in small, incremental fashion—can help inspire audiences in the short term and over time.

In the case of *Blackfish*, although the filmmakers did not explicitly tell the public what to do—and they did not advocate shutting down SeaWorld but instead called for other ways to help captive orcas[96]—the identification of Tilikum's captive home was clearly embedded in the story itself. The audience understood SeaWorld's role, and the film's narrative about orcas in captivity issued a clarion call. The public was moved and motivated to make noise and call for change. And it did, over and over.

Can *Blackfish* claim a tidy causal connection to the reported financial misfortune, public outcry, and the final SeaWorld announcement? Not precisely, but the documentary clearly contributed to the company policy change.[97] The intersection of organic and directed social action, consistent media coverage, and financial woes provided a portrait of the film's impact. The available data emerged steadily, from mid-2014 media reports about SeaWorld's financial trouble[98] to a *Washington Post* analysis later that year, which detailed a steady stock-price decline throughout the film's life cycle.[99] The accessible metrics from a publicly traded company offered encouragement for the grassroots efforts, which fit into a narrative frame that established itself early in favor of *Blackfish*. Each signal of decline, from attendance to stock price, offered a new opportunity for the ongoing Seaworld-*Blackfish* media story to renew itself and keep the issue in the public and journalistic spotlight.

The film is not without critics, however. Notably, although family members of a SeaWorld trainer who died in an accident with Tilikum did not explicitly criticize the film, they did seek to add distance between her story and the documentary. In 2014, they issued a public statement: "The film has brought a great deal of attention to the welfare of animals, and for that we are grateful. However, 'Blackfish' is not Dawn's story. Dawn Brancheau believed in the ethical treatment of animals. . . . Dawn would not have remained a trainer at SeaWorld for 15 years if she felt that the whales were not well cared for."[100] Two former SeaWorld trainers interviewed for the film later said they thought it portrayed a narrow lens and failed to illustrate an even-handed account.[101] Further, one SeaWorld employee featured on screen said her statements were shown selectively and did not represent her perspective.[102]

Regardless, the impact manifested steadily. The documentary's intimate, emotional story about a tragic orca with a name and face and back story played the central role in "the *Blackfish* Effect." But this is not a simple case study about an audience engaged with an emotional film; indeed, the online buzz about *Blackfish* and marine mammals in capacity likely far surpassed actual viewers of the film. As *Fast Company* reported in 2015, more than two years after the film's premiere, "Even if you hadn't heard of *Blackfish*, you likely saw your friends talking about whales on Facebook."[103]

Do all documentary films that interrogate social issues have the opportunity and infrastructure to coalesce visible, relatively fast structural change? No. Should all documentary films endeavor to tell stories in ways that are similar to *Blackfish*? Certainly not. Social change is not a monolithic, tidy process; it manifests as both short-term victories and long-term shifts—a slow flow of progress over time, a composition of many stories working together in concert. Corporate policy shifts do not nearly encompass the full spectrum of possibilities by which social progress reveals itself. In this case, conspicuously missing from the *Blackfish* story is the valuable role of intentional partnerships between civil society organizations and documentaries in social-change efforts; the function played here by PETA and other animal-rights organizations shows the power of the activism infrastructure, even though their campaigns were not embedded within the filmmakers' efforts.

Creatively speaking, documentaries are culturally meaningful due to the vast array of artistic approaches they may take; there is not, nor should there be, one model for evocative nonfiction storytelling or a simplistic goal for audience engagement. Similarly, the experience of empathy, while an acknowledged artifact of evocative nonfiction storytelling, is not a guaranteed or sufficient emotional response that connects unequivocally to the kind of public response that can engender social change. Connecting with characters in nonfiction storytelling is central to the documentary experience, of course, but empathy alone is not sufficient for meaningful change—it is not, in itself, a destination. Solidarity, rather, is built with a sense of shared destiny.[104]

Complexities and nuances notwithstanding, the "*Blackfish* Effect" illustrates the people-powered intersection of intimate, creative nonfiction storytelling and parallel public protest—fueled by a sophisticated activism infrastructure poised and ready to push for change. The documentary likely would not have sparked such grassroots momentum without the purposeful efforts of professional activists who understood how to create and sustain a reinforcing media narrative and torrent of unrelenting pressure, along with ways to engage the public. It's hard to deny the role of *Blackfish* in raising cultural attention about marine animals in captivity and pushing to change their fate in a meaningful way—embodied in the participatory culture's empowerment of grassroots voices who lifted up the story of an imprisoned wild creature.

I grew up in a place that often made the headlines but nothing deeper. What I was seeing from where I stood in Logan County, West Virginia, in the middle of a coal field, was that I lived in one of the most desperate, hopeless places—according to all of the media representation.

— **Elaine McMillion Sheldon**
Director, *Heroin(e)*[1]

6

Humanizing the Headlines

Documentary's Interpretive Framing

For several months in 2014, domestic violence was firmly on the radar of US news media, dominating pundit chatter and headlines for a fleeting cultural moment. Despite its scale, private physical and sexual abuse endured by millions of people, particularly women,[2] is not regular fodder for public attention and dialogue. But that year, at least, domestic violence was in the public eye.

What brought the issue back into the cultural fold was a short video of a professional football player knocking his fiancée unconscious in an elevator, an incident that leaked into public view. The clip went viral, fueling a wave of news and entertainment media attention about pro athletes for several weeks.[3] In the aftermath, the National Football League (NFL) updated its domestic violence policy and disseminated a public response,[4] including a public service campaign, "No More," broadcast during the 2014 season and the Super Bowl.[5] The cultural attention to domestic abuse was thus relegated to the confines of a sports story about professional male athletes.

Story Movements. Caty Borum Chattoo, Oxford University Press (2020) © Oxford University Press.
DOI: 10.1093/oso/9780190943417.001.0001

News frenzy though it was, the celebrity sports framing failed to aim a needed spotlight onto the larger systemic failures facing individuals who live with and survive domestic violence. Focusing narrowly on the incidents of identifiable celebrity domestic violence misses the opportunity to more diligently examine the "social aspects of the issue," such as legislation[6] and the flawed criminal justice system. A similar pattern was evident in the sensationalized media coverage of the 1994 O. J. Simpson case and assertions of long-term private violence inflicted on the retired athlete's murdered wife, Nicole Brown Simpson; research concluded that "the media continually portray domestic violence through sensationalized or cliched stories that focus on the individual abuser and victim."[7] As a composite portrait, it's a powerful narrative fabric with life-and-death implications—one that offers little efficacy for people trying to survive the vortex of fear in their own homes.

Meanwhile, in North Carolina, documentarian Cynthia Hill was hard at work for six years shaping a verité film about domestic violence with a distinctly different point of view. She was motivated by the invisibility of secret terror—a topic in which she had firsthand experience. With equal urgency, Hill wanted to shape a narrative that interrogated the flawed system that makes it more dangerous for a woman to leave an abusive partner than to stay. She reflects, "News coverage still had this very strong tone of victim-blaming to it, like somehow the woman is responsible for the abuse. . . . It becomes the women's responsibility to extricate herself from that situation, and how complicated that is on every level is something that society does not understand. I didn't want this to be a film that didn't move the needle a bit in that area."[8] This narrative, and the intimate experience of women, was missing, she thought, from the general cultural and news messages around domestic violence, as she makes clear:

> I grew up in a household where I witnessed domestic violence, so I had a desire to show what that experience was like. That was *the* reason why I wanted to make this film and why it was so important for me to get it right. . . . I didn't want it to be oversimplified. The situations women find themselves in are way more complicated than folks realize when they are looking from the outside in, and it's such a disservice to what typical news coverage does, which is to say that this was a domestic dispute or this notion that this was a love spat. It's such a disservice to what is really going on and also to the first responders who are walking into that dangerous situation.[9]

Contrasting with the news coverage of domestic abuse and its traditional focus on individual incidents or implicit victim-blaming,[10] Hill's documentary, *Private Violence*, trains its lens on the stories of two North Carolina women: Kit Gruelle, a domestic violence advocate and survivor with firsthand understanding of the trauma of abuse and navigating the system, and Deanna Walters, a young mother who finally left her husband, Robbie, after years of injury and verbal abuse. Moving well beyond one individual incident, the film invites viewers to see and contemplate a neglected angle—that is, the criminal justice system's treatment of women who face patterns of long-term, ongoing abuse. Complexity in the criminal justice system that fails women who leave their abusers—and the danger when they do—is the documentary's nerve-wracking narrative spine, transmitted through the emotional lens of two women living in the day-to-day nuances of domestic violence. Addressing the "why doesn't she leave?" victim-blaming perpetuated through repetitive news frames, one film critic noted:

> One of the triumphs of this film is that by the end of it, you will not be asking such questions. You will start to appreciate the complexity of the psychological dynamic involved in being the victim of such abuse. You will ask instead how a civilized society lets it happen. Viewers will see and hear a North Carolina prosecutor explaining to Kit that even if she took the case and won, Robbie might be sentenced to only 150 days in jail on charges of "misdemeanor assault against a woman."[11]

Private Violence premiered in January 2014 at the Sundance Film Festival, and in October on HBO, in the midst of the cultural spotlight trained firmly on the NFL (Figure 6.1). Through Hill's point of view and a verité story as witness, the documentary transmits a more complex, nuanced examination well beyond the news headlines of the time. In *Private Violence*, a different view is rendered possible through an interpretive lens that moves through the stories of women—not as victims who choose to stay of their own volition, but as individuals forced to rely on a system that fails to protect them or punishes them when they finally defend themselves. Addressing the headline-raising influence and simultaneous timing of the NFL story, and yet, its failure to interrogate the infrastructure of domestic violence, one TV critic reflected:

> And then, as the media always seem to do, we moved on to new stories, leaving the issue of domestic violence before most of its deeper truths and complexities could be explored even in this Domestic Violence Awareness Month. I was angry about that until I saw "Private Violence." . . . Let's just be grateful that Hill and HBO stayed with their story long after most other media would have packed up and moved on.[12]

Figure 6.1. In the Emmy-nominated HBO documentary, *Private Violence*, Deanna Walters, a domestic violence survivor, looks at photos of the abuse she suffered at the hands of her estranged husband. Photo by Josh Woll, courtesy of Markay Media.

Through the grassroots public engagement campaign architected by Hill and her impact producers Erin Sorenson, Un Kyong Ho, and Janeen Gingrich, *Private Violence* expanded its reach, screening at more than 100 college campuses and 120 domestic violence shelters and organizations across the country, including One Billion Rising, and the UN Mission for Peace Association— and also partnering with national and statewide groups to spark conversation, including Futures Without Violence, the National Resource Center on Domestic and Sexual Violence, the American Bar Association Commission on Domestic & Sexual Violence, multiple statewide domestic violence coalitions; and with individuals like Gloria Steinem and Bev Gooden, the creator of the viral #WhyIStayed campaign.[13] It was a film designed to be seen but also to be publicly discussed.

Private Violence exemplifies a meaningful cultural role for nonfiction storytelling that addresses social problems— its creative, interpretive ability to transmit a missing or nuanced narrative that moves beyond dominant daily news and entertainment headlines of social issues that are either polarized in the public imagination or communicated through statistics, simplified patterns, or decontextualized generalities. This chapter showcases social-issue documentaries that reveal—through creative interpretation, intimate narratives, and identifiable points of view—the human stories and neglected realities within hot-button, often divisive social issues. In so doing, this chapter argues that documentary's ability to humanize the headlines beyond daily reporting is a meaningful contribution to a society's contemplation of its social problems, particularly as we seek ways to encourage public discourse. As they creatively interrogate seemingly settled narratives, social-issue documentaries can inject a new way of seeing and provoke new conversation about social problems that matter—a crucial function in a long view of social change.

Documentaries are positioned here within a broader cultural stew of information. Contemporary social problems in the post-millennial information age are packaged and disseminated through daily headlines of news and entertainment media, repeated and redistributed across platforms. But perspectives about social issues also are shared by individuals through the niche echo chambers of social media, which offer a freedom to express but also can serve to deepen perceptions of differing opinions about political and social issues.[14] In the process of navigating the headlines in the on-demand media system, polarization can settle into sides of "for" and "against," "we" and "them"—a broad-brush binary that can leave out the intricacy that engenders human connection and compassion. While the evolving internet age has opened new avenues for expression, it has simultaneously posed challenges for civic discourse, as scholar David Karpf wrote: "As news-filtering technology improves, it becomes increasingly easy for citizens to avoid countervailing facts and opinions, polarizing the public sphere."[15] In turn, polarization poses a danger to democracy as it diminishes the ability of individuals and publics to find common ground and shared values about issues of societal importance.[16]

There's reason for urgent concern: As of 2018, research shows that Americans find it increasingly stressful to talk about public issues with people with whom they don't already agree.[17] In other words, while issues like racial justice and race relations, immigration, healthcare, and drug addiction remain high on Americans' list of "most important problems,"[18] we may be increasingly unable to talk about and work through them together. And yet, human lives and experiences do not align into tidy sides. Further, addressing the broader cultures and systems that support societally large problems—domestic abuse, criminal justice, addiction—prove chronically difficult to discuss effectively.

Against this cultural backdrop, documentaries about social challenges are certainly not a magical panacea, nor are all daily news and entertainment media reflections reductive in their coverage of social issues. But documentaries are important as public discourse—they play a symbiotic relationship with daily reporting. Documentaries package reality for public consumption through deep analysis, similar to journalism,[19] but with an artistic sensibility and point of view that deepens their emotional resonance. In *Columbia Journalism Review*, Robert Gehr asserted the essential role of creative artistry:

> Cinematic artistry is tough to beat. Print journalism, no matter how arduously reported and beautifully written, will never quite overtake film's experiential advantage. . . . While one might introduce political or humanitarian causes into the mainstream through persuasion alone, they're more effective when coupled with a stylish visual component and an identifiable point of view.[20]

Similarly, the MacArthur Foundation's journalism and media program director Kathy Im sees documentary's interpretive quality and intimacy as vital to the view it can open for a viewer:

> For me, the most powerful social issue documentaries are the ones that allow a viewer, with no proximity to the circumstances portrayed, to understand someone else's experience at a visceral level. When a person has the trust and courage to let a camera in, the human experience they share becomes part of how we understand a complicated set of issues that might otherwise be abstract. I carry in my heart the devastation and betrayal felt by the female soldiers who were sexually assaulted by their supervisors and peers and silenced by the U.S. military (*The Invisible War*), I understand and would have done the same as Barbara, who kept the unjust killing of her son buried deep inside of her (*Strong Island*), and I find renewing inspiration in Grace Lee Boggs' infectious courage and optimism (*American Revolutionary: The Evolution of Grace Lee Boggs*).[21]

The core of this argument is the idea that social problems are the lived experiences of individual people trying to get by, not abstractions framed by politicians. By humanizing the headlines of hot-button social problems, documentaries can disrupt a settled or one-dimensional narrative. They can provide an entirely new creative lens with which to look—a deeper portal into the human details and lived experiences of an issue. In this way, documentaries supply the kind of "narrative imagination" so crucial to our full capacity to include and contemplate a broad swath of human experience, to borrow philosopher Martha Nussbaum's articulation:

> Narrative imagination is an essential preparation for moral interaction. Habits of empathy and conjecture conduce to a certain type of citizenship and a certain form of community: one that cultivates a sympathetic responsiveness to another's

needs, and understands the way circumstances shape those needs, while re-specting separateness and privacy.[22]

Moving beyond daily news stories, documentaries paint expansive portraits of social issues or open the door to the intimate details of human lives and experiences in ways that can open dialogue and disrupt seemingly rote assumptions about people and their challenges. This is documentary's interpretive ability to delve under the headlines and reveal new ways to look at a story or a social problem, or to disrupt status-quo cultural narratives that miss the voices and lived realities of the people most affected.

Interrogating Racial Injustice: *13th*

No country holds more of its people behind bars than the United States.[23] The rate of imprisonment in the US remained steady throughout the 20th century, rising in the 1970s and spiking upward throughout the 1980s,[24] continuing through the 1990s.[25] Experts point to distinct contributory political moments, including the "war on drugs" that began in the 1970s and exploded in the 1980s,[26] which ushered in policies that prescribed sentencing guidelines, limited the ability of judges to practice discretion, determined mandatory minimum sentences for federal drug offenses, and reflected a disproportionately punitive stance toward crack cocaine used mostly by African Americans, relative to powder cocaine used primarily by whites.[27] Adding to the complexity, for-profit private prisons appeared on the scene in 1997 to handle the increased prison population.[28]

Beyond numbers, mass incarceration in the United States is a story about race. During the incarceration spike between 1980 and 1996, the number of imprisoned African Americans rose by 261 percent, compared to 185 percent among whites.[29] As of 2018, more than 60 percent of the incarcerated population comprises people of color, particularly African American men, who are six times more likely than white men to live behind bars.[30] And, as sociologists Lawrence D. Bobo and Victor Thompson asserted, the relatively recent "mass incarceration" term itself, with its emphasis on the sheer numerical scope, can obscure the racial reality: "While the overall U.S. rate of incarceration is up very substantially, this shift has fallen with radically disproportionate severity on African Americans, particularly low-income and poorly educated blacks."[31] A legacy of discriminatory policies that helped foster urban poverty also negatively contributes.[32]

These were not unilateral policy decisions. The conditions that enabled elevating incarceration rates were firmly aided and abetted by robust public opinion. Between the late 1970s and 1990s, the public strongly backed an increased "punitive" stance toward crime, and politicians leveraged this support to their advantage by way of policy decisions.[33] Public opinion was "a central, perhaps *the* central, consideration in the making of penal policy,"[34] wrote political scientist Marie Gottschalk. And according to research, "public opinion can also influence those directly involved in the criminal justice system, such as police, prosecutors, and judges."[35] Race is deeply embedded here. In their work, sociologists Bobo and Thompson concluded that the strongest predictor of Americans' punitive stance against crime is their degree of prejudiced feelings about African Americans—their "collective racial resentment"—particularly among white Americans.[36]

Public opinion about crime is culturally shaped, to a great degree, by media narratives. Generally, Americans learn about crime from media, not firsthand experiences,[37] and crime portrayals in news and entertainment play a crucial part in shaping widespread public perspectives about danger in the world.[38] In general, consuming various types of news and entertainment broadly leads viewers to feel less confident in the criminal justice system and more supportive of punitive crime policies.[39] Further, in news coverage, African Americans have been broadly characterized as violent,[40] and in negatively stereotyped ways as "criminal" and "dangerous."[41] Together, this powerful composite cultural portrait mixes generalized fear of crime with negative media portrayals of a group of people systemically impacted by incarceration.

Changing the direction of a decades-long mass incarceration trend, then— a social problem that evolved year after year, constructed by layer upon layer of politics, media images, and public perception—is complex. Unweaving an elaborate infrastructure is not a sole-solution problem. But the same interplay of public opinion, policy, and media portrayals is crucial. A challenge remains: How can the nuances of history and policy and research and racism be packaged into a palatable, urgent narrative—to disrupt the usual news coverage and encourage people to understand and care?

Enter filmmaker Ava DuVernay.

"The United States is home to five percent of the world's population but 25 percent of the world's prisoners. Think about that."[42] So intones then-president Barack Obama in *13th*, director Ava DuVernay's 2016 cinematic illustration of systematic racism and oppression, rendered through the complicated history and present-day reality of mass incarceration in America. *13th*, produced by DuVernay along with Spencer Averick and Howard Barish, premiered to immediate critical acclaim at the New York Film Festival in

September 2016 and on Netflix in October of that year.[43] The documentary garnered a nomination for Best Documentary Feature in the 2017 Academy Awards, won a Primetime Emmy Award, BAFTA Award, DuPont-Columbia Award, the Humanitas Prize, Critic's Choice Award, Peabody Award, and many others.[44]

The documentary takes its name from the 13th Amendment to the US Constitution, which abolished slavery in 1865, codified in these words: "Neither slavery nor involuntary servitude, except as a punishment for crime whereof the party shall have been duly convicted, shall exist within the United States, or any place subject to their jurisdiction."[45] The major argument of *13th* zooms in on the key middle clause—"except as punishment for a crime"—to diligently, artistically draw a steady line between slavery, terror and violence, dehumanizing media images, segregation, and decades of discriminatory policies, leading to the vast infrastructure of incarceration as a source of low-wage labor and form of social discipline imposed on black Americans. DuVernay expands the cultural and historical narrative of criminal justice and reframes it, as one review in the *New York Times* noted:

> As she sifts through American history, you grasp the larger implications of her argument: The United States did not just criminalize a select group of black people. It criminalized black people as a whole, a process that, in addition to destroying untold lives, effectively transferred the guilt for slavery from the people who perpetuated it to the very people who suffered through it.[46]

Connecting slavery, Jim Crow policies, urban poverty, and incarceration as a form of oppressive social control foisted on African Americans is a well-cited concept articulated by scholars,[47] including legal scholar Michelle Alexander's bestselling 2010 book, *The New Jim Crow: Mass Incarceration in the Age of Colorblindness*.[48] As a visual statement and scathing indictment, though, the narrative is expansive, intricate, emotional, artistic, and disruptive in DuVernay's hands, weaving together historical and contemporary news footage and pop culture images and animations, interspersed with interviews from historians, politicians, and scholars. The documentary also contributes an elaborate, nuanced full story that isn't readily available in dominant day-to-day news coverage about mass incarceration. In a media interview, DuVernay pointed out what she perceived as the need for a narrative "that can deepen our understanding of what it means to be incarcerated," and one that was missing from the culture: "There are so many facets of the criminal justice system that don't make their way into American television and

film. For storytellers, they're fertile ground: deeply emotional, deeply resonant human stories."[49]

Through *13th*, Ava DuVernay's depiction of the criminal justice system is
a journey through which she weaves a broad tapestry about the legacy and
ongoing structures that oppress African Americans—not only through
prison, but through the steady drumbeat of negative, dehumanizing media
images and discriminatory laws. The resulting policy implications that predominantly punish African Americans are mapped in her documentary as
an inevitable result of an interconnected structure that has imposed constant
barriers onto an entire group of the population. And in this, her framing compels viewers to see a full portrait of a destructive, suffocating system. Many
people, she said in a press interview, know and feel this reality already, but
others might not know—and she wanted to reach both ends of this audience
spectrum:

> The documentary was built for two different kinds of audiences—folks out there
> that know about this and folks out there that have never heard of it. For folks out
> there that know about it, the feedback that I've gotten and what my intention was,
> was to put it all in one place because when you see everything lined up, some of the
> things that we know from various books and documentaries of great thinkers out
> there, when everything is lined up back to back, it paints a different picture. There's
> something that's illuminated when you put it all together as a whole. So that was
> one way that I constructed the documentary. The other way that my editor Spencer
> Averick and I went about it was to the person that has heard nothing about this,
> that thinks that prison is a place where bad people go and that's that, to give them
> just a primer to think more deeply about, become more educated about, just have
> a broader base of knowledge about the criminal justice system as it stands right
> now and as it has stood for many decades.[50]

DuVernay provides varied audiences with a definitive vision with which to
view structures at work—to scrutinize systematic injustice and the complex interaction of institutional discrimination, but in so doing, to feel and
bear witness to the personal devastation to individual lives. In its composite
message, Ava DuVernay's film is not a historical documentary, even as she
stated, "We're giving you 150 years of oppression in 100 minutes. The film
was 150 years in the making. Really, it's to give context to the current moment."[51] *13th* is a living, breathing, contemporary connection that ultimately
arrives and situates itself firmly in the present day, in the context of Black Lives
Matter, compelling viewers to fully confront—some for the first time, some
confirming what they understand deeply already, according to DuVernay's

two-audience approach—how the structural parts fit together. As DuVernay said, "The final act of our picture is all about Black Lives Matter, not as some kind of dutiful, 'Oh it's the present moment, we should do something.' Every line, every frame of this film leads you to that place. Leads you to the now, leads you to the movement."[52]

But what, then, of mass incarceration in America—is the tide turning? In 2016, US incarceration rates declined to their lowest levels in two decades.[53] Data from 2018 show generally low public support for building new jails and prisons, and nearly half of surveyed Americans believe people are held in jail for the wrong reasons.[54] Leaders of both major political parties now indicate a shared desire to address America's mass incarceration problem.[55] In December 2018, bipartisan criminal justice reform legislation, the FIRST STEP Act, was signed into law, bringing with it sentencing reforms that justice advocates call a meaningful contribution.[56] As criminologist Justin Pickett wrote in 2016, "This could be a pivotal moment in American penal history. We may be transitioning from a punitive crime control agenda to one centered on rehabilitation and reintegration"—but, as he also noted, a trajectory of social change can't take place without supportive public opinion.[57]

Positioned within this context, this is the documentary's lasting legacy as it disrupts the daily headlines of mass incarceration and criminal justice. *13th* insists on interrogating racism and injustice at the heart of an ongoing system that disproportionately locks up people of color, centering the need for understanding and solidarity—and indeed, rage—at the core of an issue that often is rhetorically dominated by economics and numbing statistics, often devoid of historical context. DuVernay demands that the American people look closer—deep into our own power and culpability:

> At this point, after you see *13th*, silence in this case is consent. You know all of this. You're a forward-thinking person, you care about it. You can't just walk out into the night after you see the movie or put down your iPad after you see it on Netflix and do nothing about it. I'm not saying you have to join a march. I'm not saying you have to push for legislation. I'm saying what this film talks about is the very way that we deal with each other in the everyday. It's about our relationship to each other as it deals with race.[58]

In its full educational and artistic portrait, *13th* commands audiences to directly see—in full, stark reality—the routes by which white supremacy has created destructive mechanisms to control African American lives through every major historical gain and loss, from the abolition of slavery to Jim Crow to the civil rights movement to mass incarceration today. DuVernay tells us in no uncertain terms that racialized systems of oppression are human constructions, supported and expanded through the widespread consent of the people and their elected representatives. And in this message, history is not an appendage in the past but a disastrous living reality that will perpetuate itself until and unless a new system is shaped—just as diligently and with equal intent, from the hands of one generation to the next.

Sharing Hope in Appalachia: *Heroin(e)*

By the time the Great Recession hit the United States in the late 2000s,[59] many families in West Virginia and neighboring Appalachian states were intimately familiar with joblessness and poverty.[60] Already suffering from a decades-long industrial shift—a transition that began well before the latest downturn as the steel industry declined, manufacturing jobs changed, and coal mining decreased[61]—working-class neighborhoods found it difficult to catch a break. Where economic distress in Appalachia had typically been higher in coal-mining areas, today no communities in the region are immune; poverty has increased in non-mining localities, too.[62]

Against this backdrop, opioid addiction and death rates have reached dramatic proportions[63]—and four out of the five states with the highest rates of opioid overdose are located in the Appalachian region: West Virginia, Ohio, Pennsylvania, and Kentucky.[64] Widely labeled as a crisis, an average of 130 Americans overdose each day due to opioid use, a sixfold increase from 1999 to 2017.[65] Opioid substance use disorder—both prescription opioids and illegal heroin—impacts individuals of various backgrounds. Correlated with economic hardship and unemployment,[66] opioids also play a role "as a refuge from physical and psychological trauma, concentrated disadvantage, isolation, and hopelessness."[67]

How did we arrive here? Contributing factors point to a complex system forged in part by well-meaning intentions from the medical community.[68] Following a 1980 letter to the editor in the *New England Journal of Medicine* that downplayed the addictive nature of opioid pain medication—a claim reproduced in more than 400 medical journals—medical interest in pain management picked up through the 1990s.[69] In 1995, the newly created American Pain Society (APS), formed by a group of doctors working in cancer care, coined the idea of pain measurement as the "5th vital sign."[70] Pain management as a medical commitment, healthcare measurement system, and industry took off.[71]

That same year, the US Food and Drug Administration (FDA) approved OxyContin, a prescription opioid pain medication produced by Purdue

Pharma.[72] Purdue began a robust OxyContin marketing effort targeted at primary care doctors in the late 1990s[73] and later funded medical education materials that promoted the use of opioids for pain.[74] Prescriptions increased dramatically—by the millions.[75] In 2007, a federal court fined Purdue Pharma $634.5 million for knowingly providing misleading and incorrect information about the potential for addiction to OxyContin;[76] by that point, though, prescription opioids were firmly acculturated in the medical establishment after more than a decade on the market.[77] Years later, research confirmed the damage already done: pharmaceutical company marketing to doctors was associated with increased opioid prescriptions and overdose deaths.[78] In 2019, Massachusetts and a handful of impacted states filed lawsuits against Purdue Pharma for its contribution to opioid addiction and overdose due in part to false, deceptive marketing.[79] The same year, another prescription opioid manufacturer, Johnson & Johnson, sued by the Oklahoma attorney general for misleading marketing practices, was ordered to pay $572 million to the state of Oklahoma for its part in the opioid crisis.[80]

Despite complicated social and economic factors—and billion-dollar profits flowing into the legal opioid industry while overdose deaths accumulate—news media reflections about opioid use and addiction overwhelmingly paint a criminal justice portrait rather than a treatable public health issue.[81] So concluded large-scale research that examined 15 years of news media coverage about opioid abuse—from 1996 through 2012. As the study authors wrote, "Less than 5% of news stories overall mentioned expanding substance abuse treatment, and even fewer mentioned expanding access to evidence-based medication-assisted treatments."[82] Further, they stated, treatment and recovery options do exist, and including them in news coverage could help reduce discrimination and stigma targeted toward individuals battling substance use disorder.[83]

Such a persistent cultural message conveys little efficacy to communities and leaders trying to make change. As Dr. John Dreyzehner, a medical doctor and commissioner of the Tennessee Department of Health, who has worked for years on the opioids issue in Appalachia, wrote with a colleague:

> Framing the opioid epidemic as a crisis and an individual problem obscures the power of prevention and society's role in promoting it. . . . Such stories—which shape how we view the issue, the people it affects, and the solutions we see and support—frame addiction as a crisis of individual suffering and bad choices, where the only solution is to make better decisions and have a stronger will. But bad decisions do not explain the epidemic, and better decisions won't end it. We must change policy and practice to support people with addiction, help others resist it, and expose fewer people to addictive substances in the first place. . . . [W]e need

narratives that support the possibility of solutions. This issue is dire and deeply disturbing, but not irreversible.[84]

In 2016, West Virginia documentary filmmaker Elaine McMillion Sheldon was watching and reading media coverage about opioid addiction while she dealt with her own sadness and fear: "The bodies were piling up, and those were young bodies—and I knew those bodies. Those were people I went to school with. I had lost quite a few friends already from middle school and high school to drug overdoses."[85] The media portrayals compose a repetitive pattern of "needles and spoons," as Sheldon puts it:

> How many times can you show the destructive behavior of drug addiction before people just turn off from it? . . . I'm not against showing [drug] use at all, but I do think if you show it as a singular scene without providing the context of results for the larger community and people outside of that one person's experience, it becomes completely unrelatable. At least show some counternarrative with a person that has some vision. Show us a potential way out, like how is someone coping with this?[86]

Sparked by curiosity, urgent concern, and a desire to move beyond "addiction porn" media portrayals, as she calls them—that is, images that frame the issue as individual moral failure and hopelessness—Sheldon and her producing partner and husband, Curren Sheldon, headed across the state to Huntington, West Virginia. It was the epicenter of the challenge—the leading state for opioid deaths and a community with an overdose rate ten times higher than the national average.[87] But she chose the community for another reason: "Huntington had been the drop-in center for all media that was coming to just basically look at how bad this situation was."[88] She wanted to learn firsthand what was happening on the ground—to expand beyond what she was seeing and hearing in headlines. She found the story nearly immediately in three women who together create a community response system in Huntington: firefighter and first responder Jan Rader, West Virginia's first female fire chief; Necia Freeman, a realtor running Backpacks & Brown Bags, a missionary program for sex workers; and Family Court Judge Patricia Keller, who presides over the county's drug court as an alternative to criminal justice sentencing. As Sheldon recounts:

> When we got there [to Huntington] we found there were a lot of people doing things. Of course there's a huge issue there, no one denies that, but we also found a lot of incredibly positive people and programs that I hadn't even heard of. And

leaders—especially women leaders. It was such a different outlook than anything
I had seen and heard.[89]

In 2016 and 2017, with funding from a new Center for Investigative
Reporting fellowship for women documentary filmmakers, Sheldon crafted
a 39-minute verité short documentary, *Heroin(e),* with a title inspired by the
three lead subjects—women she calls "the helpers"—and the hope and community solidarity she found in Huntington, West Virginia, alongside its harrowing daily moments. *Heroin(e)* premiered at the Telluride Film Festival in
early September 2017, and it was released as a Netflix Original documentary
a few days later.[90] The film was nominated for a 2018 Academy Award for Best
Documentary (Short Subject)[91] and it won an Emmy Award for Best Short
Subject Documentary in 2018.[92]

On screen, *Heroin(e)* juxtaposes the daily working experiences of the three
women. By highlighting their individual efforts and the connections between
them, the film reveals what a community response to the opioid epidemic
looks like—in a concrete way, molded by compassion and rendered through
the reality of day-to-day life and decisions. The specificity of Huntington's
workforce in physical mining and manufacturing jobs is a necessary context.
Fire Chief Rader explains in the film: "A lot of people in this area got hooked
on pills through a legitimate injury and have now moved on to heroin because
they can't get pills anymore."[93] Much of the verité documentary focuses on
Rader (Figure 6.2) as she responds to emergency calls about opioid overdoses,

Figure 6.2. Fire Chief Jan Rader of Huntington, West Virginia, as featured in *Heroin(e)*.
Photo courtesy of Requisite Media, LLC/Netflix.

where she administers Naloxone (Narcan), the medication that jumpstarts breathing in overdose victims. She's unwavering about the long-term goal of treatment and recovery for people suffering with substance use disorder, as she states on screen: "The only qualification for getting into long-term recovery is you have to be alive. And I don't care if I save somebody 50 times."[94] Meanwhile, by reaching out to vulnerable women, missionary Necia Freeman painstakingly establishes the kind of trust, person by person, that helps pull them into safety. And in the Cabell County Family Court, Judge Patricia Keller's drug court program helps people with substance use disorders make their way into treatment and recovery—and celebrates them when they come out on the other side. In their roles as front-line interveners, the three women overlap and collaborate.

Beyond news headlines, a different view comes into focus in *Heroin(e)*. As a reporter from neighboring Athens, Ohio, reflected: "Many do not think of hope when they hear about America's modern opioid epidemic, but the *Heroin(e)* documentary shows how the chain of compassion holds one town together through the crisis."[95] Sheldon aims to transmit a missing narrative of efficacy, as she reflects:

> I was hoping the story could contribute hope. Because I was looking for hope. I was very discouraged by everything I was seeing. When I went to Huntington and found these women and saw what these women were doing, I personally saw a lot of hope. . . . All I wanted to do was potentially provide some hope, and not false hope, not wearing rose-colored glasses, being very real about the situation. . . . So often media shows only the misery.[96]

Since its 2017 premiere, Sheldon has leveraged *Heroin(e)* as a tool to engage the public, offering the film and discussion resources to communities in West Virginia and other parts of the country, facilitating more than 300 free grassroots screenings hosted by community groups, medical schools, elementary schools, prisons, and other organizations—particularly the places where communities are mobilizing local solutions to the opioid epidemic: "When they show the film, they don't talk about the film afterwards— they use it as a vehicle to get people in chairs to learn about what's happening in their own backyard."[97] And, according to Sheldon, "We didn't plan this, but a lot of people have been using the documentary to get people in to get them trained on using Naloxone. The West Virginia United Methodist Conference here in Appalachia did a series of screenings where they did Naloxone trainings before or after the film, and it's happened within health departments too."[98]

Fire Chief Jan Rader remains committed to her efforts in Huntington. In her perspective, the film's high profile sparked needed conversations and brought fresh visibility to the challenge. Named one of *Time*'s "100 Most Influential People" in 2018,[99] she has spoken to dozens of communities at *Heroin(e)* screenings across the country—and continues. As she reflects:

> People have reached out sharing their stories, people have decided to do things in their own community because they've been inspired. This documentary has given people permission to talk about something that's taboo. I think a lot of people craved and needed a film like this to be able to do that. . . . It's given a voice to people who didn't have one before.[100]

Can the trajectory of opioid addiction and overdose reverse course? There's no easy fix. Several years after *Heroin(e)*'s premiere, officials pointed to a series of contributing solutions along with treatment and recovery, including training first responders and others to use Naloxone,[101] a position advocated in a 2018 statement by the US Surgeon General.[102] In West Virginia, Health Commissioner Dr. Rahul Gupta talked about the need to address stigma and provide optimism, along with a full public health response.[103] In Huntington, Chief Rader sees optimism: "In 2018, we saw a 41 percent decline in overdoses here in Huntington. Our numbers for the first couple months in 2019 are even lower, so we're very hopeful. This community has come together in so many different ways to help those in need. . . . There's plenty of hope to go around."[104]

As a composite portrait, *Heroin(e)* invites viewers to see the residents of Huntington as individual people dealing with health challenges and economically challenging times, not faceless, morally bankrupt addicts, even while the documentary doesn't shy away from showing the devastation. In so doing, the film disrupts a steady cultural drumbeat of hopelessness, which can perpetuate a kind of inertia in the face of destructive odds. Even through its unvarnished depiction of a substance use catastrophe, the documentary positions its core message around the frames of humanity and compassion and recovery. Well beyond the abstractions of overdose statistics, *Heroin(e)* brings us into the story of community-based interventions and solutions—an invaluable narrative in the context of social change.

Spotlighting Community Resilience: *Charm City*

Frustration was already brewing in Baltimore on the day police arrested 25-year-old Freddie Gray. As officers placed Gray, an African American resident of the city, in the back of a police van on April 12, 2015, he was alert and conscious.[105] By the time the police transport vehicle arrived at the station, Gray was semi-conscious, his spinal cord severely injured.[106] One week later, Freddie Gray died from the fatal spinal injury he suffered while in police custody.[107] In the wake of his death and a climate of ongoing tension between police and Baltimore's black residents, community leaders and city officials called for a deeper investigation. "We need real change in the city of Baltimore and the way in which police officers engage with the community," said state senator Lisa Gladden of Baltimore.[108]

As news of Gray's coma and subsequent death and funeral spread throughout the city, peaceful protests turned into an uprising that lasted for weeks, blanketing local and national news coverage. By the time it was over, police had deployed tear gas and pepper bombs. Local businesses and cars and other property were damaged, a dominant image portrayed in mainstream news coverage.[109] The city arrested and charged six police officers in the Gray case; all were later acquitted, or charges were dropped.[110]

It was a charged series of events for Baltimore. But the city was not new to controversy or a strained relationship between police and the community, particularly its African American residents. In 2014, an investigation by the *Baltimore Sun* revealed more than $5 million in settlements paid out to Baltimore residents over four years due to allegations of civil rights abuses perpetrated by the city's police force.[111] Within a larger portrait of police and African American neighborhoods and residents, the story of Freddie Gray connects with a pattern of similar incidents, including Michael Brown, killed by a police officer in Ferguson, Missouri, in 2014; and Walter Scott, slain in Charleston, South Carolina. In all three communities, residents aired their deep anger, hurt, and frustration through protests.[112] The #BlackLivesMatter movement, which began in 2013, picked up momentum after Michael Brown's death in Ferguson, coalescing similar narratives and calling attention to a long-standing problem.[113] The wary, complicated relationship between police and many historically disadvantaged communities is a continuing morass of pain, and the new movement expressed the tension in contemporary terms.

For news consumers, the coverage in mainstream media outlets that followed Freddie Gray's death focused heavily on images of property destruction and violence.[114] The mainstream cultural narrative about Baltimore and Freddie Gray adhered to a broader schema about news coverage of Black Lives Matter activity. A 2017 study that was focused on seven mainstream US newspapers revealed, "Language of crime, lawlessness, violence, blame for nearby acts of violence, and inflammatory quotes from bystanders and official sources were often present. There was little discussion of key issues associated with the formation of BLM."[115] By failing to fully include and interrogate the protestors' motivations, the core narrative spotlights violence and clashes. In turn, news framing around volatile, sensitive issues involving race relations and policing affects public attitudes, and thus, policy.[116]

In that pivotal moment, the world saw Baltimore as a vortex of violence, destruction, and anger. But what about the community itself? When news crews left the scenes of Baltimore's unrest, how did the city's residents pick up and move forward? Documentary filmmaker Marilyn Ness and her Baltimore-based film crew were already embedded in the city when Freddie Gray was killed, and she found herself in production at the beginning of what would become the city's most violent three years—2015 through 2017. The protests lit a combustible spark of attention—and shaped a dominant media narrative. Ness recalls, "We were four months in [filming in Baltimore], and then the unrest around Freddie Gray erupted. We watched CNN and all of the world's media descend on Baltimore, film it on fire, and then just leave."[117] Prior to Gray's death, Ness had been carefully watching events of the last several years unfold through the mediated prism of tension between communities of color and police. She felt the story lacked crucial context to create deeper understanding. As she recounts:

> What we were watching particularly at the end of 2014 was this sequence of high-profile deaths of black men in police custody and you were hearing this sort of drum beat narrative on one side from communities of color saying "hey, this is nothing new, we're just recording it now." And on the police side, you were hearing "Blue Lives Matter." But none of it was getting to what is the day to day of their existence that keeps bringing them into conflict that ends with horrifying tragedy in front of an iPhone camera. That just wasn't in the headlines. You could dive deeply into the historical practices of police of racist practices, unconstitutional practices, but none of it seemed to live in the day in and day out of what it feels like to live in a community that feels excessively policed or to be a police officer working in a community that has extensive policing. That's something documentary film can do incredibly well is be in one place very patiently over a period of time and watch the world unfold around you. That's what we thought we could add to the conversation that was just sort of spinning wildly, deserving of attention but just not getting deeper than what we were seeing on the surface.[118]

Ness was motivated to tell a more intimate human story that lived in Baltimore on a daily basis—she was inspired to depart from the abstractions and generalities communicated in times of acute strife. To get it right, to authentically convey the nuances of the city and its residents, the documentary would not be quick to produce. After spending months with community leaders and police, Ness recalls a revelation:

> Whether you were with community members or police officers, they all talked about it in the same way. It was like, "What can we be doing as individuals to try to change the equation, how do communities lift themselves up?" And we realized there was more similarity than difference as they talked to us. Not to say there wasn't major tension and anger and years of distrust that had been built, but they were kind of coming at things from the same place. . . . The media will pit communities of color against police officers and vice-versa. There was a way in which everyone was singing the same song.[119]

Ness crafted a documentary story about Baltimore residents, community leaders and police trying to forge a hopeful path forward—a missing narrative amid the tapestry of media messages about the city's most dangerous chapter. In verité style crafted from hours of intimate footage, *Charm City*, produced by Ness and Katy Chevigny—which takes its title from the city's nickname (although, as Ness pointed out in a media interview, the nickname "plays two ways in that town. . . . For white communities, they call it 'Charm City,' and for communities of color they call it 'Harm City,' and so we made our 'C' flicker onscreen in the title")[120]—chronicles the change-making efforts of Baltimore residents and community leaders: "Mr. C," Clayton Guyton, an elder statesman in charge of the city's Rose Street Community Center and unofficial counselor to the neighborhood's young people; two Baltimore police officers, Officer Monique "Mo" Brown and Officer Eric Winston (Figure 6.3); Baltimore City Councilman Brandon Scott; and Alex Young, Mr. C's protégé, a formerly incarcerated young man who "graduates" from the Rose Street Community Center and goes to work at Safe Streets, a nonprofit organization that takes a public health approach to changing the course of violence on the streets, helping young people avoid the criminal justice system.[121] A review in *Baltimore* magazine noted the film's nuanced approach to its subject:

> This is a generous, insightful, and altogether humane look at our wonderful, horrible city, one that doesn't shy away from its struggles, but manages to leave some room for hope. The smartest thing Ness does is focus on a small group of Baltimoreans, each representing a different perspective on the city's woes. . . . The film makes it clear that a lot of people care—cops, politicians, neighbors—and are trying as hard as they can. No one is judged. There's a sense that we're all in this together.[122]

Figure 6.3. Officer Eric Winston of the Baltimore Police Department, as featured in *Charm City*. Photo by John Benam, courtesy of Big Mouth Productions.

Embodied in the film's primary subjects, a spectrum of both community pride and frustration reveals a more complicated—and hopeful—portrayal of Baltimore working to shape its future, but "not sugar-coating what reality is," says Ness.[123] In this way, *Charm City* provides a narrative that disrupts the steady drumbeat of doomsday, fatalistic imagery, as Officer Mo Brown mused in a news interview: "People focus on the negative. . . . We've got great things happening, our youth achieving great things, but that's never show-cased. People like going to the negative narrative, where you can sensation-alize. It makes everyone outside think we're the worst city in the world, but we have greatness."[124] And yet, the film's composite portrait, a strong focus on community and collaboration even as it reveals a breakdown of trust between residents and the criminal justice system, recognizes, as Alex Long says on screen: "The streets are going to have to cure the streets."[125]

After Ness wrapped post-production, she facilitated separate screenings with the key constituents represented in the film, including the Rose Street Community Center team, police officers, Councilman Brandon Scott, and senior leadership of the Baltimore Police Department. The impact of the sto-rytelling was clear, as Ness recalls:

> To a person, they said it represented their truth, we captured their experience to them. And many of them expressed surprised to hear what the other side was going through—that the others felt that way about the violence or they were doing that

kind of work, or that they aspired to do that kind of work. It was all an epiphany. You then realize the detrimental impact of the news just repeating the narrative about the divide means people only can see themselves in contradiction to one another and just survive it. What we found is that more often than not, they felt the same about the issues—they were troubled and heartbroken about what was happening. Through the film they could see what others were doing.[126]

Charm City premiered at the Tribeca Film Festival in April 2018 and in theaters later that year, landing on the Academy Awards nominations short list for Best Documentary Feature.[127] The film made its TV debut in April 2019 as part of the PBS *Independent Lens* documentary series.[128] Ness and her impact-producing team crafted a multi-pronged community engagement campaign shaped in large part by a May 2018 "braintrust" meeting facilitated with criminal justice experts, Baltimore community leaders, and police. The grassroots screening campaign kicked off with a 2018 Baltimore pilot effort, designed to "create an infrastructure to support Baltimore community members and police officers to engage in meaningful, healing dialogue and create a forum for identifying next steps to improve trust and safety in Baltimore," identifying major objectives—to create opportunities for dialogue between police and citizens, to facilitate community film screenings and police trainings, and to host educational screenings.[129]

Bringing disparate community factions together was the main idea. Ness worked with the Baltimore Police Academy to facilitate a training with the film, and after the experience, she says, "a huge number of them said they would opt into more training about how to interact with community members. . . . The film was a starting point for people to see one another, that there's common ground."[130] Safe Streets, the violence interruption community program, hosted a screening as a "meet and greet" in its new office at Baltimore City Hall, a convening that proved to be pivotal for police and other municipal workers to see Safe Streets' role in the community—previously not well understood. Said Ness: "That was our intention—to give people a line of sight into a world they wouldn't otherwise get to see. Can you shift perspectives and really entrenched perspectives if you can show them what things look like on the other side?"[131]

In Baltimore, efforts to curb violence continue with a focus on police and their relationships with the residents and community leaders who inhabit a sprawling, diverse metropolis.[132] As Marilyn Ness reflects on her hope for *Charm City*'s ongoing contribution: "The realistic hope is that everyone understands they have a part to play. Society has gotten comfortable with the idea that we should send a 22-year-old police officer with a gun to deal with any problem in the community—like poverty and mental illness and homelessness—and we wonder why things go wrong. You have a role to play in this—we all do—to deal with the root causes of violence."[133] In *Charm City*, Baltimore is both a singular story about an American city, but also a representation of many places where neighborhood leaders and community officials strive to create resilience, shared understanding, and a climate of peace. After uprisings come to an end, amid a racialized media narrative of destruction and division and anger, communities are left to forge a path forward. *Charm City* provides a way for various constituencies to see one another with different eyes, moving past the news headlines about a series of incidents to lift up a new cultural message about the possibility for progress.

Constructing intimate, nuanced stories about contemporary public affairs issues requires a devotion to both artistic craft and the communities at the heart of the topics. In this context, the documentaries profiled in this chapter share meaningful characteristics, beginning with the motivation of their auteurs. These films were all shaped by storytellers who explicitly wanted to tell a story that was different from the one they saw reflected in the culture around them—a culture shaped in large part by daily news reporting. By providing a holistic, expansive counternarrative, through the eyes and authentic experiences of the humans at the center of pundit-debated social problems, the filmmakers contributed to public and media discourse. The filmmakers hoped for change—and this also motivated their stories. They actively wanted their films to change conversations and improve the state of affairs for the people and problems they reflected on screen.

Community resides at the center of these documentaries. The narratives here were created by makers who share a deep personal connection to, and membership within, the community of people portrayed in the documentaries. The filmmakers or crews are local or come from these on-screen communities, which shapes the authenticity of the storytelling—and with their reflections, the stories validate the nuances that individuals and communities have long understood to be true even if they have been invisible or neglected in dominant media portrayals. With the help of public engagement campaigns that leverage documentary's dual marketplace distribution norm—that is, life on TV and theaters, but also in police stations and libraries and places of worship and schools—the stories travel into communities to foster the kind of conversation designed to chip away at the problems. These documentaries are designed for participation with the public, not just nonfiction as entertainment and education. In the long-range view of social change, seeing people matters, not merely as they are constructed in media representation on a daily basis, but within a more nuanced artistic lens.

These films are not, by tactical construction, news coverage produced from the norms, practices, and constraints of daily journalism, and this distinction matters to the stories rendered on screen. Documentaries work symbiotically with the day-to-day reporting that contributes to and shapes the public agenda. Nonfiction stories that explore and reveal nuanced social issues and people take time to produce. They require community buy-in and trust. They need time to unfold and take shape. What we see on-screen reflects the richness of the human experience and a devotion to artistic artistry that transforms a story we thought we knew—due, in large part, to the time and breathing room to find and allow the story to emerge.

By examining complex social problems through an artistic lens, documentary storytellers can creatively agitate a seemingly settled or generalized cultural narrative about contemporary public affairs. They help to rupture the construction of a social problem as a binary of one side or another, and they remind us of the human condition that lives at the heart. Through a process of creative interpretation with human narratives at the fore, these kinds of documentary stories offer a new lens with which to see and contemplate persistent social issues that may have come to feel rote, automatic, settled, generalized, or polarized, thus stifling the opportunity for fresh dialogue or intervention. The narrative disruption of intimate documentary storytelling is vital to sparking public conversation and participation—and ultimately, social progress with an eye toward justice.

When people talk about films as a tool for social change, I talk about the incipient drumbeat that films can insert into a cultural conversation and have a lasting effect. The qualities of those films that make them works of arts and journalism and social commentary are hearing voices that challenge me and challenge my belief system and make me question my belief system and my privilege, hearing stories of communities or individuals I'm never going to have a chance to interact with in other ways, breaking down social and cultural barriers— films that allow me to make up my own mind through the experience of watching and don't tell me what to think.

— **Simon Kilmurry**
Executive Director
International Documentary Association[1]

7

Shaping Laws

Documentaries and Policy Engagement

In January 2012, a searing independent documentary film, *The Invisible War*, exploded onto the cultural scene, opening the public door to a shocking reality—sexual assault in the US military, an issue framed by the filmmakers as "one of the United States' most shameful and well-kept secrets."[2] Through copious research and interviews with more than 70 survivors, director Kirby Dick and producer Amy Ziering crafted their scathing investigation and visual indictment of an insular military culture that had not, according to the film's premise, effectively addressed the challenge.[3] The US Department of Defense estimated that approximately 26,000 US military service members had experienced sexual assault in 2012.[4] As one survivor states on screen, "If this is happening to me, surely I'm not the only one."[5]

With an audience of institutional decision makers and policy change in mind,[6] the documentarians—working with their team of impact and engagement strategists—shaped the film's outreach and screening campaign to reach

Story Movements. Caty Borum Chattoo, Oxford University Press (2020) © Oxford University Press.
DOI: 10.1093/oso/9780190943417.001.0001

Capitol Hill and the Department of Defense directly, aiming to encourage pol-icymakers and influential military leaders to investigate and alter the official infrastructure inside the reporting, enforcement, and punishment for sexual assault in the US military.[7] As director Kirby Dick recalls, "As we went around doing the research, it became clearer and clearer that the most important and the first major reform was to take sexual assault out of the [military] chain of command because the conflict of interest is so abhorrent. . . . [T]hat became the rallying point for reform."[8] Given the team's focus on institutional change, producer Amy Ziering, the architect of the documentary's public engagement campaign, described the strategy to a reporter as "a grass-top, rather than a grass-roots, approach."[9]

Media coverage, public buzz, and critical acclaim followed. The next year, after a broadcast premiere on PBS, *The Invisible War* won a 2013 Peabody Award, and it was nominated for the 2013 Academy Award for Best Feature Documentary; it also won a 2014 Emmy Award for Best Documentary (Figure 7.1).[10] From 2012 to 2014, throughout the course of a strategic outreach campaign that included more than 1,400 community film screenings along with Capitol Hill showings,[11] signs of policy interest emerged. For Senator Kirsten Gillibrand (D-NY)—who held a 2013 congressional hearing on the

Figure 7.1. Lieutenant Elle Helmer at the Vietnam War Memorial, US Marine Corps, from *The Invisible War*, a Cinedigm/Docurama Films release. Photo courtesy of Cinedigm/Docurama Films.

issue, proposed legislation, and continues vocal policy efforts in Congress after becoming chairwoman of the Senate Armed Services subcommittee on personnel[12]—the awareness and beginning of her legislative commitment ignited when she watched *The Invisible War*, as she said in a press interview:

> [The documentary] tells the stories of men and women who survive these brutal rapes, and then had to survive having their command turn their back on them. It was the second victimization that really crushed their spirits and crushed their souls. And my fury watching these stories unfold was so strong I just said, "I just had to do something about it."[13]

Watching an intimate, human-narrative-centered documentary film expanded her legislative agenda, which continues years later.[14] Ultimately unable to pass the sweeping reform contained in the 2013 Military Justice Improvement Act, although she came close,[15] Gillibrand has successfully advanced bills in Congress that include reforms suggested by the documentary.[16] But the issue is deeply complex, and structural solutions will likely unfold over years to follow. There is no quick fix, but *The Invisible War* played an unquestionably outsized role in capturing public attention, setting a media and policy agenda, and generating considerable concern on both sides of the political aisle within the ranks of Congress and the Department of Defense. Director Kirby Dick describes the bipartisan outcome as a deliberate editorial strategy:

> There have been so many documentaries that critique the military, and for very good reason, but we saw absolutely no change [from those films]. They were taking a very obvious anti-military position. We were not going to take that position. Our subjects talked about how they loved the military again and again. I think that gave lawmakers pause—the military wasn't getting attacked. The other thing we did was make this bipartisan. We had as many Republican members of Congress in the film as Democratic members of Congress. That, too, allowed it to not be dismissed. . . . When Senator Gillibrand took up the issue in hearings, nearly every member of that committee watched the film, and there were six or seven representatives from the military praising the film. Only a couple of years earlier, no one [from the military] would speak about this.[17]

The story of *The Invisible War* illustrates the symbiotic connection between policymakers and truthful, evocative documentary storytelling in the information age. Reflecting on the distinctive narrative proposition of creative nonfiction storytelling, Dick says: "The thing about documentary that's really unique is you're able to convey the information and more analytical presentation at the same time as the emotional experience of the survivors, and they become infused into this one experience. I think that becomes very powerful."[18] In this context, policymakers leveraged a critically lauded, intimate nonfiction story as an awareness and engagement tool, and the film provided a human-centered source of new insight to spur legislative interest and action. *The Invisible War* garnered media attention, public conversation, and policymaker dialogue, all of which is valuable and necessary to move a legislative process that takes place both behind the scenes and on the public stage.

This chapter argues that contemporary documentaries can play a unique and vital role in the policymaking process due to their narrative approaches—human-centered narratives that expand beyond facts and statistics and ideological sides—and the collaborative, cultural nature of the policymaking process. Beyond political timing, the road to changing or making new laws is paved by legislators who champion an issue, along with supportive or oppositional public opinion and pressure. Policy change—technocratic though the process may seem to the people it is designed to represent—is meant to be executed as an expression of the public interest. At its core, policy reflects human experiences, and stories are essential.[19] With its emphasis on spotlighting the human condition, social-issue documentary storytelling plays a clear role in illuminating the real lives behind numbers and charts, and in elevating culturally resonant issues at particular moments in time. Documentary storytelling is naturally positioned to not only investigate little-seen stories but also to jolt awake publics and a specialized group of professionals whose decisions impact daily life: policymakers and their staffs. While documentary films have resided within political or policy change efforts prior to the digital era,[20] the practice of leveraging nonfiction stories to advocate for change may be more effective and powerful in the networked internet age.[21]

Through the strategies and policy outcomes of the documentary film teams included here, this chapter reveals how the filmmakers, policymakers, legislative staffers, and advocacy groups formed collaborative "policy subnetworks"—that is, microcosmic professional communities engaged in shaping policy that include interest groups, researchers, and legislative staffers, along with policymakers themselves[22]—that resulted in successful legislative change in response to documentaries. Contemporary documentary film projects have configured policy and grassroots engagement machines that have enraged publics and policy professionals alike, moving them to tears and making calls for change inevitable. In some cases, the filmmakers evolve into leaders of temporary movements for social change. In other scenarios, policymakers and advocacy groups find strategic ways to integrate a film into their existing campaigns to move a social justice issue forward.

At the core of the process, documentary stories can provide a way of seeing that unlocks the paralyzing gridlock of facts, statistics, and long-standing myths or assumptions about people and problems. Documentary films can also expose social problems long relegated to obscurity, or those that are new on the cultural horizon—documentary's monitorial function. The filmmakers profiled here did not do the work alone as they sought to shape grassroots forces built by community and civil society groups—a vital function of an informed democracy that comes together to change what is unjust, united by a common goal. The stories in this chapter reveal documentarians' collaborative efforts on the journey to passing new laws, changing the lives of ordinary people in the process.

Seeing Forgotten Women: *Sin by Silence*

Inside the California Institution for Women, a group of inmates—known to the world through their convictions as murderers of their abusers—came together first in the late 1980s to fight for justice after surviving years of trauma and violence in their own homes. Years later, they captured the attention of documentary filmmaker Olivia Klaus, who told their story in her 2009 film, *Sin by Silence*, co-produced, co-written, and edited by Ann-Caryn Cleveland:

> Against the system and against the odds, the women of Convicted Women Against Abuse have risen to expose the stigma of the cycle of domestic violence. Through their stories of terror and hope, the viewer can begin to understand the cycle of violence, the signs of an abuser, and how each and every one of us is responsible for changing the tragedy of domestic violence.[23]

For director Klaus, the story of battered women serving upward of 20 years in prison for protecting themselves from their abusers lodged itself into her brain and refused to be dismissed. It was a story that demanded to be told, and it ignited through her strong connection to women who had been forgotten—locked away in the seemingly intractable black hole of a vast criminal justice system—but who began to believe that she might finally be the person who would listen. "I started on this journey way back, and it was because one of my best friends opened up to me that she was in an abusive relationship and needed help. I had no idea how to help her, and it shattered my world. I started the work of helping her with an escape plan and learned there were no real answers," recalls Klaus.[24]

Her search for answers led to a conversation with an expert on domestic violence, Elizabeth Leonard, who advised Klaus to talk to the real experts—women in prison who had self-organized themselves as an advocacy cooperative behind prison walls, the only path they could imagine as a pathway to their exoneration. From within the California state prison system, the women of the Convicted Women Against Abuse (CWAA) had been fighting for their lives to understand and change a system that did not consider the conditions of their abuse in sentencing.[25] Their precise circumstances varied, but they all shared a similar back story—months and years of escalating, life-threatening abuse at the hands of their spouses or intimate partners.

Because California state law at the time did not allow the women's prior and ongoing abuse conditions to be considered as factors in trials or sentencing, they were sentenced as first- and second-degree murderers. To Klaus, this seemed like re-victimizing the survivors through the prison system. Once the women were behind bars, they became invisible, disposable, never to be heard from again. Klaus started a volunteer position with the women inside the correctional facility, and her interest in their stories deepened. Four years later, the women asked her to consider telling their story publicly. Pooling their funds from $.10/hour wages inside the prison, they raised the first $1,000 to make the documentary film, to share stories that had never been told and they feared were long forgotten.[26]

Her main subject, Brenda Clubine, was a domestic violence survivor who had been imprisoned for 26 years for second-degree murder, from the age of 21. The founder of Convicted Women Against Abuse, released in 2008 as a result of her own tireless legal advocacy, Clubine became an indispensable spokesperson for her story and those of other women in similar situations. Her story, revealed on camera in *Sin by Silence*, was abhorrent:

> In 1983, after eleven restraining orders filed against her husband, and countless visits to the police department and hospital, Clubine hit her husband over the head with a wine bottle while fleeing for her life. Brenda was convicted of second degree murder with a 16-years-to-life sentence. The judicial system at this time simply did not understand nor did they take the time, to weigh the substantial history of domestic violence Clubine experienced.[27]

More than seven years after a personal quest to find answers to help a friend, leading to a collection of shockingly untold stories, Klaus's documentary feature film, *Sin by Silence*, premiered in 2009 on the film festival circuit,[28] and on

Investigation Discovery in October 2011,[29] ensuring a broad audience. Klaus knew the law-changing impact she wanted to make, and she understood that film festivals and a broadcast premiere would not be enough. She needed to activate the public.

Advocacy around domestic violence and its grim relationship to the criminal justice system, both within California and around the country, was not new by the time *Sin by Silence* was released. Interest groups, attorneys, survivors, and families had been engaged in the issue for years. But they didn't have the ability to share the intimate stories of the women—at least not in a documentary. To Klaus, that was the missing element: "Grassroots advocates and groups finally had a way to share the stories of these women, which they didn't have before."[30] As her core awareness and outreach strategy, Klaus launched a grassroots engagement tour of the 10 states with the most troubling domestic abuse statistics, visiting hundreds of community centers, university locations, town halls, and other locations throughout the country over the next several years. In each state, Klaus partnered with coalitions that were part of state chapters for the National Coalition against Domestic Violence. Together, the filmmaker and a growing network of civil society groups and community leaders hosted screenings to make sure they "hit every target audience we could," according to Klaus.[31]

The untold stories of the women, forgotten by policymakers and news media alike, connected deeply. In California, where the on-screen stories of *Sin by Silence* took place, the impact was immediate. After a community screening at the University of San Francisco, a member of the audience sent a copy of the film to California State Assemblywoman Fiona Ma (D-San Francisco and San Mateo Counties), chair of the Domestic Violence Select Committee for the California State Assembly. Ma promptly got to work on legislative change after urging Klaus to screen the film for the Domestic Violence Caucus in Sacramento. It was this moment, according to Klaus, that provided the tipping point to set the complex policy process in motion: "The legislative change really started there at that screening, because every legislator who watched it wanted to do something about the issue [after watching]."[32]

For Assemblywoman Fiona Ma, watching the film was a professionally defining moment. To her, the documentary was a shocking, visceral, emotional, immediate charge to make change. "We [staffers in my office and I] watched the film and we knew immediately we had to do something about this issue; we had no idea this was happening. The elected officials and their staff that saw the film were sympathetic. . . . This had vast bipartisan support—Republicans and Democrats."[33] The incarcerated women's new legislative champion worked quickly and urgently. Ma reached out to Heidi Rummel, a Los Angeles–based public interest attorney and law professor at the University of Southern California who was deeply engaged with domestic violence policy in California. With the help of an unusual new team—filmmaker Olivia Klaus, film subject Brenda Clubine, and a coalition of domestic violence organizations in the state—Rummel, along with the California Habeas Project, helped to craft two eventual pieces of legislation championed by Assemblywoman Ma, titled the *Sin by Silence* bills: AB 593 and AB 1593, which allow expert testimony in jury trials about the effects of long-term intimate-partner domestic violence, and require that parole boards "give great weight to any information or evidence that proves the prisoner experienced intimate partner battering (IPB) and its effects at the time the crime was committed," respectively.[34] The AB 1593 summary statement outlined the vast, untold scope of the problem:

> Currently, over 7,000 women are imprisoned in California's state prisons, the majority of whom have survived domestic violence. Several hundred women in California are serving time for killing their batterers and hundreds, if not thousands more, are serving time for domestic violence-related crimes. A California state prison study found that 93% of the women who had killed their significant others had been battered by them; 67% of these women indicated the crime resulted from an attempt to protect themselves or their children.[35]

Alongside Olivia Klaus, Assemblywoman Ma became a vocal and energetic champion for the film, the women's stories, and the proposed legislation. She hosted screenings, hearings, and meetings with traditionally oppositional groups, and she leveraged media opportunities about the film to build awareness of the issue and push the proposed legislation forward. It was a story-centered legislative advocacy campaign. Without the intimate documentary storytelling and the window into the women's lives and experience, the issue might have been presented with the usual inanimate statistics and policy briefs, relegating the story to the dusty annals of criminal justice history. According to Ma, a seasoned policymaker,

> A fact sheet would not have moved me. The movie is powerful because it humanizes what the issue is. For me, the film was the big driver. If someone had just handed me stats about 7,000 women sitting in prison who needed my help, it wouldn't have been the same, compared to us saying "we need to help Brenda." The documentary was strong and powerful because it gave us a broader scope and opportunity to actually hear and see these women's stories.[36]

As the legislative efforts progressed, Klaus and *Sin by Silence* followed the direct trajectory of the advocacy, supporting local public community engagement by distributing additional footage and shorter versions of the film. In this way, the producers created ongoing moments to generate and regenerate public attention and outcry about the issue, and to stimulate media attention and coverage in every community. As champions and intimate spokespeople, Klaus and on-screen main subject Brenda Clubine became a two-woman community engagement machine (Figure 7.2). "Olivia would show up at any hearing, any screening, anything we needed. If we can't get our star witnesses to show up, then our bills are going to die.... [E]very time they shared their story, it really moved us along," says Ma.[37]

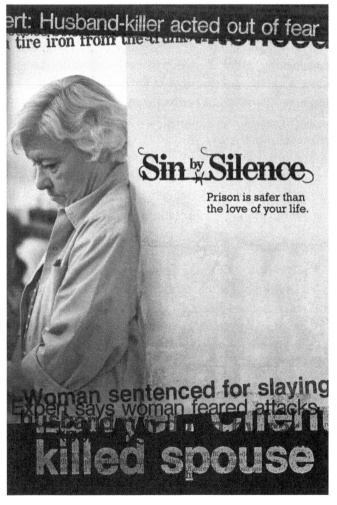

Figure 7.2. *Sin by Silence* movie poster. Image courtesy of Olivia Klaus.

The months evolved slowly, from screening to screening, community to community—filmmaker and film subject, policymaker and staff, working to smooth a rocky path to legislative change. Ma and her office worked directly with Klaus and the massive grassroots list of supporters she had amassed through local screenings around the state. As public support intensified its visibility, support for the legislation moved through the California House and Senate. Klaus turned up her efforts to support the final push with the governor, who still needed to sign them into law: "We met with everyone in the governor's office, giving them copies of the film, hosting a screening just for the governor's office and bringing Brenda [the main film subject], and engaging all of our grassroots lists of supporters to bombard the governor's office with letters and calls."[38]

On October 2, 2012, hundreds of grassroots screenings and public support letters later, the two *Sin by Silence* bills became laws signed by California Governor Jerry Brown. Both laws went into effect on January 1, 2013.[39] Assemblywoman Ma lauded the achievement, recognizing the immediate opportunity to change the story for thousands of women: "Today, we give hope to approximately 7,000 victims across the state who have survived domestic violence, who believed the system had failed them, and will now have an opportunity to speak out against injustice."[40]

Olivia Klaus, after years of work to spotlight untold stories—deeply intimate portraits of survivors—wrote in a public statement, "Years ago when I started this journey, I had no idea what change would come through creating *Sin by Silence*, but I knew I couldn't give up hope that we could make a difference to help free incarcerated, battered women. The passing of the *Sin by Silence* bills brings together a decade long journey of work to help right the wrong in this world."[41] For Brenda Clubine, who continues her advocacy on behalf of abused women throughout the country, particularly those who are incarcerated for protecting themselves, the film started a movement:

> Olivia had a dream, and her dream carried her through, and her tenacity just kept her going. I can't even begin to imagine how many times doors were slammed in her face, and people thought these women are just getting what they deserve because women don't commit violent crime. I guess being able to have seen this kind of an impact in my lifetime has been incredible. Just to see how people's minds have changed really matters, and to know women are now saying "enough is enough."[42]

Throughout the long journey—crafting the film, architecting the public engagement campaign, acting as a public spokesperson for the legislation and the women's stories—director Klaus's motivation could not be quelled, and her determination did not waver. The synergy of the documentary, the filmmaker as artist and strategic policy collaborator, an influential member of the California State Assembly, and a legal expert, alongside a massive public outcry of support through their community campaign, changed the law. Years later, the impact of the documentary and its legislative campaign continue, as Olivia Ma wrote in 2017 for the Huffington Post:

> The emotional journey I experienced while watching the "Sin by Silence" documentary inspired me to help other survivors by introducing AB 593 and AB 1593, my "Sin by Silence" bills. . . . On this five year anniversary of the bills' passage into law, I'm proud to say two other states, Oregon and New York, are focusing on similar legislation. I remember Glenda Virgil, who, in 2013, was the first woman from the film to be released as a result of my bills. I was able to give a voice to the voiceless and give these women a fighting chance for justice. It was the right thing to do.[43]

A Marine's Journey for Justice: *Semper Fi*

In 1997, after seeing a TV news report about a possible investigation of Camp LeJeune and potential chemical contaminants, retired Marine Corps Master Sgt. Jerry Ensminger—devoted to the Corps for more than 25 years—began a long quest to uncover the truth about the 1985 death of his nine-year-old daughter, Janey, from a rare form of cancer. After living with his young family for many years at Camp Lejeune, armed with a growing suspicion that the Marine Corps may have known and failed to provide information about dangerous chemical contaminants in the water supply, Ensminger devoted himself to finding answers. Steadily, he pieced together a strong dossier of materials to investigate—shocking to the former drill instructor who had "lived and breathed the 'Corps' and was responsible for indoctrinating thousands of new recruits with its motto Semper Fidelis or 'Always Faithful.'"[44] He began to transform his heartbreak into action, the beginning of a long journey to expose the truth and fight for the thousands of Marines and their families who were affected—many through losses as devastating as his own. As Ensminger reflects, "No amount of money would bring Janey back, and no amount of money will help her, either. There were still a lot of people out there affected by this and need help. That's always been my main focus."[45]

In 2004, the *Washington Post* published a story about Ensminger's efforts, "Tainted Water in the Land of Semper Fi."[46] Documentary filmmakers Rachel Libert and Tony Hardmon, who had already heard about Ensminger from his sister while working on a different project, read the story and set out to track him down. As a social-issue documentary team, they knew immediately this was a story that needed to be told. "There's this environmental message coming from such an unexpected source. He was not an environmentalist before this happened. We thought this message could really preach beyond the choir. You can be invested in the story of this man and his passion, even if you didn't connect with that issue," says Libert.[47] Recognizing that a documentary film could amplify his efforts, Ensminger agreed to let Libert and Hardmon follow his efforts to push for justice. The legislative goal was to secure healthcare for the thousands of Marines and their families who had been harmed by the toxic water contamination. The documentary film—*Semper Fi: Always Faithful*—a growing grassroots community effort, and Ensminger's one-man efforts melded into a small force.

Jerry Ensminger's journey captured the attention of US Representative John Dingell (D-MI), who served at the time as the ranking Democrat on the House of Representatives Energy and Commerce Committee. Dingell and his office had been working for several years on environmental regulation issues related to Superfund and other toxic contaminants.[48] His staff invited Ensminger to meet and testify about his daughter to the full Energy and Commerce Committee. Ensminger recalls that Dingell's office "looked like something out of the Smithsonian. We had the meeting, and he got down to brass tacks. I stopped him. I had pictures of Janey when she was undergoing treatment and her gravestone, and I said, 'This is why I'm here.' And he said, 'You're absolutely correct, and we have to stop this from happening in other places.'"[49] The documentary film team captured it all.

Ensminger's testimony solidified a role for his story and created powerful connections for him on Capitol Hill. As Ensminger continued to work with Dingell's office, he and the film team knocked on other doors in Congress. They focused on North Carolina, home to Camp Lejeune. A meeting with Senator Richard Burr (R-NC) led to Burr's office assigning a senior staffer to work with Ensminger. The slow policy work unfolded over the next several years. While Jerry Ensminger became an unexpected Capitol Hill expert, documentary filmmakers Libert and Hardmon established connections with issue advocates in order to build a strong grassroots infrastructure while they continued filming. The filmmakers understood that they needed to cultivate relationships with issue advocacy groups to help provide facts for the storytelling, to amplify Ensminger's efforts on Capitol Hill, and to create an infrastructure for eventual outreach to the public and policymakers.

While they filmed, they worked with strong advocacy supporters— particularly the Environmental Working Group (EWG) and the Project on

Government Oversight (POGO)—to help them reach other congressional offices, to distribute press releases and alerts to their members, and to help set up
Capitol Hill screenings. Heather White, then executive director of the EWG,
assigned a policy expert in her office to work directly with Ensminger and the
film team, who were already working diligently with congressional staffers in the
offices of Senators Kay Hagan (D-NC) and Richard Burr (R-NC). As savvy DC-
based advocates and policy experts, White and her team amplified the efforts
directly by drumming up public support. White, the experienced issue advocate,
understood the power of story in the policy process, as she stated:

> Every story needs to be personal. The conversation needs to be values-based, not
> technological, and needs to be bipartisan as much as possible. . . . Policy analysts
> have to become storytellers—we just have to, it's how we persuade, it's how we
> tell stories and it's how we get to the right outcome. If we can't encapsulate these
> technical, complex issues in a meaningful storytelling way, we won't be effective.[50]

The advocacy groups did more than just educate and activate their own
members and constituents. They acted as sophisticated, trusted expert guides
into the professional policy sector, working between elected officials who saw
the world through diametrically opposed partisan viewpoints. Inspired and
outraged by Jerry Ensminger's story, distinct groups—strange bedfellows
of progressive environmental justice groups, conservatives, and military
families—came together in pursuit of a common goal.

The heart and soul of the effort, though, was the human story and the
film's command of factual information. The documentary was not seen as
a one-sided advocacy vehicle, a key to its influence and impact. The film's
even-handed, factual approach to the story—and its powerful human
center—allowed members of Congress from both sides of the partisan aisle to
get involved, bypassing the usual ideological gridlock. "I've seen a lot of partisan activist groups really flame out—some in frustration or some who make
it conspiratorial—but they did this exactly the right way to ultimately be effective, even in a polarized world," says Dick Frandsen, then-lead staffer from
Representative Dingell's office.[51]

Semper Fi: Always Faithful, produced by Libert and Hardmon along with
Todd Wider and Jedd Wider, premiered in April 2011 at the Tribeca Film
Festival and on MSNBC in February 2012. The film was shortlisted for the
2012 Academy Award for Best Documentary Feature, and it was nominated for a 2013 News & Documentary Emmy Award.[52] By the time the film
screened on MSNBC, the earlier momentum of the proposed legislation had
halted. The resulting news coverage, public outcry, and timing of the TV

premiere was key to pushing the legislation over the edge, according to interviews with the filmmakers and legislative staffers. The amplified community created by the symbiosis of media coverage, advocacy groups, and public pressure in the form of letters, emails, and calls to Congress was the key to final policy success. The story of Jerry's unrelenting investigation, which "led to the shocking discovery of a Marine Corps cover-up of one of the largest water contamination incidents in U.S. history,"[53] could not be ignored.

More than a quarter-century after Jerry Ensminger lost his daughter, Janey, 15 years after his justice crusade began, and eight years of documentary filmmaking later, the legislative moment finally arrived. In August 2012, President Barack Obama signed into law *The Honoring America's Veterans and Caring for Camp Lejeune Families Act of 2012,* also known as the Janey Ensminger Act.[54] Ensminger and the filmmakers were invited to the White House for the signing ceremony. The law, based on Senator Burr's legislation, provides healthcare for the Marine Corps veterans and their families who lived or worked at Camp Lejeune from January 1, 1957, through December 31, 1987, and who have a condition linked to exposure to the toxic chemicals as listed in the legislation.[55] For Jerry Ensminger, the documentary film was essential to changing the law, and his journey was worth it, although it will never be enough: "I got a crash course in civics. If someone had told me I'd be doing all this when I retired in 1994, I'd say you were crazy."[56]

Hidden Injustice:
Playground: The Child Sex Trade in America

By the time she started producing *Playground: The Child Sex Trade in America*, a feature-length film that premiered in 2009 at the Tribeca Film Festival, director Libby Spears knew a great deal about the topic of child sex trafficking. She had spent the better part of a decade investigating the sex trafficking industry in other parts of the world, including Thailand and South Korea.[57] But what she learned there was crucial to the film that focused a spotlight at home in the United States. Her research revealed that a problem typically framed in international terms—as a troubling state of affairs in faraway places—was directly shaped by activities within the United States, "influencing the global demand and growth of the sex trafficking industry."[58] Spears shaped her documentary to push back against a lack of public awareness about the United States' role in a global tragedy and the cultural framing of child sex trafficking victims as "prostitutes," both of which were barriers to change, as the film synopsis states: "Challenging the notion that the sexual exploitation and trafficking of children is limited to back-alley brothels in developing countries, the documentary feature film, *PLAYGROUND: The Child Sex Trade in America*, traces the phenomenon to its disparate, and decidedly domestic, roots."[59]

Although her original production plans had focused on the international scope of the issue, she shifted her lens to the United States as conversations with advocates like Ernie Allen, CEO of the National Center of Missing & Exploited Children, revealed that the issue of children exploited and trafficked domestically was misunderstood and unseen to the American public or its leaders. Understanding that a documentary that focused on statistics alone would be insufficient, the film team chose to tell the story of one young person, Michelle Brown. In 2004, while directing *Playground*, Spears founded a new organization, the Nest Foundation, dedicated to ending the sexual exploitation of children.[60]

The filmmakers, including producers Jeff Vespa, Martha Adams, and Stefan Nowicki (and a powerful team of executive producers including Abigail Disney, George Clooney, Grant Heslov, Lauren Embrey, and Steven Soderbergh) did not have policy change in mind as they produced the film and worked diligently to ensure the accuracy of their facts and stories. But as they approached the end of the editing process, according to Spears, "it became clear that the film could have a tremendous impact in addressing laws that we encountered in the making of the film—laws that disproportionately criminalized victims and the lack of policy advancements that earmarked funding for resources, services and shelters."[61]

The filmmakers began to engage local communities and issue experts with the movie trailer even while the final documentary was in the editing phase. The strategy was useful for starting initial discussions and helping to shape a likely impact strategy; as their understanding deepened, the filmmakers shifted deliberately, moving away from a plan to raise general public awareness to imagining policy change. After they completed the documentary, Spears and her team began a grassroots screening tour as the film played in film festivals, and the ideas for public engagement evolved. Along the way, conversation by conversation, meeting by meeting, the team learned of a glaring legislative opportunity: At the time, no federal or state legislation decriminalized the children themselves—the victims—which, in a ripple effect, limited the opportunity to help them officially. According to Spears and her team:

At the time, there were no laws that differentiated between adults who willingly engaged in sex work, and children who were being forced to sell themselves. Because children were being arrested and treated like criminals, there were no services available to them. The most important thing that needed to happen for policy change was for minors to be recognized as victims, then resources would be made available to them.[62]

The film team formed partnerships with three nonprofit organizations that were expert advocates and policy specialists on the issue of exploited children: Polaris, the National Center for Missing and Exploited Children, and ECPAT-USA. Spears and her team supported their policy change objectives with screenings and events, which helped spark new understanding from policymakers themselves, who had not seen anything like *Playground* focused on the United States.

Interest among federal policymakers was immediate. When two senators—Senator Ron Wyden (D-OR) and Senator Dick Durbin (D-IL)—saw the film at a screening hosted by Senator Barbara Boxer (D-CA), both took early action to address the issue. Senator Durbin hosted one of the first US Senate hearings focused on child sex trafficking in the United States, citing *Playground* as the inspiration. On February 24, 2010, Senator Durbin opened the hearing, called "In Our Own Backyard: Child Prostitution and Sex Trafficking in the United States," by introducing Libby Spears and the film:

Recently I saw a powerful documentary, along with Senator Wyden—it was actually at the home of Senator Boxer who invited us over. It was a documentary entitled "Playground," and it was directed by a visionary filmmaker named Libby Spears, who is with us today. . . . I would like to show, if I can, a short, 4-minute excerpt from this documentary which had such a profound impact on Senator Wyden and myself. . . . Libby Spears, thank you. I know when we met you said that you had started your research on this issue looking overseas at the international trafficking, and somebody said you ought to look at home. And I am glad you did and opened our eyes to this, and thank you for your inspiration that led to this hearing today, and I hope it leads to new laws that will protect these children and deal with them in the right, humane way. This documentary opened the eyes of Senator Wyden and myself and many others—Senator Boxer. It is estimated that over 100,000 American children became sex-trafficking victims last year and every year.[63]

According to the filmmakers, Wyden credited the documentary with playing a vital role in building support for bipartisan legislation he introduced along with Senator John Cornyn (R-TX).[64] Introduced in March 2011, the Wyden-Cornyn Bill, known formally as the Domestic Minor Sex Trafficking Deterrence and Victims Support Act, provided funding for essential services like shelters for child victims of domestic sex trafficking, training for law enforcement, and calls for states to treat minors as victims, not criminals.[65] In January 2015, Senator Cornyn introduced the Justice for Victims of Trafficking Act; the bill, sponsored by original co-sponsors Senators Ron Wyden (D-OR), Mark Kirk (R-IL), and Amy Klobuchar (D-MN), became law in May 2015.[66]

Along the way, the film was screened at both public events and closed-door sessions with federal decision makers, including an FBI screening for 450 special agents; the Luxor International Forum, the first global gathering with particular focus on highlighting the pivotal role of the business community in anti- trafficking efforts, attended by 400 participants from more than 30 countries; a hearing before the Senate Committee on the Judiciary, Subcommittee on Human Rights and the Law; the Judicial Conference for US judges; Senator Wyden's human trafficking congressional briefing; and a screening for federal judges.[67]

The film provided both a narrative reimagining—reframing—of the core issue itself, while also serving as an educational and mobilization tool. To the experts and advocates working on child sexual exploitation in the United States, issue reframing was not a mere semantics challenge but one of the most fundamental barriers to change. Prior to the legislation around the issue, exploited minors were referenced within the context of "child prostitution," a failure to recognize their status as victims, not willing participants. ECPAT-USA's executive director Carol Smolenski sees the film's role in shifting the narrative as key:

> In some ways, *Playground* was part of a movement that was already taking place. It came out as the shift was just starting to take place and it contributed to that shift. Services are usually developed at the local level, and it contributed to that. It also really contributed to a recognition by law enforcement that these were not bad kids but kids that needed help. The film is a completely different way of looking at it.[68]

But, like many social justice issues, the policy opportunity was not unfolding solely on the federal level. The issue was differentially addressed, and yet urgently, on the state level, and the role of the film in supporting expert advocacy organizations' policy work was valuable, strategic, and timely. By the time *Playground* was produced, humanitarian organizations—including leaders like Polaris and ECPAT-USA—had been engaged for years in the hard work of advocating state laws to help minors.[69]

The state-level "Safe Harbor" laws "have two components: legal protection and provision of services," although they are enforced differently on the state level; they provide the crucial official recognition of children as victims, not as prostitutes.[70] The timing of the film was optimal and strategic for state-level public and policymaker education. According to ECPAT-USA's Smolenski, *Playground* became the indispensable strategic tool to show the public and state legislators that the children were victims and survivors—and without the human portrayal of an intimate, misunderstood challenge, the ripple effect of state laws would have faced a greater uphill battle. *Playground* was leveraged for the state-level Safe Harbor laws beginning with the crucial first state. According to Smolenski, the issue expert and advocate, the film played the crucial role in helping and urging the public and elected officials to see the problem differently:

> When New York was considering a Safe Harbor Law, I remember hearing that one of the legislators said "we don't want those kids on our block" and I knew we really needed to do education. . . . We needed to show that it wasn't just one kind of girl that was being trafficked—it's not just an urban poor people phenomenon, not just black but also white. It's so gratifying for me to see people really "get it" for the first time. There has been so much more awareness now by child protective service workers, more resources, more ways to help these children.[71]

The first state-level Safe Harbor law went into effect in New York in 2010.[72] Safe Harbor laws have now passed in 34 states as of 2015,[73] up from 18 states in 2013.[74]

For the issue of child sex exploitation in the United States, *Playground* was distributed at an optimal, crucial time in an ongoing advocacy movement for policy solutions. It was a moment during which real momentum—in both awareness and a willingness to demand change—had begun for the public and elected officials at multiple levels of government. Although the documentary focuses on intimate human stories, its command of factual information and experts was essential to the film's reception by elected officials. Notably, *Playground* was not perceived as partisan advocacy but instead as a well-researched, accurate film—not a one-sided ideological essay. According to Joel Shapiro, former senior aide to Senator Wyden of Oregon, "Libby became an expert. She was working with tremendously experienced people. She had very qualified experts that she interviewed and spoke to. . . . It's very easy to dismiss films that are seen as partisan."[75]

At the same time, Spears's narrative lens on the social problem was vitally important for policymakers and advocates—the documentary did not advocate a particular solution. Recalls Carol Smolenski, "I actually don't think the film showed real concrete solutions. It was more upstream than that and showed the problems. We could use the film to show our own recommendations about the solutions and what should happen. . . . We could not have adopted the film if it had advocated for solutions that we knew wouldn't work."[76] For her, the opportunity to work with documentary storytelling in policy engagement efforts completely changed her perspective about the importance of storytelling as a strategic, essential policy tool: "*Playground* was the only movie that really showed this issue. [Without it] I wouldn't have had any other way to tell engaging case study stories about this issue. It doesn't take much effort to watch, and it's engaging and compelling—we really needed it to help shift this issue."[77]

The documentaries profiled here coalesced the machinery of policy toward legislative success through a collaborative process with human narrative at the core. The filmmakers located themselves in the hands of connected policy networks that conferred credibility to the films through their association, and in turn, incorporated the documentary narratives into ongoing efforts for public education and policy engagement. Disparate professionals—advocacy and issue experts, policymakers and staffers, and filmmakers—formed distinct policy sub-networks[78] with the films' narratives at the epicenter, acting as a kind of "situated knowledge," or the articulation of lived human experience as a component of the policymaking process.[79] The advocacy leaders, policymakers, and their staffers activated their members and constituents, and they acted as expert policy guides, pointing the filmmakers in strategic directions to maximize their films' policy potential and reach, and they helped amplify media coverage. In so doing, the policy networks leveraged the films as persuasive, nonpartisan material, and they positioned the documentary filmmakers as spokespeople for their stories.

These were not overnight policy successes, though. Consistent themes emerge to help illuminate how these documentaries and teams were successfully able to parlay intimate human stories, rendered creatively and artistically, into changing laws. First, the documentaries provided new stories alongside nonpartisan command of facts—not propaganda. For all advocates and policymakers, focusing on partisan-framed unrealistic solutions, even unwittingly, would have meant the films likely wouldn't have been endorsed by issue experts and policy leaders. The documentaries were seen by policy professionals as nonpartisan—an articulation of facts and revelation of human stories that did not take explicit ideological, partisan positions on legislative solutions. Policymakers and issue experts did not see the documentaries as propagandistic, essay-style expressions, but as journalistic, intimate, artistically-rendered portrayals of human lives. In a culture of partisan gridlock, human-centered, truthful narrative and the explicit rejection of ideological doctrine were key to the art and business of successful policy engagement. The films reached beyond partisan choirs.

These nonfiction films are also emotional and intimate, which matters for engaging policymakers and the public. The human-centered narrative of the three social-issue documentaries was a primary element of decision-making influence. The collective immediate emotional response to the stories was motivating. Advocacy leaders, policymakers and their staffers described watching these movies as the experience of seeing a human issue for the first time, or in a new way. In turn, these lenses prompted specific policy initiatives. Seeing the real-life impact on human lives through documentary narrative was crucial.

Contemporary documentary films can play a vital role in the policy process by providing the most valuable lens of all—the human one. Regardless of the precise configuration of story and community, or artistic choices, the nonfiction movies profiled here fueled powerful tipping point moments and sparked the active engine of publics because they captured hearts and emotions in ways that policy briefs and fact sheets could not. They bypassed ideological, partisan gridlock through a connection focused on real people. In the information age, characterized by digitally engaged civic engagement, social-issue documentaries are positioned to harness the attention and commitment of publics and specialized professionals whose decisions impact daily life—policy experts and decision makers—because they illuminate stories about the shared human condition.

As we express ourselves, we have journalistic obligations, but I also
think we have cinematic obligations—or at least aspirations—and that
has to do with the depth of storytelling, the level of craft, and how a
film unfolds. I care about all those things deeply, and I don't find them
to be mutually exclusive in any way.

— **Laura Poitras**
Director, *Citizenfour*[1]

8

Interrogating Hidden Truths

Investigative Documentary

When National Security Agency (NSA) whistleblower Edward Snowden covertly reached out to documentarian Laura Poitras in January 2013, she was
already intimately familiar with the risks posed by the vast network of surveillance capabilities controlled by the US government. In the shadows of the
September 2001 terrorist attacks, and the energized political rhetoric of national security matched by the unprecedented tracking capabilities of the digital era, Poitras had fashioned herself into an expert in digital encryption.[2] It
was a necessary tool of the trade for a filmmaker whose artistic and journalistic curiosities were sparked, at least partially, by illuminating the dynamics
of state-sanctioned power.[3]

Poitras had become part of the story by 2013 (see Figure 8.1). For years
following the 2006 premiere of *My Country, My Country*, Poitras's Academy
Award–nominated feature film about the Iraq War, US border agents had de-
tained her repeatedly—upwards of 40 times.[4] Her whereabouts and activities

Story Movements. Caty Borum Chattoo, Oxford University Press (2020) © Oxford University Press.
DOI: 10.1093/oso/9780190943417.001.0001

Figure 8.1. *Citizenfour* director Laura Poitras filming an NSA construction site in Utah, 2011. Photo by Conor Provenzano, courtesy of Praxis Films.

were tracked and filed in a trove of data, a consequence of her identity as a filmmaker asking inconvenient questions.[5] By the time Snowden made contact, Poitras was already working on a documentary about Wikileaks, filming Julian Assange and plunging deep into the complexities and murky details of digital surveillance.[6] As Poitras reflects:

> The issue of surveillance had been on my mind before I started that film, partly because I was put on a watch list and I was intensely aware of it. . . . It's this looming danger and threat that I feel, and that I don't experience the world is paying attention to, and it's really scary, and I know it's being used as a tool of power. And we're not questioning or challenging how that power is going to be deployed on populations.[7]

Snowden's contact was revelatory, though. Over the following year, Poitras crafted an intimate documentary feature film, *Citizenfour*, that chronicles her encrypted correspondence with Snowden, whose knowledge and disclosure of the National Security Agency's secret surveillance of American citizens constituted, as scholar Lisa Parks noted, "one of the most significant acts of whistleblowing in U.S. history."[8] Unspooling over eight covert days in the Mira Hotel in Hong Kong—along with veteran investigative journalists Glenn

Greenwald and Ewen MacAskill—Snowden's inside knowledge of the NSA surveillance program added layers to the reporters' existing understanding, even while global news outlets broke his story.[9]

The human drama that centers Edward Snowden in an unfolding saga of political intrigue propels *Citizenfour*'s narrative, and the film is an unprecedented harbinger of a new age. It reveals the surveillance and privacy issues unwoven through a whistleblower's leak, but Poitras also urgently points documentary filmmakers and journalists to the potent peril of the digital world order: "For me, it's obviously a film about the dangers of mass surveillance. And it's also a film about journalism and threats to journalism, and a film about sources and threats to sources who come forward to expose government wrongdoing."[10] Indeed, "the film becomes a meta-document that communicates its own fraught process of production," noted media scholar Daniel Grinsberg.[11] *Citizenfour* is, then, simultaneously a marker in time and warning system for investigative documentarians working in a digital climate of risk.[12]

In October 2014, after more than a year of editing, encrypting files, moving her physical location, and storing duplicate footage in multiple locations,[13] Laura Poitras premiered *Citizenfour* at the New York Film Festival and the BFI London Film Festival several days later, followed by other festivals.[14] In February 2015, *Citizenfour*, produced by Poitras along with Mathilde Bonnefoy and Dirk Wilutzky, won the Academy Award for Best Documentary Feature; it premiered the following day on HBO, and later that month on Channel 4 in the United Kingdom.[15] The film is widely lauded by critics and award-granting organizations as an act of public service and a crucial interrogation of democracy.[16] In the tradition of whistleblowing journalism, in Poitras's words, "The public has a right to know more about what the government is doing in terms of security and surveillance."[17]

Both Poitras's production practices and editorial point of view are meaningful in shaping a thoughtful contemplation about the role and influence of investigative documentary that is both artistic and journalistic, incurring unique peril while it reveals and critiques power in the digital age. Indeed, danger was compounded by Poitras's status as an independent documentarian working in an investigative capacity—not an employee of a news or entertainment company. She recalled in a media interview: "I felt isolated and solitary. I work with people to make films, but I don't have a newsroom sitting behind me to talk about these things. I was kind of out there, engaging with the source and not knowing."[18] She forged her own path. Digital mechanisms to protect footage, privacy, and sources were available by 2011; Poitras was diligent about learning and developing full expertise in the new privacy and encryption tools,[19] eventually also training other documentarians to use digital security measures.[20]

While independence posed risk, it also empowered Poitras's artistic creativity and allowed a cinematic, human expression of a complex, technological challenge. In this way, the film's editorial perspective departs from the stringent objectivity conceit of investigative journalism—*Citizenfour* clearly transmits Poitras's personal point of view and her own narrative. As she said in a media interview: "It was pretty self-evident that I had participated in these events, and it [the film] had to be told from a subjective point of view. But that doesn't mean that it's not still journalism. Just because I'm telling it from a subjective point of view, it also needs to be told with the same fact-checking, journalistic responsibility that you had in any other films I've done in the past."[21] She maintains her adherence to truth and accuracy, with the license of artistic freedom that allowed the duality of her own narrative and Snowden's to coalesce in a gripping, creative story.

Beyond its moment in the public spotlight, *Citizenfour* motivated a new initiative that will evolve the practice and influence of contemporary cinematic investigative documentary storytelling. Inspired by *Citizenfour*, Field of Vision, a film unit of the First Look Media organization, was co-created by Poitras and launched in 2015 as "a filmmaker-driven documentary unit that commissions and creates original short-form nonfiction films about developing and ongoing stories around the globe," producing "cinematic work that tells the stories of our world from new perspectives."[22] Field of Vision co-creator and executive producer Charlotte Cook explains the vision:

> Field of Vision was started under the idea of two things. One was how can we bring artistic filmmaking language into the news cycle? And what would that look like, and could—at a political time when people get apathetic as they get bombarded with the same kind of narratives—an artistic viewpoint disrupt that and actually help a subject matter purely through craft and language? The second part was that we were founded by a group of filmmakers who'd made different kinds of films and realizing that having an outlet for short-form filmmaking really helped people keep earning money, but also to be able to explore their own craft, because when you make a feature length film, you have to stick with the approach you start with, whereas for the short, you can play.[23]

In 2018, Field of Vision announced a new fellowship for emerging documentarians, offering them newsroom resources—legal support and a research team—while upholding the creative, artistic practices of nonfiction filmmakers operating amid threat and opportunity.[24] The influence of

Citizenfour's approach to investigative, cinematic documentary continues and expands, then, embodied in the gaze and grit of future filmmakers and the stories they will tell.

Citizenfour exemplifies a particular classification of contemporary investigative nonfiction films and the impulses of filmmakers who produce them—to interrogate and expose hidden truths, weaving stories with the artistic license of cinema. Creative investigative documentary makers examine topical realities and employ many of the practices and intentions of investigative journalism; at the same time, they make editorial decisions to shape artful films—including an evident point of view, with cinematic choices in cinematography, editing, music, graphic art, pacing. This chapter argues that investigative documentary serves as an essential component of democratic discourse, offering a unique depth and emotional resonance that expands traditional investigative journalism. And yet, the two—investigative journalism and investigative cinema—work in tandem. It's not "either or," but "both and." Within a larger cultural exchange of information, investigative documentary makers balance creative artistry with journalistic practices while they navigate risk and security concerns in precarious times, and they play a vital role in democratic functioning by fostering public awareness and conversation.

It's a meaningful cultural moment for filmmakers motivated by this instinct. On the one hand, the practice of watchdog journalism in newsrooms around the country has declined in the digital economy, along with dwindling reporter numbers in general.[25] Investigative journalism has been hit hard.[26] As Field of Vision's Cook reflects:

> The difficult thing when it comes to investigative documentaries is that traditionally over history, those topics had been covered by news outlets. But then suddenly all their investigative departments were going, and it was evident to those of us who were keeping an eye on this that documentary filmmakers were going to pick up that slack. And they did so without any of that institutional support—without the legal support and without protection of any kind, and we've seen instances of filmmakers really being hurt by that. Trying to find that balance is something we really care about.[27]

On the other hand, an evolution for investigative journalism is unfolding, with new possibilities for ways of doing business and mechanisms for funding, production, and distribution. "While investigative reporting has drastically diminished in traditional and mainstream newsrooms, it has rapidly expanded into different forms and combinations in web ventures and at universities throughout the world," wrote professor and journalist Brant Houston.[28] Crucial to the future are robust economic models and courageous institutions that can support and publish material that speaks truth to power; as longtime investigative journalist Charles Lewis noted, "What is needed are new, sustainable economic models for in-depth news and a new, much greater ownership and management commitment to publishing it 'without fear or favor.' "[29] The investigative films produced by Field of Vision, as well as other independent documentary filmmakers—showcased on outlets from the *Guardian* to the *New York Times* to Vice Media—are positioned in the context of this evolutionary juncture.

Investigative nonfiction cinema shares characteristics with investigative journalism, and yet it is distinct in meaningful ways. ProPublica's Richard Tofel describes investigative journalism as "journalism that seeks to reveal something that someone with some modicum of power (a person, group or institution) seeks to keep a secret."[30] Further, the desire to expose and interrogate is intentionally meant to challenge power; investigative journalism "is adversarial and populist, challenging the powers that be. It brings with it moral judgments."[31] It is "a way of seeking reform within the system. It is one of democracy's safety valves."[32] Laura Poitras describes her own motivation as both artistic impulse and a desire to understand—alongside a theme of investigating power—rather than focusing on a reform outcome:

> I find that I get absolutely compelled by the film. It's not like an obligation or a social need to do good, but I want to understand something. I want to understand how something is happening and I want to learn. . . . And it often revolves around a repeated theme of interrogating power—exposing it, holding it to account, and challenging it. For instance, with the Iraq War, I just felt this profound sense of despair, and that the media was failing, and that the country was heading down an incredibly dark path, which I think we've continued to go down, unfortunately.[33]

And yet, investigative reporting is produced within the confines of formal rules, norms, and practices of journalism, with an emphasis on sharing multiple sides of a story, and with the ideals of objectivity and neutral editorial voice. Creative documentary storytelling often decidedly takes a point of view. How, then, can we describe the practices of creative investigative documentary makers who craft cinematic films that uncover and challenge power, expose injustice, and inform the public? Investigative documentarians work from journalistic standards of truth, employing fact-checking mechanisms and verifying sources. But these filmmakers don't view an evident editorial point of view as oppositional to truth and accuracy—and fairness. Creative investigative documentary filmmakers make artistic choices that can highlight emotional impact or provide a deep view into a particular perspective, even inserting themselves into the story, as in the case of *Citizenfour* and Laura Poitras's narrative within the unfolding of Edward Snowden's saga.

Veteran documentarian and journalist Carrie Lozano, director of the International Documentary Association (IDA) Enterprise Documentary Fund for cinematic, creative investigative documentaries—who holds a unique vantage point given her professional experience in both investigative journalism and independent documentary—reflects:

> Departure from the two-sides paradigm [of journalism] is really important in independent investigative documentary film. Most independent film does have a point of view and I think that's critical. . . . What is really important is—is the film fair? Is there enough other documentation for you to make your case? Just because you're being fair doesn't mean you don't have a point of view. . . . That's a critical part of journalism that should be maintained if we're going to have integrity.[34]

In a groundbreaking 2015 report, *Dangerous Documentaries: Reducing Risk When Telling Truth to Power*, scholar Patricia Aufderheide's interviews with more than 50 contemporary investigative nonfiction storytellers and journalists revealed that creative investigative documentary makers agree strongly with reporting practices and beliefs codified in various journalistic codes of standards—that is, dedication to public interest motivation, transparency, accurate representation of oneself, truth, and accuracy.[35] And yet, investigative documentarians depart from the journalistic standard of attempted objectivity, as she wrote in the report:

> They [documentary filmmakers] certainly believe in fairness and accuracy. But filmmakers also believed that their job was often to tell a story from a particular point of view, and to capture the richness of that experience, not to report an issue from different sides. . . . The difference highlighted in this last point reflects, we believe, different cultural experiences and training rather than a fundamental disagreement over values and purpose, or even methods. Journalists and non-fiction filmmakers have historically worked in overlapping but different networks.[36]

Creative investigative documentary storytellers are motivated by a sense of public purpose and moral outrage. They share this drive with investigative journalists, who operate from a strong sense of right and wrong, prioritizing ethics over rules;[37] working to expose wrongdoing;[38] and providing a sense of conscience by spotlighting the interplay between the powerful and victims.[39] As Lozano says of independent investigative documentarians: "I do think the motivation is to change the public conversation around a really important issue."[40] An element of moral storytelling and a desire to make change is embedded in investigative documentary, as is the value of an independent editorial voice. In my own study of documentary filmmakers in United States, *The State of the Documentary Field: 2018 Survey of Documentary Professionals*, documentary makers indicated two top elements as the most meaningful aspects of their work: the ability to make a positive impact on social issues, and independent creative voice.[41] Creating investigative documentaries outside newsrooms is, in fact, what makes them unique and valuable as "a critical piece of our storytelling culture," as Carrie Lozano articulates:

> Independent documentarians can access stories that wouldn't easily be told within a newsroom. That can have to do with the relationship-building, that might have to do with time involved, that might have to do with just the sheer cost of doing that work. They can access stories that I think journalists can't quite access. And creativity—independents are really scrappy and really creative, and that creative storytelling is what touches people. You can have ten investigative reports in the paper and we all read them and we're all horrified, but we're not necessarily emotionally touched. I think the power of creative independent documentary film is to really touch people deeply or to just be really provocative and make them think and see things in a different way..[42]

But what about dangers to investigative documentary makers—and the potential hazards that exist *because* they are independent? Risk is high for investigative nonfiction media-makers who seek to question authority and the status quo. Journalists are under constant threat around the world, and so too are investigative documentary storytellers—with distinctive areas of peril that can originate, at least in part, as a consequence of their editorial independence, thus threatening their ability to produce and disseminate stories that may be inconvenient to powerful institutions and individuals. As scholar Daniel Grinsberg wrote, "Obstacles such as censorship, restricted access, legal action, and seizure have all prevented the dissemination of critical arguments. They have also motivated an immeasurable, but undoubtedly substantial, amount of self-censorship throughout documentary history."[43]

Risk is compounded outside the newsroom, and for makers without journalistic training, says Lozano: "Independent filmmakers do have real journalistic challenges. . . . There are three big buckets—legal, safety, reporting—that pop up pretty regularly as areas of risk."[44] Investigative documentary filmmakers don't have the same legal, budgetary, or risk-assessment resources as in-house journalists when they work in hostile environments or critique government power. Potential danger to their personal safety and security, and their sources, is real. Compounding the traditional threats investigative documentarians have faced for decades, "contemporary documentarians like Poitras must now also contend with the risks posed to digital information and communication technologies (ICTs)"[45]—and all such technologies, like laptops and smartphones that are essential to filmmaking, pose "a calculated risk for documentarians,"[46] wrote scholar Daniel Grinberg. Absolute security for data, footage, and correspondence with sources and subjects is profoundly difficult to guarantee.

Contours of risk and practices of investigative documentary filmmakers have endured for decades and will continue, but the internet-based system poses an unprecedented set of new opportunities and challenges. Leaders in the documentary field have noticed. In 2015, the Double Exposure Investigative Film Festival, the first contemporary annual convening to spotlight the intersections between creative investigative documentary and investigative journalism, premiered in Washington, DC, and continues to expand.[47] In 2017, partially inspired by the 2015 *Dangerous Documentaries* report published by the Center for Media & Social Impact, the International Documentary Association, with funding from the MacArthur Foundation, launched the Enterprise Documentary Fund, which funds and provides journalistic resources to independent creative nonfiction storytellers working in an investigative capacity.[48] As IDA's executive director Simon Kilmurry explains:

> In the past few years, we have seen a kind of renaissance in investigative documentary. . . . I thought our documentary community brought a unique lens into this investigative work because of the length of time they could spend on a topic that could allow the kinds of nuance and complications of life to come out. Unlike traditional journalists at *The New York Times* or *The Washington Post*, they were not afraid of embracing emotion and art. *The New York Times* does a great investigative piece that's well-written and grounded. *The New Yorker* balances the long-form essays that are suffused with solid journalism but also an artistry that understands a creativity behind it. . . . For me, it's an equivalence there when I look at the kinds of documentary films that balance the creativity and investigation.[49]

Embodied in these programs and others, we can visualize a future for the continuing, evolving practice of documentary filmmaking that investigates authority and reveals injustice through artistic modes of expression. How this storytelling is constructed—and the influence of this documentary approach in its ability to foster public dialogue—is the remaining focus of this chapter, which spotlights two films made by investigative documentary filmmakers who balance creativity, art, risk, journalistic practice, safety, privacy, accuracy, and the public's right to know about hidden truths lurking in dark corners.

Trial by Homophobia: *Southwest of Salem: The Story of the San Antonio Four*

In the early 1990s, before they were indelibly designated "the San Antonio Four" in the media eye, Elizabeth Ramirez, Cassandra Rivera, Kristie Mayhugh, and Anna Vasquez were four best friends taking care of each other during the busy days of their 20s. As the young women graduated from high school and began their adult lives in San Antonio, Texas, they created a close-knit family together. Liz, Cassie, Kristie, and Anna also were well acquainted with the stigma of being gay—homophobia was alive and well in a particular time and place.[50] Still, they carried on with the usual quarter-life preoccupations of jobs and families and love stories and the future. Cassie and Anna were a couple raising Cassie's two children from an earlier marriage. Liz and Kristie were roommates, friends, and lovers. It was an inseparable quartet centered around Liz's and Kristie's apartment, a hub of activity and community.

A self-described family person, Liz didn't hesitate when her brother-in-law—her sister's ex-husband—asked if his daughters could stay with her for a few days in 1994. For a week, Liz took care of her nieces, then aged 7 and 9, while Kristie, Cassie, and Anna spent time in the apartment as usual. It was an unremarkable stint, "doing routine, mundane things such as shopping and going to Arby's for lunch," as the women would later recount.[51] Months later, they learned that the two girls had shared elaborate stories of sexual assault at the hands of the four women—abuse that took place in the apartment, according to the children. The long saga of an unexpected life chapter began at that moment for Liz, Anna, Cassie, and Kristie. As Anna later recalled, "I just couldn't believe it."[52]

Despite their shock at being accused of an unthinkable crime, the four women cooperated fully with police and investigators. They were convinced the truth would come to light quickly—the girls' stories, after all, were inconsistent,[53] and in prior years, Liz had rejected love letters and romantic advances from her brother-in-law, who she thought was particularly unhappy about her attraction to women.[54] But as the months and years went by, the situation escalated all the way to criminal court. In Liz's trial, the first of the group, the pediatrician who testified in the case, Dr. Kellogg, presented her interpretation of physical evidence and also speculated about satanic abuse of the girls, fitting with a cultural context in the 1980s and '90s. The fact that the women were gay became an explicit theme in the courtroom; a clearly derogatory perspective revealed itself in testimony that included lines of questioning like: "Insertion of objects into the vagina is consistent with a gay sexual lesbian relationship—sexual relationship, isn't it?"[55] Debbie Nathan, co-founder of the advocacy organization National Center for Reason and Justice and an expert in the case, noted: "There was homophobia in the police department, among the investigators. There was homophobia in the trial, and there was homophobia in the whole city."[56]

In 1997, Elizabeth Ramirez was found guilty of aggravated assault of a child and indecency with a child—a prison sentence of 37.5 years.[57] In 1998, Cassandra Rivera, Kristie Mayhugh, and Anna Vasquez were found guilty of the same charges, each sentenced to 15 years in prison.[58] As Nathan would later reflect, the case of the San Antonio Four, as they were publicly known at that point, represented "one of the last gasps of the satanic ritual abuse panic" of the 1980s and early '90s that had convicted primarily gay daycare providers of satanic sexual abuse of children.[59] And so it was that the four women—working-class lesbians without the money or connections to fight for a deeper look into their cases—were absorbed into the complex web of the American prison system, locked away, and virtually forgotten.

The women sat in prison for years before a Canadian professor and researcher, Darrell Otto, began digging around. In 2008, after learning their stories and conducting his own research, he contacted Nathan. Interest in their innocence and potentially wrongful convictions picked up. In 2010, Michelle Mondo, a reporter from the *San Antonio Express-News*, published a deep investigation about the story, pointing out inconsistencies in the courtroom testimony and a clear homophobic bias against the women.[60] Attorneys at the Innocence Project of Texas, a legal organization that fights for new trials and exoneration of wrongly convicted individuals, launched a new investigation shortly thereafter.

At that juncture, with new momentum sparked by an expert advocate, a dogged legal team, and a renewed public spotlight sparked by local investigative journalism, the documentary about the four women was born. Determined to call attention to their story, expert advocate Debbie Nathan contacted Austin-based documentary filmmaker Deborah S. Esquenazi, a native Texan and former intern with *The Village Voice* investigative reporting team. Nathan shared the court testimony with Esquenazi, along with little-seen home video footage of the four women from the early 2000s (Figure 8.2). Esquenazi recalls: "It was clear that the media, when reporting on these four women, never told the story of the women themselves. . . . I'm looking at the home video tape and seeing this beautiful makeshift family and all the ways they are being torn apart."[61]

She was immediately inspired to tell their story, by then—13 years after the first conviction—a narrative also focused on the women's fight for release and exoneration with the support of the Innocence Project. As Esquenazi reviewed court documents and videos, she was convinced of their innocence and two other truths: There was more to the women's story than what had been permitted or framed in the court proceedings, and she was well equipped to share the kind of personal, intimate nuance required to shape the narrative. As she recounts the inciting moments and her moral connection to the story:

> At the end of our conversation [Debbie Nathan and Esquenazi], she said, I think it would be really good for you because it's a case about four lesbians. I thought, "what does she mean by that?" I was not out yet. I didn't come out until I made the film. She clearly knew. She sends me the [court] transcripts, and when I read the transcripts from Elizabeth's trial, I was just pretty stunned. When I got to the voir dire [jury selection transcript], I thought, "this reads like a piece of fiction." People

Figure 8.2. Anna Vasquez and Cassandra Rivera in early home movies, as featured in *Southwest of Salem: The Story of the San Antonio Four*. Photo courtesy of *Southwest of Salem* documentary.

easily admitting that they don't feel comfortable around gay people. They're on the jury and they said that. . . . Then I see the [home video] tape, and the tape just kills me. . . . At that point, I just knew. That was the origin—that really tugged my heartstrings and I thought "now I know what I know, and I can't go backwards." I just don't think I would have been able to sleep.[62]

Over the course of the next several years, Esquenazi, who calls herself an investigative filmmaker, dug into the case and crafted the documentary, *Southwest of Salem: The Story of the San Antonio Four*, which centers its story around her interviews with the four women in prison, the previously unseen home videos that depict a loving group of friends, and their search for inconsistencies and evidence that could release them from prison sentences that stretched years into the future. Esquenazi captures the women's pain and a sense of their shock as they recount the rampant homophobia in the courtrooms and the injustice of their cases. In one interview in the film, with tears in her eyes and a wavering voice, Anna Vasquez recalls, "According to the people in court, this is what gay people do. That's what they said."[63] As one film reviewer later wrote, the documentary opened a narrative that was unseen at the time of their convictions:

> The four come across as likeable young women who had overcome much (low-paying jobs, rejection by parents) to find their small but supportive community. Being gay and working-class may be the best explanation for how they wound up convicted of such unthinkable crimes. As Mayhugh remembers it, prosecutors at the trial spoke as though homosexuality and child molestation went hand in hand; the fact that four gay women lived together, in this conservative part of the country, seemed to set the stage for "cult-like activity."[64]

As the film team and the Innocence Project continued their work along parallel tracks, the story took a dramatic turn, all captured in the documentary. Major revelations revealed the women's innocence. In 2012, one of Elizabeth Ramirez's nieces, now a grown woman, recounted her testimony on camera to Esquenazi and the attorneys, who had tracked her down. Her father had threatened her and her sister when they were little girls, she told them. Esquenazi shared the audio of the conversation with local reporters to keep the story alive, a turning point in the filmmaking itself. As she said in a press interview: "Once that happened, a buzz about it started in San Antonio and Austin. Local networks started asking our documentary team, 'Are you willing to share any of that footage?' . . . Maybe sharing your documentary footage upfront isn't necessarily common, but my goal was to get these women out of prison. In fact, that was sort of when the film became a part of the process of getting these women out of prison."[65] A short time later, the physical evidence of the girls' alleged sexual assault was reconsidered due to a new state "junk science law" that permitted new trials for cases convicted with the help of flawed science.[66] With the most damaging two pieces of testimony debunked, the women were granted new trials, beginning with Ramirez. By November 2013, Liz, Cassie, Kristie, and Anna were free women, released after more than a decade behind prison walls.[67] The documentary reveals, and intervenes in, the full journey.

Southwest of Salem: The Story of the San Antonio Four, produced by Esquenazi along with Sam Tabet, premiered at the Tribeca Film Festival in April 2016, followed by screenings and accolades at many additional festivals and a theatrical run, later garnering a GLAAD Media Award for Outstanding Documentary, a Peabody Award, and an Emmy nomination.[68] In October 2016, the documentary premiered on Investigation Discovery as part of the network's true-crime investigation series.[69] And yet, the quest for the women's full exoneration continued. Esquenazi's work was not over. Public attention was fundamental and necessary, as Innocence Project of Texas attorney Jeff Blackburn says on camera: "People think that these cases are won or lost in court. They're not. They're won or lost in the public's mind. Without real support and mobilization of that support, we will not win this thing."[70]

Launched from the first festival and television premiere of the documentary, Esquenazi and her film impact team, along with the Innocence Project of Texas, provided ways for the public to sign petitions, contact the district attorney's office, and keep awareness and pressure in the public eye through social media and news coverage, along with grassroots screenings of the film.[71] On November 23, 2016, the women were exonerated of all charges in the Texas State Criminal Court of Appeals; Judge David Newell wrote in the majority opinion: "Those defendants have won the right to proclaim to the citizens of Texas that they did not commit a crime. That they are innocent."[72] As documentarian Esquenazi reflects: "This is the dream of every journalist, to blow open a kind of Watergate and that kind of feeling of what it would be like to be this under-resourced, closeted girl helping this case? That was definitely in my mind. As we got farther and farther into it, it started becoming a reality and people joined the fight. We saw the audience also take the story and ingest it and consume it and make it their own. That really helped."[73]

The documentary about four innocent women reveals meaningful insights about investigative, creative nonfiction storytelling—and its value in the democratic process involved in seeking justice. Journalistic practice was integral as Esquenazi gathered data, secured permission to film in the courtroom, reached out to sources, and scoured archival research and primary documents. And yet, the departure from strict journalistic rules was also valuable. Working from a place of alleged objectivity seemed, to her, to be inauthentic to the story, even while she pursued accuracy and fairness. She was motivated by the morality of injustice, explicitly pushing for reform and change—like an investigative journalist—but the creative license opened up by a distinct point of view allowed the intimate, emotional portrayal that departed from the existing narrative. As Esquenazi says:

> We all know that this idea of objectivity is false, and we all come to the table with our points of view and our ancestry and our race and our social identities—and it's bullshit. For me going backward would be hard. Because that's denying that I come with all of these identities to the table. But why would I deny those? Those are real, that's my identity. Let's put that on the table and say that's my point of view, and let's move into a different realm to talk about things. . . . [I]t is ridiculous to give the most powerful people a point of view after they've oppressed and there's evidence of that. . . . Why do we give them a platform and not properly hear from those who have been victimized?[74]

Esquenazi believes her documentary provided an intimate, nuanced portrait of the four women and their stories precisely because of her own identity and the lens she brought to the topic and her relationships with them—a departure from the norms of attempted neutrality in classic journalistic practice: "If I were a white, straight male filmmaker, how would this film had been different? It might have been more of a *60 Minutes* story. It's clearly because of my own self-oppression, my own internalized homophobia, my own experience growing up as a first-generation immigrant in Texas that I need to tell this story from this point of view. . . . Because of agency and representation, I knew I was going to tell a story from their point of view."[75] As an integral part of her production process, Esquenazi worked with queer communities in Texas to screen raw footage as she gathered it. She credits this approach as vital to the final film:

> One of the reasons *Southwest of Salem* was able to do what it did was we would sit down with gay women and trans people of color and watch and bear witness to these stories and talk about them. . . . It was so powerful to get people to echo back what they are seeing and then experiencing in their own lives. . . . [W]e did this for two years. By the time we applied for Sundance [production funding] we had done 14 of these screenings. I credit the queer community in San Antonio and Austin for making this happen.[76]

For Esquenazi, editorial independence opened up areas of risk, and yet was integral to the storytelling itself. She was not working inside a news or entertainment company while she made the film—editorial and production decisions were her own, as were the relationships with Elizabeth, Anna, Cassie, and Kristie. At the same time, funding was difficult to raise. She faced the potential for legal risk, and as an independent investigative filmmaker, she didn't have the resources to seek or maintain legal support. But the intimate access afforded to the film's audience, Esquenazi notes, comes from her independent artistic, journalistic sensibilities. Even details about production infrastructure were meaningful given the peculiarities of the context—featuring deep conversations with women already situated in vulnerable positions in prison, as she says: "Netflix now says you need a specific 4K Red camera to make documentaries. I can't imagine making *Southwest of Salem* with that camera. I used a shitty little camera to make me disappear. . . . I don't think the San Antonio Four would have opened up the way they did [otherwise]. . . . If we were a crew of four people plus the correctional officers, they would have been unwilling to share what they shared."[77]

Southwest of Salem: The Story of the San Antonio Four interrogated a forgotten story through a process and set of relationships that worked together to seek justice. It did so with artistic vision and a filmmaker's distinct point of view—and trusted connections forged with the film's subjects. The documentary did not work alone to bring about change, even while it played a clear part in the eventual fate of the four women. *Southwest of Salem* notably supplied an emotional, intimate, human portrayal that investigated new ideas and evidence alongside the crucial work of local investigative journalists, an expert advocate who brought together various constituencies, a dedicated legal team, and queer communities who supplied their perspectives and lived experiences to authentically shape the narrative. In so doing, the movie illuminated a dark corner of injustice and provided a counternarrative to disrupt a seemingly settled "official" narrative—a destructive, homophobic perspective shaped in the courtroom—that had never been truthful at all.

Exposing the Voyeurs: *The Feeling of Being Watched*

When James Comey took the helm of the Federal Bureau of Investigation (FBI) in 2013, he expressed his admiration for Dr. Martin Luther King Jr. by assigning agency employees to read King's "Letter from a Birmingham Jail" and directing them to visit the Martin Luther King Jr. Memorial in Washington,

DC.[78] He viewed the FBI's famed surveillance of King as "shameful"—a troubling chapter for an organization that had strayed far off course.[79] At the time, the FBI's COINTELPRO program, a massive counterintelligence program that operated from 1956 to 1971 under the auspices of investigating the Communist Party of the United States, had broadened its tracking well into major domestic organizations and individuals involved in the civil rights movement[80] and broadly surveilled communities and organizations operating toward social justice goals,[81] while also tracking terrorist organizations like the Ku Klux Klan. But, as historian Jeffrey O. G. Ogbar wrote, discriminatory surveillance was institutionally entrenched by that point—not, in fact, an isolated scenario:

> The campaign against King is best understood as a continuum of government policies that pre-date King by decades. The FBI had been, like other American institutions, inextricably tied to the ideology of white supremacy. In the 1930s, everything from the military to restaurants officially discriminated nationwide. Challenges to that archaic and endemic belief were almost always considered subversive. . . .
> FBI agents worked with journalists to plant stories in order to discredit leadership and organizations. Across the country, the Bureau collaborated with local police to repress targeted groups. Sharing resources and intelligence, activists were arrested, fired from jobs, expelled from schools and lost business contracts. COINTELPRO even used switchboard operators and postal workers to spy on citizens, with or without court order.[82]

More than a half-century later, a contemporary FBI director seemingly saw value in reminding a new generation of federal agents about the perils of misplacing citizens' civil liberties. It was a rare rebuke of FBI conduct within its own ranks. Tracking black civil rights leaders, however, was hardly a singular phenomenon—the new director might have pointed to any number of such chapters in the history of government surveillance used "to track Americans who were perceived as enemies."[83] Citizen surveillance in the United States is widespread in the internet age, but the right to privacy is disproportionately applied across population groups when it comes to government activities. In their 2017 report, *The Disparate Impact of Surveillance*, Pulitzer Prize–winning investigative journalist Barton Gellman and policy colleague Sam Adler-Bell wrote:

> We do not need a unified theory of privacy to show that, in each of its meanings, marginal communities enjoy far less of it in practice. In some contexts, poor people and people of color have legal rights to privacy, but no means to exercise them;

"paper rights," as Karl Llewellyn called them.[84] In other contexts, the government justifies extraordinary surveillance in superficially general language that applies exclusively, or close to exclusively, in minority neighborhoods. In still others, the government denies a disfavored class a privacy right, even in principle, that other Americans freely enjoy.[85]

Well beyond tracking leaders and organizations, probing deep into neighborhoods, "historically, government surveillance has often been used to wrongly target, and surveil communities of color," according to the American Civil Liberties Union (ACLU).[86] Groups with "elevated risk" for entrapment in post-9/11 terrorism sting operations include undocumented immigrants, racial minority groups, religious minorities, and individuals with low socioeconomic status.[87] The attacks of 9/11 launched a climate that precipitously increased the mandate and resources to investigate Muslim American communities.[88]

Evidence of Muslim Americans under watch has been laid bare for public view—or some of it, at least. In 2011, a series of Pulitzer Prize–winning investigative reports from Matt Apuzzo and Adam Goldman of the Associated Press—which became part of their 2013 book, *Enemies Within: Inside the NYPD's Secret Spying Unit and Bin Laden's Final Plot Against America*—broke open the story about widespread official surveillance of Muslim Americans by the New York Police Department (NYPD) in collaboration with the Central Intelligence Agency (CIA).[89] According to their investigation, the NYPD infiltrated student groups, places of worship, and neighborhoods without any connections to crime or terrorism.[90] Revealing the stress to Muslim American neighborhoods living under an assumed surveillance state, "the reporting also brought to light the coercion tactics used to leverage Muslim Americans to inform on members of their local communities," wrote scholar Sara Kamali.[91] New York, however, was hardly the only site under government-sanctioned tracking. Elsewhere in 2011, civil liberties organizations sued the FBI over surveillance in California mosques; the FBI violated worshippers' First Amendment rights, said the Council on American-Islamic Relations and the ACLU, and the widespread damage to the relationship between government authorities and American Muslims was acute.[92] The stories abound.

None of this felt particularly revelatory to filmmaker Assia Boundaoui. Growing up in the 1990s and early 2000s in the suburban Chicago community of Bridgeview, Illinois, Boundaoui lived for years with a gnawing feeling that she—and her family and neighbors—were living under a voyeuristic gaze, "and even though not a single person in my community has ever been convicted of anything related to terrorism, we still feel like we're being watched."[93]

She recalled waking up to men on a telephone pole outside her house in the early hours of the morning, curious knocks and visits from people in dark suits who knew her neighbors' names, and stories shared in hushed tones by members of her tight-knit Muslim American community, where life revolved around family and faith.[94] With journalistic training and experience, Boundaoui was determined to investigate the whispered mystery of her own neighborhood. She knew, however, that her authentic narrative would be a more nuanced exploration than a detached examination. Her take on the scenario would require a deeply personal probe of her own story and suspicions, which began well before the events of 9/11 heightened government-sanctioned scrutiny of Muslim Americans. As she expresses her motivations:

> I always had in in my mind that I wanted to tell the story about the place where I grew up and I wanted to get to the bottom of why everyone in my community felt like they were under surveillance. . . . I felt like the FBI looked at all of us like we were a bunch of terrorists, and their question would be "are you or are you not terrorists?" and my question is "did the FBI violate our civil rights in these decades of surveillance?" That's my question. . . . This film is not just an investigative film but also a personal film where I tried to cope with and reconcile what two decades of surveillance has personally done to me and my family.[95]

Five years in the making, Boundaoui's documentary film, *The Feeling of Being Watched*, produced by Jessica Devaney, chronicles her firsthand journey as she investigates suspected FBI activity in her hometown of Bridgeview, Illinois. Unknown to her at the start of production, the FBI had, indeed, planted itself in her neighborhood for years, part of a long-running investigation into alleged ties between community members and funding for terrorist operations in the Middle East.[96] Bridgeview was a prime target in a counterintelligence operation called "Operation Vulgar Betrayal, a major probe into 'terrorist financing' launched in late 1996 by the FBI's counterterrorism unit."[97] The documentary follows along—a hybrid of cinema verité, personal narrative, and investigative journalism—as Boundaoui begins asking her neighbors about their experiences. Her task is not easy, as she says in the film, because "a lot of people in my neighborhood have stories about being watched, but most of them are afraid to talk out loud about it, especially when there's a camera around."[98] Simultaneously, in the story on screen and off, she launches a dogged research and reporting process to find evidence of government surveillance, leading her to the truth about Operation Vulgar Betrayal and its laser focus on Bridgeview's families.

In a unique portrayal of journalistic practice in a creative documentary film, Boundaoui files multiple Freedom of Information Act (FOIA) requests to seek FBI surveillance documents about her own family, along with her neighbors and friends. Months pass, denial after denial, as official return letters from the US Department of Justice detail the ways in which this department plans not to comply fully with the FOIA requests, citing administrative challenges, national security concerns, or questioning the public interest value of her request. As the film reveals, the Department of Justice finally agrees to send records—but piece by piece, stretching over years. The documentary unfolds with scenes of Boundaoui and her family and friends enjoying daily activities—dinners, roller-skating, birthday parties—as she files a lawsuit to gain timely access to the suspected surveillance records. Her computer is hacked by suspected government bodies along the way.

More than a year later, a court victory requires the Department of Justice to turn over 33,000 pages of records about Operation Vulgar Betrayal to Boundaoui—finally shedding light on the massive surveillance operation dating back to the mid-1980s, rooted in her Bridgeview hometown but without a single conviction related to terrorism. A graphic in the film reveals: "In nearly twenty years of investigating, the FBI field office in Chicago collected information on more than 600 American Muslim mosques, schools, businesses, charities and individuals across the U.S."[99] Although the FBI documents are 70 percent redacted, they confirm Boundaoui's suspicions and raise questions about whether the surveillance continues. The lasting damage and the fraying of community fabric is profound, as she said in a media interview: "You can trace a direct line between the tactics the FBI was using in our community and the negative effect."[100]

As a composite narrative, Boundaoui constructs the documentary to expand audience introspection well beyond the investigative details about a community under FBI surveillance. It is simultaneously an interrogation of a one-dimensional cultural image of Muslim Americans over time, as she explains:

For decades, Muslims and Arabs have been portrayed in popular culture as villains, terrorists, backwards, oppressive, there are all these tropes. This manifests also in local and national news and media. When you grow up constantly seeing projections of yourself as villainous and criminal, it starts to have a really negative impact on how you see yourself. There are millions of American Muslims who have also grown up this way, never seeing themselves reflected back in the culture. The point of this film in terms of public service is to show a representation of a culture that is nuanced and reflected and for other Muslim Americans or people of color who have similarly been profiled by the government to see themselves reflected back with nuance. . . . The secondary effect is for the mainstream American public to can get a representation of American Muslims on their own terms, a view of that experience from the inside looking around instead of from the outside looking in. It serves both of those purposes.[101]

The Feeling of Being Watched premiered at the Tribeca Film Festival in April 2018, followed by grassroots community screenings at universities and 30 festivals throughout the year, including Hot Docs, Blackstar, Camden International Film Festival, Chicago International Film Festival, and the Human Rights Film Festival.[102] Beginning in May 2019, Boundaoui and the film team—including producer Jessica Devaney, co-producer Anya Rous, and impact producer Ahlam Said—facilitated a theatrical run in a dozen cities. The film's community value is central to the entertainment marketplace and grassroots distribution strategy, not adjacent to it, as producer Devaney explains:

For *The Feeling of Being Watched* theatrical release, we decided to rely only on organic bookings and avoid the "pay to play" four-walling of theaters required by awards. We launched the film at home in Chicago and in LA, along with a handful of our target impact cities, using the theatrical release to raise the profile of the film to support our community engagement work, which will launch in tandem with our broadcast.[103]

Boundaoui and her production team architected the impact campaign for communities that had lived in silent fear under the possibility of surveillance (see Figure 8.3). Place by place, beginning in October 2018 with a first town hall screening in Bridgeview, people shared their own surveillance stories. Policy conversations, long-range conversations, and workshops about government accountability are central to the public dialogue as the film moves forward. As co-producer Anya Rous describes the community events: "These workshops incorporate both a conversation around healing, and some skills and tools about protecting communities in the face of this targeting and building stronger community relationships, and it's all informed by the local organizations."[104]

In October 2019, the documentary premiered on PBS's *POV* independent nonfiction storytelling series.[105] In parallel, the film team and the *POV* engagement team launched a community tour and free screenings in 10 cities with

Figure 8.3. *The Feeling of Being Watched* movie poster. Image courtesy of Watched Film, LLC.

large Muslim American populations, each followed by town hall convenings with local partners and mental health practitioners facilitating conversations about the documentary, and, as Boundaoui notes, "about collective trauma—and what surveillance has done in our communities personally and collectively, and how we should start healing from that trauma."[106]

The Feeling of Being Watched illustrates crucial motivations and practices involved in investigative documentary filmmaking. The artistic form itself is noteworthy, a mix of verité and personal narrative combined with a pointed exploration unfolding on screen. A review in the *Columbia Journalism Review* highlighted the film's journalistic contribution, given the little-known FBI surveillance initiative it reveals: "She [Boundaoui] found evidence of a massive pre-9/11 FBI counterterrorism investigation, conducted during the 1990s and 2000s and code-named 'Operation Vulgar Betrayal.' The operation had been mentioned in previous news reports, but often with few details."[107] Boundaoui notes her use of journalistic tools and journalistic ethics to tell the story, but she also reflects: "Increasingly I just call myself a filmmaker. I use journalistic practices and I do journalism and I don't know about calling myself a journalist. I feel like it has so many limitations."[108] Personal point of view and creative license were central to her motivations and process:

> When you say my point of view is from the inside, that generally delegitimizes you within the framework of journalism because we have this idea that objectivity and distance and anything up close to a story can't be truthful. I always say I don't believe in objectivity, I believe in transparency. We all have points of view, we have positionalities where we stand that inform the way we see the world, and the most honest thing you can do is be honest about where you're standing and be honest about your process. If you're honest about your process, you don't have claim to be objective to be truthful.[109]

Editorial independence was similarly meaningful to the film. On the one hand, Boundaoui's journalistic skills and artistic sensibilities combined with her personal story to render an intimate film that resonates with communities like her own. Editorial independence was key. As she reflects: "We've had tons of documentary films, news films about 'the terrorists within,' and you know, that kind of story—it's very prevalent. We've heard a lot of stories of folks from the outside the community telling stories of Muslims in the U.S. and [they are] always consistently framed around terrorism. . . . This was a story I needed to tell."[110]

At the same time, her status as an independent storyteller—not a journalist working as an employee of a media institution—may have hindered her ability to secure FBI files about Operation Vulgar Betrayal through her FOIA requests. In Boundaoui's lawsuit against the FBI, 2017 court transcripts show that the Department of Justice initially denied her request for fee waiver because she had "not demonstrate[d] [her] expertise in the subject area, [her] ability, and/or [her] intention to effectively convey the information to the public."[111] Boundaoui notes this challenge and risk for independent filmmakers speaking truth to power: "Look at things like the government responding to my FOIA requests—they just dismiss us. Not being tied to an institution is really risky. . . . It became important that we had a big law firm representing us in case something happened. And the grants also become really important, like having funding from the Ford Foundation and the International Documentary Association [Enterprise Documentary Fund] was important to raise the profile of the film and keep us safe."[112]

Boundaoui views her journalistic practice in documentary filmmaking not as dogma or formula, but as a helpful guide: "The journalism is all in the process. I think of journalism as a set of tools—you can use them in any kind of creative film. The way you tell the story can all be creative, but if you use a certain set of tools it makes it journalistic. . . . The use of primary sources is very important and the mark of an investigative film. . . . The ethics involved are very important, and any filmmaker can learn the ethics of interviewing people who are vulnerable and marginalized, how you reduce harm."[113] And yet, her lived experience provides the documentary's cinematic pulse and the crucial center of the community engagement campaign that publicly interrogates the myriad issues within it—airing the collective trauma and breakdown in community solidarity and individual psychology, year by year, that takes place when a group of neighbors understands it is viewed as suspicious and dangerous. *The Feeling of Being Watched* is, at its core, a counternarrative and investigation offered amid a tapestry of cultural storytelling about Muslim Americans—a lens rendered possible from the depth of an inside perspective.

Cinematic investigative documentary storytelling takes shape through various approaches, created by makers who want to interrogate and expose hidden truths. Journalistic practices, tools, skills, and training are valuable to this group of makers. Fact-checking and accuracy, ethics, and responsible conduct with sources and subjects are imperatives. Risk, safety, and legal threats also are vital considerations for creative documentary filmmakers who may not have formal journalistic training to prepare them, or the institutional backing to help in times of trouble. Data security, legal resources, threat modeling, access to research and archival information, relationships with notable institutions, and financial resources are crucial for documentary stories that investigate power and illuminate dark corners. Recognizing the challenge, the International Documentary Association joined forces with the University of Missouri's Jonathan B. Murray Center for Documentary Journalism in 2018 to launch *Mapping the Documentary Journalism Landscape*, an online resource guide "designed to help filmmakers find information and make decisions that journalists make every day," covering topics like First Amendment rights, accountability and transparency with sources, public information resources, copyright and fair use, and journalism codes of ethics.[114]

Despite their appreciation for journalistic skills and tools, filmmakers who produce artful investigative documentary films are not bound by the imperative to showcase reality as neutral observers serving up information from various perspectives— "the view from nowhere," as some critics articulate.[115] This impulse is not artistic freedom *in place* of truth, however, but transparency about whose truth is seen—explicitly naming the gaze from which the story is told. The three films profiled here—*Citizenfour, Southwest of Salem: The Story of the San Antonio Four*, and *The Feeling of Being Watched*—reveal the filmmakers' commitment to authenticity as they unapologetically craft artistic investigative stories through evident points of view rather than assumed objectivity. These decisions were necessary for truth-telling, according to these filmmakers. As Assia Boundaoui wrote for *Documentary* magazine in 2019, "Had I mistakenly gone on to make a 'journalistically objective' film, it would have been far less truthful than the blisteringly personal, investigative film I ended up making."[116] This chapter argues that artistic freedom and editorial voice enhance the storytelling—giving agency and authentic voice to stories and perspectives that remain marginalized or unseen. At the same time, it's naïve to imagine that an impulse toward creative freedom can't be exploited for ill; artistic sensibility is not an excuse to distort truth.

Documentaries that investigate troubling realities are not solo media actors in the public sphere, of course. Creative documentary films interrogate social problems alongside journalistic revelations, and while cinema and journalism vary in degrees of artistic freedom, they work together. Deep investigative journalism and daily news together play an unquestionably irreplaceable, indispensable role in providing a public record and keeping issues alive in the public eye, while investigative nonfiction filmmaking opens space to permit different ways of seeing. Creative investigative documentary stories play a vital part in democratic discourse by providing distinctive, emotionally resonant, artistic cultural perspectives to consider and discuss, even while they are crafted with journalistic practices. Highlighting this interplay is important in noting the symbiotic role documentary can play alongside the agenda-setting function of investigative journalism and day-to-day reporting.

In the hands of creative documentary makers, hidden truths are interrogated well beyond theaters and TV screens. Filmmakers' moral motivations for reform, which match investigative journalists' inclinations, often push them to take their films deep into community through explicit grassroots public engagement screenings and campaigns. These stories are architected to investigate, entertain, inform, and spark real private and public dialogue, combined with efforts of organizations already doing the groundwork. In this way, creative investigative documentaries can become part of ongoing movements and efforts for justice. Nonfiction cinema joins forces with publics and civil society, providing lenses into stories that may not be considered—or validating points of view that may be deeply felt in communities even as they are too often rendered invisible in the mainstay of a larger media machine.

I think having a space in which the independent voice is protected and elevated is the thing that defines an open society—it is the thing that can lead to a more healthy democracy, because almost by definition there will be a multiplicity of perspectives and independent voices. . . . It's artists who often say the most difficult things, the most provocative things, the most challenging things. How do we continue to protect them in times such as these?

—Tabitha Jackson
Director, Sundance Film Festival[1]

9

Imagining the Future

Why Documentary Matters

The business and art of documentary finds itself at a curious cultural juncture marked by paradoxical opportunity and challenge. On the one hand, the participatory media era has, in a dizzyingly fast pace, helped to democratize access for a broad swath of storytellers through evolving technology and platforms. The transforming contemporary media ecology has welcomed new audiences across an expanding list of media outlets and content distributors. Global distribution is no longer a documentary anomaly. Commercial networks, from HBO to Netflix to Hulu, are pouring money into nonfiction storytelling production, distribution, and promotion—thus, the documentary "golden era" moniker,[2] a phrase alternately loved or loathed in the field.

And yet, an influx of commercial financing and vast audience potential does not necessarily guarantee the civic values of intimate nonfiction stories, as in the tradition of documentary that interrogates reality through oft-ignored lenses and sparks public discourse—at least not categorically. Then again,

Story Movements. Caty Borum Chattoo, Oxford University Press (2020) © Oxford University Press.
DOI: 10.1093/oso/9780190943417.001.0001

documentary makers themselves embed civic values and motivations into the content of their work, regardless of how it is exhibited. It's too early to say what will become of this boom time for nonfiction film and TV, but history reminds us that leaving documentaries *solely* to market proclivities does not fully foster a rich diversity of voices and viewpoints. After all, when it comes to the media marketplace "the commercial logic driving this system isn't troubled by democracy."[3] As the International Documentary Association's Simon Kilmurry reflects, historically speaking, "public television has been the place most unafraid of taking on social issue topics that at the time were considered the most controversial and featuring marginalized communities. This public commons function, underpinned by a set of values that are not solely market-driven, is a very precious space."[4] Similarly, documentary scholar John Corner asserted in 2002:

> Television documentary producers have often produced work that entertains, sometimes in surprising and subversive ways, sometimes with populist calculation. However, when a piece of work in documentary format is entirely designed in relation to its capacity to deliver entertainment, quite radical changes occur both to the forms of representation and to viewing relations.[5]

Documentaries that probe social challenges and realities, particularly independently produced ones, are disruptive because they reflect creative vision and perspectives that are often invisible elsewhere in the media landscape. The documentary field needs a well-diversified system of funding and revenue and distribution—across commercial, public, and philanthropic sectors—to ensure that storytellers can make a living and audiences can discover their work. A future vision for documentaries and their role in democracy and the media landscape maximally benefits from reinforcing structures working together—and from the innovation and leadership of documentary field leaders and decision makers who endeavor to understand how each sector benefits the other.

As for public engagement in social problems, these metamorphic times also are marked by anxiety about civic participation and unease about the future of democratic functioning in the internet-based information system. Ideological polarization in an age characterized by on-demand niche media choices threatens the pursuit of shared values and constructive public discourse. Like-minded echo chambers enabled by social media pose detrimental consequences for democracy even as they strengthen constituencies that are united by shared beliefs. The very foundation of the information age— the commercial underpinning of internet-based content and distribution—is not designed to be concerned with the public interest, civic values of the public sphere; as scholar Matthew Hindman wrote, "Digital media are just as dependent on a few corporate gatekeepers as ever. . . . [T]he attention economy has doomed most of our civic hopes for the web."[6] Encouraging people to even see different points of view—much less find common ground and values—is a fundamental challenge now and in the future, a tough road contrained by the same technological forces that have opened access to previously marginalized storytellers. And yet, as scholars Nick Couldry, Sonia Livingstone, and Tim Markham presciently wrote in the fledgling days of social media: "Against these concerns at the decline of democracy, we must register an important counter-argument. What if, instead of declining, political orientation is simply taking new, more dispersed forms?"[7] Rather than disengagement, public participation is being transformed:

> In the face of voter apathy and the supposed decline of civil society, we are witnessing a range of initiatives to engage audiences in public fora, often aided by new technological forms of interactive and participatory media. The familiar, mass communication model—with its centralised organisation, elite gatekeepers and established relations with institutions of power—no longer has a monopoly, with new opportunities emerging for the public to communicate, connect, and deliberate online.[8]

Looking to the future of our complex evolving reality, we would do well to avoid subscribing to a false binary of either doom or an idealistic notion of full expansion for public engagement with social challenges. Indeed, in his writing about democracy and public participation in a transforming networked era, scholar Henry Jenkins implored that we see and understand two contradictory truths that are simultaneously in play: On the one hand, media are more consolidated than ever and trust in institutions dwindles while surveillance invades our privacy, but on the other hand, digital communication mechanisms have expanded the ability to see and hear from other voices "using networked communications toward our collective interests . . . with grassroots media being deployed as the tool by which to challenge the failed mechanisms of institutional politics."[9]

Contemporary documentary and civic practice reside squarely in this complicated reality. This is not to suggest that documentary storytelling is a magical solution to the future of democratic functioning, but rather, to reinforce the unique and indispensable cultural role documentaries play in the media landscape as they artistically showcase lives and social problems with depth and nuance, creating space for private reflections and public dialogue. As the future marches forward, structural conditions need focus and attention to ensure that social-issue nonfiction storytelling progresses in a meaningful way, retaining characteristics of creative freedom, artistic innovation, and civic value. Within this context, as the final stop in this book's journey, particular themes are imperative to probe and advance: representation and diversity, the changing marketplace, and the central role of a professional nonfiction community equipped to uphold civic values and practices. These themes are critical to contemplating why documentary matters.

Diversity and Representation in Documentary Storytelling

Whose experiences do we see on screen—and who is telling their stories? Honoring a full spectrum of lived experience in documentary storytelling is imperative, particularly given the reality of a broader entertainment and news media system that fails to fully reflect the lives of people who have been historically marginalized by virtue of race, ethnicity, socioeconomic status, sexual orientation, religion, gender, gender identity, physical ability, or regional location. Questions about who is validated to tell viable documentary stories—what stories are told by which storytellers, whose stories achieve critical recognition, which filmmakers are able to make a living—are inseparably intertwined with economics, public validation through cultural awards and attention, funding, and the social capital built through access and relationships with industry decision makers. As documentary professor and filmmaker Renee Tajima-Peña reflected in *Documentary* magazine in 2016, the vitality of the contemporary media age does not necessarily mean equitable, pluralistic representation in documentary will be inevitable. Industry leaders, decision makers, and mentors must be diligently committed, as she wrote:

> Forging a truly diverse documentary field takes work on all levels, from the big picture to the grassroots. Some of the core principles of pushing for diversity—leadership, funding, programming—haven't changed since the race-based activism of the '60s and '70s. At the same time, everything has changed. New technologies have opened doors, but have also amplified digital divides. And there's the global market, and how documentarians of color interface with transnational production. The contour of the racial divide today is complicated by intersections of class, gender, sexuality and citizenship. The time calls for alliances and a discussion of racial diversity that is strategic and inclusive. The drive for racial justice in

documentary demands consciousness—of inequality and privilege, of others and of our own.[10]

The story about diversity in the current documentary landscape is complicated. On the one hand, women are now the leading decision makers across many major nonprofit and commercial documentary industry organizations, among them Justine Nagan at POV, Courtney Sexton at CNN Films, Raney Aronson at PBS Frontline, Sally Jo Fifer at ITVS, Tabitha Jackson at the Sundance Film Festival (and formerly the Sundance Institute Documentary Film Program), Lisa Nishimura at Netflix, Molly Thompson at Apple, Nancy Abraham and Lisa Heller at HBO Documentary Films, and Sheila Nevins at MTV Documentary Films, to name a few. My 2018 *State of the Documentary Field* study showed that new documentary filmmakers who have entered the field within the past 15 years of the digital era are more likely to be people of color and women,[11] an insight also reflected in cultural recognition bestowed onto a dynamic cadre of talented contemporary documentary filmmakers of color like Dawn Porter, Ava DuVernay, Yance Ford, Grace Lee, Deborah Esquenazi, Nadia Hallgren, RaMell Ross, Bing Liu, Stephen Maing, Violet Feng, and Assia Boundaoui, among others. And yet, as Tajima-Peña urgently posited: "Some filmmakers of color have reached or even broken through the glass ceiling, but how do we move from individual to collective gains? How do we push for real programs and investment in diversity during a time of retrenchment and racial polarization?"[12]

Her point is well taken, as on the other hand, numerical data show a persistent imbalance. According to my 2017 study, *Oscars So White: Gender, Racial, and Ethnic Diversity and Social Issues in U.S. Documentary Films (2008–2017)*, which examined the makers of shortlisted films in the Best Documentary Feature category of the Academy Awards for a decade (150 total films), 87 percent of honored documentary directors were white and 13 percent were people of color, and 75 percent of short-listed directors were men and 25 percent women; the pattern is similar for documentary producers lauded by this top cultural recognition in the field.[13] Additionally, as I wrote, "notably, of the 25 Academy shortlist-recognized documentary feature film directors from racial and ethnic minority groups over a full decade, five were recognized in 2017 alone,"[14] indicating, perhaps, some consciousness-raising in the #OscarsSoWhite moment amid an otherwise persistent pattern. To add complexity to the portrait of representation, almost 7 in 10 of the decade's documentary feature films recognized on the shortlist of the Academy Awards were social-issue stories (69 percent) compared to 31 percent pure "entertainment slice-of-life" stories (like biopics or other character portraits). As I concluded in the study,

> the perspectives of women and members of marginalized racial and ethnic groups barely register. Considering that women and racial and ethnic minority groups are disproportionately impacted by contemporary social justice issues portrayed in many of the Academy Award–shortlisted documentary feature films—such as racism, gender-based violence, environmental justice, and poverty—this represents a stark paradox indeed.[15]

The Academy Awards are hardly the only measure of documentary representation even if the shortlist provides a measurable opportunity to examine gender, racial, and ethnic diversity—a composite surrogate that reflects the years of support, relationships, marketing power, and financing that goes into producing and distributing a documentary film of such high caliber. Some of my other research shows similar patterns with different units of analysis. One such 2018 study found that documentary storytelling produced for public TV is generally more diverse—looking at racial, ethnic, and gender representation—than commercial TV documentaries.[16]

Funding and seeing the stories produced by filmmakers across the country—not just those made within the entertainment and news industry hubs of New York and Los Angeles—also is crucial to rendering visible a fuller tapestry of life. A separate study, which examined a decade (2007–2016) of the 400 US-focused documentary films partially financed and co-produced by the Independent Television Service (ITVS), revealed that ITVS-funded documentary makers hailed from 33 states in the United States and from both rural and urban regions of the country.[17] Other sources of documentary diversity data are elusive, given the complexity and messiness of documentary filmmaking as an industry that includes independent makers and in-house producers across media organizations. A strong focus on representation that includes but also looks beyond race, ethnicity, and gender—including sexual orientation, gender identity, socioeconomic status, and disability—remains a perennial pursuit in contemporary documentary across stories that interrogate social issues *and* those that don't.

Explicit, intentional leadership and innovation is vital. As Renee Tajima-Peña pointed out in her #DocsSoWhite reflection in *Documentary* magazine, the "race-conscious political and cultural activism of the 1960s and '70s incubated pioneering organizations that created long-lasting models to increase diverse representation and opportunity in documentary—including training, mentorships, production opportunities, financing—including

Los Angeles' Visual Communications, Philadelphia's Scribe Video Center, New York's Third World Newsreel, the public media Minority Consortia."[18] Today, those efforts are joined by newer organizations, institutions, and leaders who create opportunities for diverse storytellers through funding, training, mentoring, and network-building, including the Southern Documentary Fund, Firelight Media's Documentary Lab, Kartemquin Films' Diverse Voices in Docs (DVID), Chicken & Egg Pictures, the Diversity Initiative at Sundance, ITVS's Diversity Development Fund, Working Films, and the continuing work of the National Multicultural Alliance, comprising the five organizations who together support, fund, and represent diverse voices in public media (Center for Asian American Media, Latino Public Broadcasting, Vision Maker Media, Black Public Media, and Pacific Islanders in Communications). Supporting diverse nonfiction stories is crucial, as Latino Public Broadcasting executive director Sandie Viquez Pedlow reflects, because of the cultural reflection gap that exists in the media landscape: "When you look at documentaries, we go beyond what is being reported in the media. These are the personal experiences of people. These are the personal struggles, this is the history that maybe people haven't seen or haven't heard about, or maybe hasn't been reported."[19]

Power also lives in the hands of a new generation of documentary makers and leaders who are creating professional networks and opportunities. At the 2016 Getting Real convening hosted by the International Documentary Association, in consultation with Renee Tajima-Peña and the Ford Foundation's Chi-hui Yang,[20] filmmakers S. Leo Chiang and Grace Lee launched the Asian American Documentary Network (A-Doc) as "a national network that works to increase the visibility and support of Asian Americans in the documentary field."[21] Co-founder Chiang acknowledges the legacy and ongoing efforts of the original multicultural organizations started in the last century—and progress toward lifting up the voices and work of Asian American documentary professionals—and simultaneously emphasizes the need to look across the entire lifecycle of documentary: "Yes, funders are supporting diverse stories, but are the distribution platforms on board to put full effort to get these stories out? Or do they still consider these stories 'niche' and 'regional' and are putting efforts behind the traditionally mainstream stories?"[22] This question, too, remains an ongoing pursuit as the marketplace shifts and new network decision makers emerge (Figure 9.1).

Similarly, in 2018 at the Sundance Film Festival, Brown Girls Doc Mafia (BGDM), "an organization advocating for women and non-binary people of color in the documentary industry,"[23] went public after filmmaker Iyabo

Figure 9.1. A-Doc members at the 2017 A-Doc working meeting hosted at the Ford Foundation. Photo courtesy of A-Doc.

Boyd started it in 2015. The group had grown to a membership of 2,400 by the end of 2018.[24] As she said in a media interview, "Brown Girls Doc Mafia was formed to tackle a myth that has been repeated in industry conversations, hiring discussions, festival programming meetings and funder circles: that there aren't many filmmakers of color worth paying attention to, especially not women of color."[25] BGDM, which was sparked initially by Boyd's participation in a 2015 Doc Society Good Pitch convening, hosts workshops, master classes, and retreats for its members—and focuses on increasing visibility for women and non-binary people of color in film festival spaces, as Boyd explains:

> Festivals are kind of the place where folks network, where you make genuine friendships that turn into creative collaborations, where funders put a face to a name or begin to put you on their tracking lists, where the field is talking about issues that are critical to the development of what we're doing—interactions that are critical to how the doc industry works. . . . My experience on the funding side was realizing there are so many critical conversations that are happening in those spaces that women of color just weren't having access to. And that was a financial barrier and a cultural barrier.[26]

The group continues to expand influence through building social capital for women and non-binary people of color, creating community and focusing on changing images on screen. As Boyd reflects:

> Even beyond the audience, this is about humanity. It's about expression in story-telling. I often say that in the future when the aliens finally come and look back at what humans were doing, I'd like them to be able to see the impressions that women and people of color and non-binary people had in our human culture. All of this work are the cave paintings of our current time. . . . In a bigger sense, it's about representing who we are as all people, and having that be a fair and accurate representation.[27]

With parallel motivation, in 2018, filmmaker and audio engineer Jim LeBrecht curated a group of documentary makers from the disability community to share their perspectives, challenge institutional barriers, and dismantle con-straining stereotypes, beginning with his public writing: "Over the years, we've seen the emergence of filmmakers from underrepresented communities, which has brought nuance and authenticity to documentary films. However, one community is still far behind. I'm talking about my community: the disa-bled community."[28] In September 2018, in response to the advocacy LeBrecht started with a post on the global documentary online community site, The D-Word, earlier that year,[29] the International Documentary Association hosted a panel and the first-ever gathering of documentary makers with disabilities as part of its biennial Getting Real convening (Figure 9.2).[30]

According to LeBrecht, who speaks of "a history of disability not being part of diversity and inclusion efforts," documentary industry recognition of—and engagement with—the disability community is vital for both the careers of the makers and the authenticity and quality of stories on screen:

> The lens is clearer and brighter and has greater definition when it comes from someone within that community. Case in point: we have been doing interviews from people in the disability community in our documentary [*Crip Camp*, directed by Nicole Newnham and LeBrecht] and one person said "I wouldn't be talking like this to someone who was not disabled. I might not trust them to understand my words and what I'm saying here. I might not talk to a non-disabled filmmaker the same way."[31]

Ultimately, the consequences of representation—or lack thereof—are pro-found for social progress when we consider the capability of media inclu-sion to confront negative stereotypes and show a fuller spectrum of lived

Figure 9.2. Cheryl Green, Jason DaSilva, Day Al-Mohamed, Jim LeBrecht, and Lawrence Carter-Long speak on "The Ramp Less Traveled" panel at the International Documentary Association's 2018 Getting Real convening. Photo by Laura Ahmed, courtesy of the International Documentary Association (IDA).

experiences, or the same power of media invisibility to reinforce stereotypical tropes and dominant systems of power. In a 2017 blog post that captured widespread attention from documentary professionals, Firelight Media's Sonya Childress stressed the importance of challenging a view of "the other" who elicits empathy and instead examining structural systems of power. Further, she wrote, with a sole focus on empathy, we can be distracted "from more strategic uses of film: to validate and empower those who rarely see their experience on screen, to convene disconnected people and movements, and to build alliances and power. The power when we—the marginalized 'others'— use film to speak to our own communities or across identity and issue silos to build common ground and strategize solutions."[32] A distinction exists between eliciting empathy for individuals as a desired outcome and promoting solidarity against the structures that perpetuate injustice, as "inviting solidarity charts a course for large-scale social change," according to journalism scholar Anita Varma.[33]

Opportunities exist to meaningfully expand the documentary eye as new audiences discover the form. The process of asserting cultural citizenship is under way—that is, historically marginalized groups and individuals are "taking control of a public image created by others to maintain hierarchies; it is about empowering otherwise marginalized social identities, a means of locating and asserting oneself within a specific social, cultural, and political matrix in order to counteract inequitable treatment, develop community, acquire rights, build identity, and experience a sense of shared cultural belonging."[34] Despite the seemingly open field of transforming media ecologies, audience shifts, and signs of progress, history tells us that benign non-discrimination isn't sufficient to fully open the documentary landscape to champion stories from and about a diverse array of lived experiences. The field's future will instead be shaped by the deliberate intentions and commitment of its leaders and decision makers—and storytellers demanding and making change— working together to shape the evolving marketplace for creative nonfiction stories that spotlight a broader portrait of global lives.

Documentary's Changing Marketplace and Platforms

Four years after its first documentary acquisition, Netflix did not come to the 2017 Sundance Film Festival to play. A week of movie screenings and millions of dollars later, the streamer grabbed up a pile of both scripted and nonfiction independent entertainment content, including the $5 million-dollar purchase of *Icarus*, the Russian doping investigation that would go on to win the 2018 Academy Award for Best Documentary Feature.[35] The buzz in the documentary field was palpable—enthusiastic and cautiously optimistic. Following documentaries' hot social currency, Netflix jumped into the nonfiction industry game and headed straight to the front of the acquisitions line.

Was this the beginning of a robust new marketplace and economy for documentaries, including social-issue stories—or at least a major milestone along an inevitable route? Will this financial pattern mark an upward trajectory for independent documentary investment from the wildly expanding streaming entertainment universe? It's complicated. Unquestionably, documentary helps satisfy a voracious appetite for digital storytelling content that can appeal to niche and global audiences from the likes of Netflix, Amazon, Apple, Hulu, and others on the horizon. There's no question that documentary offerings have expanded dramatically within this century. But unequivocally predicting documentary's imminent economic engine is a fool's game; it moves too quickly to pin down. At the same time, contemplating the future of documentary storytelling and its role in the public sphere requires an ongoing scrutiny of the transforming media industry—its influence can't be overlooked. What will an expanding commercial documentary market-place mean not only for the economics of nonfiction film and the sustainable careers of filmmakers, but also the stories served up to vast audiences? Challenges, opportunities, and questions abound.

To wit, just one year later, the story was different at the Sundance Film Festival. In 2018, Netflix and Amazon, the big independent documentary buyers just a year prior, left the festival almost empty-handed—although they arrived with documentaries of their own, produced in-house, to premiere.[36] As Anthony Kaufman wrote in the trade publication IndieWire:

> Documentaries are hotter than ever, but their production and distribution is in constant flux. In 2017, major companies were shelling out huge dollars to acquire documentaries, dramatically shifting the scales for the budgets and value of non-fiction. Then everything changed at Sundance 2018, when contrary to expectations, Netflix and Amazon deescalated the marketplace they had super-sized a year before.[37]

An immediate domino effect was evident as Netflix and Amazon receded from their headline-making financial investments in independent documentary acquisitions; Kaufman wrote: "It's clear that their recent absence from the market has had impact—deals have taken longer to close and the price-tags have been reduced."[38] The head-whipping speed of change between 2017 and 2018 in the Sundance Film Festival's streamer buying shifts captures only one small snapshot in time, and one corner of the documentary marketplace, and yet, it exemplifies the larger trend of uncertainty—both promise and questions—for the future of nonfiction storytelling in the public sphere.

The long-term strategy of streaming entertainment outlets and their relationship to documentaries is unknown. Then again, acquisition of independent nonfiction storytelling is only one piece of the pie as Netflix commissions new work from documentary filmmakers. A question to track, then, is what kinds of stories will be commissioned by streaming powerhouses—Netflix, Hulu, Amazon, Apple—and by which documentary talents? And how will the trends and a rich supply of documentary stories ripple out across legacy media outlets, both commercial and public?

Forecasting a consistent economic trajectory from commercial streaming networks and the resulting implications on legacy outlets is, thus, tricky business. But if any lessons can be gleaned from parallel developments in scripted entertainment—or documentary history—it's that the new platforms bring fresh competition to legacy media institutions like HBO, MTV, and PBS; new financial resources; and a mandate to capture the imaginations of wide domestic and global audiences. Entertainment players are looking for big views, prestige, and profit. What might this trend mean for the kinds of documentary stories that thrive in the new media world order? Again, it's complicated, but predictions about form are already on the table, as Anthony Kaufman outlined in a trade story:

> With more commercial entities intent on making and releasing nonfiction, it's an exciting time. But similar to Hollywood's cooption of indie film in the 2000s, much of that energy is going towards predictable places—celebrity-focused films, true-crime, pop culture scandals, docu-thrillers, and light entertainment—leaving everything else in the lurch, or at least, more restrained financing and distribution prospects.[39]

Kevin Iwashina, a powerhouse nonfiction content agent at Endeavor Content and president of the International Documentary Association's board of directors, sees the scenario in two ways, according to media interviews. On the one hand, an expanding documentary market will bring more production funding and distribution opportunities for smaller documentaries. And with the flood of documentaries available, a strong position for smaller independent distributors can emerge, as he said in a 2019 media interview: " 'I think public broadcasters and international channels will have more opportunity to acquire quality films as supply increases,' he said, while 'independent distributors will be able to position themselves as a quality alternative to larger distributors given their precision in marketing.' "[40] On the other hand, it's also likely that documentary filmmakers will face demands on their storytelling topics and approaches, as he said, with "increased pressure on documentary filmmakers to make their projects commercial 'character-driven' narratives or very high concept. . . . One can no longer focus on just an 'issue,'" even if, as he says, the "premium documentaries" will continue to be those films that expand knowledge and provide entertainment value together—captivating, engaging, and thought-provoking at once.[41] Scholar John Corner asserted a similar prediction in 2002 about a hybrid of substance and audience appeal embedded in documentary's trajectory: "Whatever the pattern finally to emerge, producers with a commitment to the popular audience that goes beyond profitability but that can nevertheless also generate profits will clearly be an important factor in documentary's survival."[42] In the contemporary media marketplace, artistic entertainment value and social consciousness co-exist in the hands of innovative documentary artists, as Field of Vision's Charlotte Cook reflects: "We've seen films like *The Act of Killing* and *Strong Island* that have really taken it [the artistry] to the next level. Those *are* the films that really strike a chord with people because they hadn't seen anything like it before. We're kind of all learning constantly as an industry."[43]

As documentary storytellers look forward, it's too simplistic to reduce entertainment industry marketplace trends and their implications to a binary of absolute positives and negatives when it comes to social justice stories. After all, one of the most important contemporary social-issue documentaries—Ava DuVernay's *13th*, commissioned as a Netflix Original and nominated for an Academy Award—exploded onto the cultural scene in 2016, sparking new dialogue about racial justice through its international distribution.[44] In 2018, an independent film acquired by Netflix, Yance Ford's *Strong Island*, a personal and artistic investigation into the racial motivations of his brother's killing, vied for the Best Documentary Feature honor at the Academy Awards.[45] In 2019, pioneering documentary directors Julia Reichart and Steven Bognar struck a global distribution deal with Netflix—to reach 190 countries—for their independent film, *American Factory*, which won the Academy Award for Best Documentary Feature in 2020, the first offering from Barack and Michelle Obama's Higher Ground Productions.[46] Also in 2019, *Roll Red Roll*, director Nancy Schwartzman's true-crime-style investigation of rape culture through a high school football sexual assault story, premiered theatrically, opened the PBS *POV* season in June, and launched internationally on Netflix while Schwartzman directed a grassroots impact and educational engagement campaign with the film.[47] We might optimistically look at this moment, then, as a culmination of so many decades of development—a juncture in which social-issue documentary practices are now driving audience demands and production assumptions for new stories, at least in part.

Indeed, the values and ethos of deeply intimate, artistic documentary storytelling also are on clear display in two of 2018's exemplary, form-advancing independent documentaries licensed and distributed by the commercial streaming network Hulu, directed by makers of color—the investigative police documentary, *Crime + Punishment*, directed by Stephen Maing, winner of the International Documentary Association's 2018 Courage Under Fire Award[48] and a 2019 News & Documentary Emmy Award for Outstanding Social Issue Documentary;[49] and *Minding the Gap*,[50] the Oscar-nominated, Peabody Award–winning skateboarding coming-of-age story and portal into domestic abuse directed by Bing Liu. A closer look reveals a symbiotic relationship between philanthropy and the public media sector, editorial independence, and wide audience distribution. Both documentaries, while distributed on a commercial media outlet with vast viewer reach, were funded by public media and philanthropic resources. Maing's film was partially funded through an International Documentary Association Enterprise Fund grant for independent creative investigative documentaries supported by the MacArthur Foundation;[51] and Liu's was a co-production with POV/American Documentary and the Independent Television Service (ITVS), with funding from the Corporation for Public Broadcasting and the Sundance Institute Documentary Film Program.[52] Both filmmakers maintained editorial independence as they made their films.

As these documentaries illustrate, looking toward the future calls upon filmmakers and industry leaders to recognize the interplay between editorial independence and peak artistry, and the potential reach and financial support of commercial operations alongside a robust public media sector. As they expand their documentary offerings and investments, commercial outlets are wise to look carefully at the circumstances that birth evocative, intimate nonfiction stories that capture audience attention—they are shaped by the authentic voices of storytellers working with creative vision and artistic control. A well-resourced hybrid system of commercial, public, and philanthropic funding and distribution can serve documentary storytellers well, and weakness in any of the three is detrimental to makers' ability to make complicated stories and ensure that audiences can see them.

In parallel, the documentary field evolves as the larger media system transforms with participatory forms and platforms, opening new ways to interact with audiences and communities. As documentary scholars Kate Nash, Craig Hight, and Catherine Summerhayes wrote in *New Documentary Ecologies*, their book about documentary's interactive future forms:

> As new media technologies and new forms of communication emerge, contemporary documentary makers are engaging in a continual process of reworking the documentary project. They (and inevitably we, as audiences) are reimagining what documentary might become: non-linear, multimedia, interactive, hybrid, cross-platform, convergent, virtual, immersive, 360-degree, collaborative, 3-D participatory, transmedia or something else yet to clearly emerge.[53]

Public participation is the centerpiece of documentary's interactive and virtual reality forms, which are centerpiece features of major film festivals, including the globe's largest nonfiction festival, the International Documentary Festival Amsterdam (IDFA). As one of several exemplars, Tribeca Immersive, hosted at the Tribeca Film Festival, programs a full slate of virtual reality films every year.[54] The Sundance Institute's New Frontier program, which launched in 2006, provides leadership, network-building, and funding for documentaries in an evolving technology landscape.[55] MIT's Open Documentary Lab chronicles the development of documentary projects in virtual reality and other interactive forms.[56] Short-form documentary programs also are on the rise, from the Tribeca Film Institute's If/Then Shorts program, which aims to discover underrepresented voices,[57] to the *New York Times* Op-Docs project.

As the future unfolds, finding adequate, consistent distribution for interactive documentaries to reach broader audiences is still a pursuit—not nearly settled business. Ingrid Kopp, who programs Storyscapes at Tribeca Interactive, sees growth in immersive documentary distribution and exhibition through "dedicated location-based experiences (LBEs), galleries, museums, art spaces and libraries"; in the industry blog and newsletter *Immerse*, she wrote about the imperative for financial investment in emergent storytelling:

> To state the obvious, we need a robust ecosystem where work is being both funded and distributed. . . . Beyond tech, funding and financing are needed to support the ecosystem for sure—but across the board so that all the dots are connected from workshops and training, to production, to distribution and audience building.[58]

Still, optimism is on the horizon for platform experimentation in documentary. Expanding the marketplace and pushing nonfiction storytelling into spaces where current and future audiences reside, in 2017, ITVS launched Indie Lens Storycast, a subscription-based free docuseries hosted on YouTube, produced by ITVS, *Independent Lens*, and PBS Digital Studios.[59] In 2019, the long-running independent documentary series on PBS, *POV*, launched POV Spark, a nonfiction storytelling program focused on interactive, immersive documentaries, including a series of Instagram stories and virtual reality programs.[60]

Underrepresented storytelling voices and the public may converge in these interactive spaces, well beyond traditional feature and TV documentaries, if current data are any indicator of the future. According to our *State of the Documentary Field* study, perhaps not surprisingly, newer documentary filmmakers (those who entered the field within the past 15 years) are more likely to be working in emerging technology and short-form documentary than legacy-generation makers.[61] These newer documentary filmmakers also are more likely to be women and people of color, thus adding to the portrait of nonfiction storytelling and its future interrogation of a fuller landscape of the human experience.

Regardless of the changes in the documentary marketplace, the influx of new players in commercial entertainment, and the promise of evolving platforms and audiences and media outlets, making a financially viable career in nonfiction storytelling remains challenging. The economics of documentary work are tenuous and inconsistent, creating conditions of struggle for independent artists, journalists, and organizers who wish to pursue this work as a career. Our 2018 survey of primarily US-based documentary filmmakers revealed stark evidence: only 22 percent said their most recent film made enough revenue to cover unpaid production costs and make a profit, and 56 percent said their most recent film made less than $25,000 in revenue.[62]

Sparked by data and documentary professionals' public airing of hardship, a growing cry to shape new economic paths and revenue streams for nonfiction storytelling has transformed into dedicated industry discussions about "documentary sustainability," with panels and convenings and research, including spotlights at the 2016 and 2018 Getting Real convenings hosted by the International Documentary Association.[63] Deliberate exploration is under way in the field. The National Endowment for the Arts, after holding a closed-door summit of documentary leaders in February 2017 on the topic, issued a report that responded to the urgency and conversations coming from documentary communities around the country.[64] Regional gatherings—like the 2018 "Heartlandia" documentary summit in Missouri[65] and the 2019 "Localism Works" convening in Washington, DC, as part of the AFI Docs film festival[66]—are raising local issues in the search for sources of funding, revenue, and infrastructure that allow documentary makers to stay in the business for the long term. In related fashion, as community conversations coalesce at field convenings, documentary makers and strategists are spotlighting issues like mental health challenges in the work, as the International Documentary Association noted in a 2019 reflection: "The struggle that undergirds sustainability is not just financial. It's emotional and psychological and physical. And, as we've witnessed over the past few years, it can take your life."[67]

Along parallel lines, in 2016, six documentary producers—Nina Chaudry, Beth Levison, Marilyn Ness, Dallas Rexer, Ann Rose, and Beth Westrate—came together to form the Documentary Producers Alliance (DPA) to self-organize and advocate for producers' financial viability, among other concerns.[68] The DPA now includes more than 100 members, each of whom has produced at least two documentary projects for film or TV.[69] In 2019, after months of work, the DPA released its "Best Practices in Crediting Guidelines," an advocacy and governance document that defines previously loosely defined terms and tiers of producer credits, disavowing the practice of "selling" certain producer credits to financial investors; the guidelines were endorsed by 24 organizational leaders in nonfiction storytelling (including the Center for Media & Social Impact, which I direct).[70] As DPA's self-organized advocacy continues, conscious implementation of the guidelines by filmmakers and industry decision makers—which will help the economics of documentary producers immediately and over time—remains.

Documentary's "golden era," then, is complex. Without question, documentary storytelling has reached a new level of public consciousness and sparked critical interest and acclaim in unprecedented ways. The value of new audience discovery and vast reach is undisputed. Anticipation about evolving platforms and interactive modes of documentary expression continues to build. Emerging makers are bending original storytelling forms and creating exciting new ways to express reality through creative visions. The balance of creativity, editorial independence, commercial pressures, and financial viability will not only continue but lives at the very heart of documentary's future as an industry, a practice of making art, and a mechanism to engage people and communities in public dialogue.

Civic Values in Documentary Communities

Documentaries reside along a broad spectrum of practices and approaches, with differing objectives on the part of their makers. For storytellers who produce creative nonfiction film projects that interrogate social challenges with a commitment to accuracy and truth-telling, making a difference in the world is a meaningful driver, but not one that competes with or impedes creative vision and the desire to make compelling art.

Within the field of makers who share this impulse, it's notable that documentary storytellers and leaders often refer to "the documentary community"—rather than using more clinical occupational terms like "profession"—as they talk about values, ethics, learnings, and collaborations with one another. Because documentary makers hail from a variety of professional identities, with a range of formal or informal training experiences, they master and shape nonfiction storytelling partially by connecting with one another—a true "community of practice" in which peer learning and norms are central to the development of practices and ways of doing business.[71] Without formal articulations like journalistic codes of conduct, norms around ethics and values are strongly initiated, encouraged, and enforced as documentary people interact with and acquire information from each other.

Contemplating nonfiction storytellers and leaders as a professional community—comprised, of course, of smaller networks based on modes of practice, collaborations, regional locations, identities, and other characteristics—is meaningful to understanding the future trajectory of documentary. As evidence, we need look no further than the rich conversations and ideas that have emerged and coalesced since 1999 on The D-Word, a self-organized online community sounding board and resource center that "hosts discussions about the art, craft, business and social impact of documentary film," with close to 17,000 members across 130 countries.[72] Documentary professionals debate ethical questions, raise topics of importance, form collaborative teams, wrestle with economic dilemmas, and celebrate triumphs on The D-Word—but also at film festivals and documentary convenings, happy hours and coffees, and informal gatherings.

The strength of documentary communities will be meaningful to shaping the future of the art form and the business. As they have for decades, community members must work together—not as individual small voices, but as a collective force—to meet challenges and shape practices as marketplace trends morph and move (Figure 9.3). Notable documentary initiatives have launched within nonfiction storytelling convenings as makers and leaders come together as community amid a social movement ethos, as in the case of A-Doc, Brown Girls Doc Mafia, disabled community advocacy, documentary career sustainability work, accountability in documentary process, and more. Celebrating and protecting documentary's ethics and civic norms will be important as new makers enter the field, new audiences discover the form, and evolving platforms shift industry patterns.

Figure 9.3. Documentary professionals participate in the "Decolonize Docs" discussion at the International Documentary Association's 2018 Getting Real convening. Photo by Laura Ahmed, courtesy of the International Documentary Association (IDA).

Since its earliest days, evolving through the direct cinema movement of the 1950s and 1960s, and into community media of the 1970s and beyond, documentary has shared and promoted ideals of civic culture—a desire to encourage democratic participation and information for the public good, with "shared commitment to the vision and procedures of democracy."[73] Practicing civic culture values—that is, reflecting images of people and ideas to spark civic imagination that inspires social progress, and providing ways for the public to participate[74]—is not a theoretical enterprise in documentary work. It lives in the practical realities of deal-making, such as considering educational distribution and grassroots screening rights in arrangements with streaming-only outlets, for example, which enables documentary film teams to continue to bring nonfiction stories directly into communities to spark dialogue and mobilize people.

In the same spirit, ethics remain central, and they are deeply embedded in the integrity of documentary process—unearthed, discussed, and negotiated among makers, who do not have codified professional standards and codes from which to draw. Although nonfiction storytellers share ethical values, research conducted by Patricia Aufderheide concluded that "filmmakers routinely denied that they could ever articulate ethical standards because of the enormous diversity of situations they experience. Filmmakers believed they should maintain the highest standards of integrity in their relationships with subjects, viewers, and makers."[75] The ethos of civic culture and ethical commitment is carried out in production practices and will be deeply interrogated now and as the field moves forward, as the Sundance Institute's Tabitha Jackson reflects:

> It's also how we think about how films are made, not just what they are made about and who's making them, but literally how they're made, how the making of work impacts communities, how everything you do is, in some sense, kind of a political act. There is so much to think about in the structures of production which goes beyond identity and representation but is part of the thinking. As a field, we have been able to look out and observe and critique the world and make films about social justice. But now we are asking ourselves more intentionally "is our practice itself just?" The marketplace absolutely doesn't need to be concerned about that, but it's what we are here for. How do we—with limited resources but incredibly strong community—push those things to the forefront and facilitate the ease of making them manifest? The work will reflect it.[76]

A robust future for documentary stories that reveal and interrogate reality—told from a full array of lived experiences and identities—will be constructed within this convergence of documentary representation, forms, audiences, markets, ability of makers to make a sustainable living, and a strong community of practice that celebrates and upholds the ethics and values of a civic culture that believes in reflecting and shaping a more just world. This future is not an abstract provocation but a destiny to actively assemble with every new piece of data, distribution deal, financial investment, film festival, community convening, and celebration of social progress.

Why Documentary Matters

Documentary is a vital, irreplaceable part of our storytelling culture and democratic discourse. It is distinct among the mediated ways we receive and interpret signals about the world and its inhabitants. We humans, despite our insistence to the contrary, make individual and collective decisions from an emotional place of the soul—where kindness and compassion and rage and anger originate—not only from a rational deliberation of facts and information. By opening a portal into the depth of human experience, documentary storytelling contributes to strengthening our cultural moral compass—our normative rulebook that shapes how we regard one another in daily exchanges, and how we prioritize the policies and laws that can either expand justice or dictate oppression. Finding connections with our fellow humans requires this nuanced, intimate view.

This matters, of course, because democracy is not a passive system. Justice is not a quick destination. Social change does not happen in singular tidy moments, even if the markers of advancement can reveal themselves in ways that are concrete and meaningful: a court victory, a policy change, a new law, a changed organization. The journey to social progress—expanding equity rather than shutting it down—is a complicated ebb and flow that can trickle slowly or race furiously forward or reverse course. It requires constant attention from ordinary people and leaders. Justice insists that we see places and people and their problems and triumphs in all of their messy humanity—their heroism and their villainy and even their daily mundanity. And in the act of seeing, social problems and realities are not abstractions but the experiences of people trying to get by. Democracy functions through this lens.

Telling stories about how lives are lived is not ancillary to democratic functioning and social progress—but embedded at the core. Through storytelling, we reflect the people we find valuable, the realities we deem worthy of cultural attention, the challenges worth solving. In documentaries that dig under the surface of what we think we know, or what we have not seen reflected in media portrayals, we find the possibility to connect and expand our literacy about human lives, to fuel solidarity that can come from a recognition of shared destiny and humanity. Experiencing a person's story is not—as an end goal—sufficient for structural social progress, but it *is* a means by which we can motivate conversation and civic practice toward realizing that solidarity. Ultimately, democracy requires the active participation of publics who believe their engagement matters.

What qualities set documentary apart from other forms of mediated storytelling and information? How does documentary connect to social progress? Social-issue documentaries are art for cultural resistance, a source of civic imagination, and a mechanism for social critique. What lies at the heart of documentary storytelling, regardless of format or artistic choice, is people. Humans are wired to connect with others. Artistically, documentary storytelling is uniquely equipped, relative to its close cousins and antecedents—journalism and fiction film—to provide the emotional, creative window into real lives, people, perspectives, and intimate moments. Documentary can advance a point of view and auteur's lens, a creative freedom not traditionally granted to the formal business of journalism, at least in the strictest articulation of journalistic norms and practices of attempted objectivity. The intimacy of the human experience exemplifies documentary storytelling's potency and ability to reach deep into emotions, and often, to compel calls for change on urgent social issues. However, in documentary, finding and showcasing facts—that is, reflecting real life truthfully—is not oppositional to art. The creative, artistic documentary license—the choices that affect music, characters, edit pacing, scenes, relationship of maker to subject—is central to the genre's emotion-generating connection with its audience. Creative documentary challenges us to process realities beyond the binary construction of contemporary politics or the recitation of facts and events provided by daily news. Documentary offers factual insights, yes, but also depth and complexity and emotional resonance. We need both—deep artistic storytelling of documentary and information-provision supply of news reporting—to make sense of the world. And we need the kinds of stories, richly enmeshed in the daily lives and struggles of our fellow humans, to establish compelling narratives and understandings that are not so easily dismissed by partisan ideological framing.

The contemporary ideals of documentaries and democracy and social change are embodied in the creative machinations and civic motivations of storytellers who are compelled to share deeper truths about the world while they capture us through their art. Progress comes partially from accumulated cultural power and recognition, built story after story, an additive process that shapes our understanding of reality. But this cultural force also dwells in the efforts of organizations, leaders, and ordinary people who recognize the capacity of nonfiction film stories to function in particular ways: to represent marginalized voices, reveal ignored stories and perspectives, imagine different realities, artistically re-interpret simplistic frames of social problems, correct damaging narratives and provide counternarratives that add nuance and depth to dominant media reflections, grab and hold attention, open dialogue, train a critical eye on injustice, mobilize people to engage in meaningful activities to make change, and foster community solidarity.

These are, of course, hopeful, optimistic ideas within the networked era and its global connectivity. Constraints and challenges abound. Nefarious actors will continue to exploit a variation of documentary forms to manipulate audiences in ways that disregard the truth in service of political gain. Freedom of creative expression is threatened all over the world. Documentaries can show life and problems in ways that are unpredictable, and the impulse to shut down art and journalism is acute when power is questioned and critiqued. This reality is not new even though the infrastructure of the internet provides fresh mechanisms to shutter open expression while it has expanded its potential reach; barriers will persist. But these challenges, too, fuel documentary fortitude and motivation. Documentary storytellers will, as they have for decades, forge ahead, evolving the form and practices and social influence, meeting the provocations and injustices that will continue. And in ordinary lives, documentaries will find and transmit extraordinary, illuminating tales—revealing and shaping reality through story movements that empower people and inspire social change.

Interviewees

Interviews were facilitated by phone or in person (two interviewees completed questions via email) from June 2018 through July 2019, except the interviews for Chapter 7, as noted below.

Patricia Aufderheide, *Documentary: A Very Short Introduction*
Assia Boundaoui, *The Feeling of Being Watched*
Iyabo Boyd, Brown Girls Doc Mafia
Caitlin Boyle, Film Sprout
Sonya Childress, Firelight Media
Dan Cogan, Impact Partners
Leo Chiang, A-Doc (emailed responses)
Charlotte Cook, Field of Vision
Brenda Coughlin, Sundance Institute Documentary Film Program
Gabriela Cowperthwaite, *Blackfish*
Jessica Devaney, *The Feeling of Being Watched*
Kirby Dick, *The Invisible War*
Abigail Disney, Fork Films
Jamie Dobie, Peace Is Loud
Deborah Esquenazi, *Southwest of Salem: The Story of the San Antonio Four*
Sally Fifer, Independent Television Service (ITVS)
Beadie Finzi, Doc Society
Maxyne Franklin, Doc Society
Katie Galloway, *The Pushouts*
Stephen Gong, Center for Asian American Media
Holly Gordon, Participant Media
Judith Helfand, *The Uprising of '34*
Cynthia Hill, *Private Violence*
Kathy Im, MacArthur Foundation (emailed responses)
Tabitha Jackson, Sundance Film Festival (Director of the Sundance Institute Documentary Film Program at the time of this book interview)
Simon Kilmurry, International Documentary Association
Jim LeBrecht, *Crip Camp*
Sheila Leddy, Fledgling Fund
Loira Limbal, Firelight Media
Carrie Lozano, International Documentary Association
Jennifer MacArthur, Borderline Media
Christie Marchese, Picture Motion
Louis Massiah, Scribe Video Center
Elaine McMillion Sheldon, *Heroin(e)*
Cara Mertes, Ford Foundation
Molly Murphy, Working Films
Justine Nagan, American Documentary, Inc. and POV
Stanley Nelson, *The Murder of Emmett Till*
Sheila Nevins, MTV Documentary Films

Marilyn Ness, *Charm City*
Sandie Viquez Pedlow, Latino Public Broadcasting
Rick Perez, Sundance Institute Stories of Change
Laura Poitras, *Citizenfour*
Gordon Quinn, Kartemquin Films
Jan Radar, Fire Chief, Huntington, West Virginia *(Heroin(e))*
Anya Rous, Multitude Films
Ellen Schneider, Active Voice
Marcia Smith, Firelight Media
Shirley Sneve, Vision Maker Media
Erin Sorenson, Third Stage Consulting
Lina Srivastava, Creative Impact and Experience Lab
John Valverde, YouthBuild
Jenni Wolfson, Chicken & Egg Pictures
Marc Weiss, founder, POV

Chapter 7 (Shaping Laws: Documentaries and Policy Engagement):

Interviews with filmmakers, film subjects, policymakers, staffers, and nonprofit executives were conducted by Caty Borum Chattoo and Will Jenkins between December 2015 and November 2017, as featured in an earlier publication of this material: Caty Borum Chattoo and Will Jenkins, "From Reel Life to Real Social Change: The Role of Contemporary Social-Issue Documentary in U.S. Public Policy." *Media, Culture & Society* 41, no. 8 (November 2019): 1107–1124. doi:10.1177/0163443718823145.

Documentary and Democracy Landscape: Profiled Organizations and Initiatives

These documentary-focused organizations and initiatives are referenced in the book given their relationship to major themes: documentaries and democracy, representation and community engagement, and the changing marketplace for nonfiction storytelling. This is not an exhaustive list of all distribution outlets, media companies, or production organizations involved in documentary storytelling.

A-Doc (Asian American Documentary Network)
Active Voice
AFI Docs Impact Lab
Brown Girls Doc Mafia
Center for Media & Social Impact
Chicken & Egg Pictures
Corporation for Public Broadcasting
Doc Society
The D-Word
Film Sprout
Firelight Media
Fledgling Fund
Ford Foundation JustFilms
Fork Films
Global Impact Producers Assembly
Good Pitch (Doc Society)
Impact Partners
Independent Television Service (ITVS)
International Documentary Association (IDA)
Just Vision
Kartemquin Films
MacArthur Foundation
National Multicultural Alliance: Center for Asian American Media, Pacific Islanders in Communications, Vision Maker Media, Black Public Media, and Latino Public Broadcasting
New Day Films
Participant Media
Peace Is Loud
Picture Motion
POV (PBS)
Scribe Video Center
Southern Documentary Fund

Sundance Institute Documentary Film Program
Sundance Institute
Vulcan Productions
Women Make Movies
Working Films

Filmography

Bag It
Blackfish
Bully
Charm City
Citizenfour
Crime + Punishment
Freedom Riders
Girl Rising
Harlan County, U.S.A.
Harvest of Shame
Heroin(e)
Hoop Dreams
Minding the Gap
Playground
Private Violence
Semper Fi
Silverlake Life: The View from Here
Sin by Silence
Southwest of Salem: The Story of the San Antonio Four
Strong Island
Surviving R. Kelly
13th
The Armor of Light
The Feeling of Being Watched
The Invisible War
The Pushouts
The Murder of Emmett Till
The Uprising of '34
Tongues Untied
Unrest
Wal-Mart: The High Cost of Low Price
When I Walk
Whose Streets?

Notes

Chapter 1

1. Kazuo Ishiguro, "My Twentieth Century Evening—and Other Small Breakthroughs," Nobel Lecture (speech), December 7, 2017, https://www.nobelprize.org/prizes/literature/2017/ishiguro/25124-kazuo-ishiguro-nobel-lecture-2017/. © The Nobel Foundation 2017. Used with permission of The Nobel Foundation.

2. Sheila Nevins, in-person interview with author, August 22, 2018.

3. Jerry Useem, "Should We Admire Wal-Mart?" *Fortune* 149, no. 5 (March 8, 2004): 118–120, http://proxyau.wrlc.org/login?url=https://search-proquest-com.proxyau.wrlc.org/docview/213299414?accountid=8285.

4. Russell Mokhiber and Robert Weissman, "The Ten Worst Corporations of 2004," *Multinational Monitor* 25, no. 12 (2004): 8–21, http://proxyau.wrlc.org/login?url=https://search-proquest-com.proxyau.wrlc.org/docview/208876772?accountid=8285.

5. Useem, "Should We Admire Wal-Mart?"

6. CNN, "No Smiles for Wal-Mart in California," *CNN Money*, April 7, 2004, https://money.cnn.com/2004/04/07/news/fortune500/walmart_inglewood/; Mokhiber and Weissman, "The Ten Worst Corporations of 2004"; Jonathan Nelson, "Taking on Wal-Mart; Retail Giant Played Tough with County and Won. But More Communities Are Standing Up to the Chain and Its Supercenters," *Columbian*, March 14, 2004, http://proxyau.wrlc.org/login?url=https://search-proquest-com.proxyau.wrlc.org/docview/253216867?accountid=8285; Jonathan Nelson, "Wal-Mart's Growth Prompts New Wave of Activists in Oregon, Washington State," *Knight Ridder Tribune Business News*, March 15, 2004, http://proxyau.wrlc.org/login?url=https://search-proquest-com.proxyau.wrlc.org/docview/463678439?accountid=8285; Hector Becerra, "CALIFORNIA; Clerics Speak Out on Wal-Mart; Some Parishioners Complain to Cardinal Mahony, Saying that Vocal Opposition to Discount Store Has No Place in Church [HOME EDITION]," *Los Angeles Times*, October 30, 2004, http://proxyau.wrlc.org/login?url=https://search-proquest-com.proxyau.wrlc.org/docview/421923836?accountid=8285; Jason Thomas, "Greenwood, Ind., Opponents Score Victory against Proposed Wal-Mart," *Knight Ridder Tribune Business News*, March 23, 2004, http://proxyau.wrlc.org/login?url=https://search-proquest-com.proxyau.wrlc.org/docview/463722822?accountid=8285.

7. Damon Smith, "Filmmaker Fires a Shot at a Corporate Giant; Robert Greenwald Turns His Activist Eye on Wal-Mart [Third Edition]," *Boston Globe*, November 20, 2005, http://proxyau.wrlc.org/login?url=https://search-proquest-com.proxyau.wrlc.org/docview/404988161?accountid=8285; Henry Jenkins, Sam Ford, and Joshua Green, *Spreadable Media* (New York: New York University Press, 2013), 169.

8. The formal name of the company, circa 2005, was "Wal-Mart." The title of the film reflects that style. Several years after the film was distributed, the company changed its smiley-face

logo—which had been parodied in the documentary's graphic art, including the movie poster—and its name from "Wal-Mart" to "Walmart."

9. Ken Eisen, "New Wal-Mart Documentary May Be a Sign of Upheavals to Come," *Grist*, November 23, 2005, https://grist.org/article/eisen1/; "WakeUpWalMart.Com Releases New 30-Second Ad: 'Who Is the Most Corrupt in America?'" U.S.Newswire, November 9, 2005, http://proxyau.wrlc.org/login?url=https://search-proquest-com.proxyau.wrlc.org/docview/451308444?accountid=8285.

10. Manuel Castells, *Networks of Outrage and Hope: Social Movements in the Internet Age* (Cambridge: Polity Press, 2012).

11. Paul R. La Monica, "Revenge of the Netflix?," *CNN Money*, February 25, 2005, https://money.cnn.com/2005/02/25/technology/netflix/.

12. Martha Nussbaum, "Chapter 10: Democratic Citizenship and the Narrative Imagination," *Yearbook of the National Society for the Study of Education*, 107 (2008): 143–157, doi:10.1111/j.1744-7984.2008.00138.x, 147.

13. John Corner, "What Can We Say about 'Documentary'?" *Media, Culture & Society* 22, no. 5 (September 2000): 681–688doi:10.1177/016344300022005009, 682.

14. Nick Fraser, "Why Documentaries Matter," *The Guardian*, March 19, 2011, https://www.theguardian.com/tv-and-radio/2011/mar/20/documentaries-brian-cox-nick-fraser.

15. Erik Barnouw, *Documentary: A History of the Non-Fiction Film,* 2nd rev. ed. (New York: Oxford University Press, 1993), 5–7. .

16. William Stott, *Documentary Expression in 1930s America* (Chicago: University of Chicago Press, 1973), 67–69.

17. Neil Gabler, *An Empire of Their Own: How the Jews Invented Hollywood* (New York: Crown Publishers, 1988), 2–7, 54–57, 74..

18. Stott, *Documentary Expression in 1930s America*, 9; Bill Nichols, *Introduction to Documentary*, 2nd ed. (Bloomington: Indiana University Press, 2010), 6.

19. Patricia Aufderheide, *Documentary: A Very Short Introduction* (New York: Oxford University Press, 2007), 2.

20. Aufderheide, *Documentary: A Very Short Introduction*, 27.

21. Nichols, *Introduction to Documentary*, 6.

22. Stott, *Documentary Expression in 1930s America*, 9.

23. Brian Winston, *Claiming the Real II. Documentary: Grierson and Beyond* (London: Palgrave Macmillan, 2008), 20.

24. Stott, *Documentary Expression in 1930s America*, 172.

25. Jane Gaines, "Radical Attractions: The Uprising of '34," *Wide Angle* 21, no. 2 (1999): 101–119, 10.1353/wan.1999.0019

26. Aufderheide, *Documentary: A Very Short Introduction*, 2–3.

27. Michael Chanan, *Politics of Documentary* (London: Palgrave Macmillan, 2008), vi.

28. Nichols, *Introduction to Documentary,* 143.

29. Chanan, *Politics of Documentary*, 23.

30. Barnouw, *Documentary: A History of the Non-Fiction Film*, 297–298.

31. Bill Nichols, *Representing Reality* (Bloomington: Indiana University Press, 2010), 3–4.

32. Michael Renov, ed., *Theorizing Documentary* (New York: Routledge, 1993), 21.

33. Stott, *Documentary Expression in 1930s America*, 15.

34. Thomas Waugh, *Show Us Life: Toward a History and Aesthetics of the Committed Documentary* (Lanham, MD: Scarecrow Press, 1984), xiv.

35. Thomas Waugh, *Show Us Life*, xiii.

36. Kate Nash and John Corner, "Strategic Impact Documentary: Contexts of Production and Social Intervention," *European Journal of Communication* 31, no. 3 (2016): 227–242, https://doi.org/10.1177/0267323116635831, 227 .

37. Caty Borum Chattoo, "Documentary and Communication," in *Oxford Bibliographies in Communication*, ed. Patricia Moy (New York: Oxford University Press, 2018), doi: 10.1093/OBO/9780199756841-0207.

38. Nichols, *Introduction to Documentary*, 1.

39. Nichols, *Introduction to Documentary*, 2.

40. Jeffrey P. Jones, *Entertaining Politics: Satiric Television and Political Engagement* (Lanham, MD: Rowman and Littlefield, 2010), 39.

41. Borum Chattoo, "Documentary and Communication."

42. Jenni Wolfson, in-person interview with author, June 13, 2018.

43. Ellen Schneider, phone interview with author, June 29, 2018.

44. Marcia Smith, in-person interview with author, June 11, 2018.

45. Gordon Quinn, phone interview with author, June 30, 2018.

46. Simon Kilmurry, phone interview with author, March 25, 2019.

47. Caty Borum Chattoo, Patricia Aufderheide, Kenneth Merrill and Modupeola Oyebolu, "Diversity on U.S. Public and Commercial TV in Authorial and Executive-Produced Social-Issue Documentaries," *Journal of Broadcasting & Electronic Media* 62, no. 3 (2018): 495–513, https://doi.org/10.1080/08838151.2018.1451865, 499.

48. Stanley Nelson, phone interview with author, May 16, 2019.

49. Sally Fifer, phone interview with author, July 25, 2018.

50. Simon Kilmurry, phone interview with author, March 25, 2019.

51. Jonathan Kahana, *Intelligence Work: The Politics of American Documentary* (New York: Columbia University Press, 2008), 15.

52. Aufderheide, *Documentary: A Very Short Introduction*, 53.

53. Tabitha Jackson, phone interview with author, May 20, 2019.

54. Patricia Aufderheide, *Dangerous Documentaries: Reducing Risk When Telling Truth to Power* (Washington, DC: Center for Media and Social Impact, 2015), https://cmsimpact.org/resource/dangerous-documentaries-reducing-risk-when-telling-truth-to-power/.

55. Abigail Disney, in-person interview with author, August 29, 2018.

56. Justine Nagan, in-person interview with author, June 13, 2018.

57. Gordon Quinn, phone interview with author, June 30, 2018.

58. Winston, *Claiming the Real II. Documentary: Grierson and Beyond*, 54.

59. Owen Gleiberman, "Film Review: Dinesh D'Souza's 'Death of a Nation,'" *Variety*, July 20, 2018, https://variety.com/2018/film/reviews/death-of-a-nation-review-dinesh-dsouza-1202890451/.

60. Caty Borum Chattoo and Bill Harder, *The State of the Documentary Field: 2018 Study of Documentary Professionals* (Washington, DC: Center for Media and Social Impact, 2018), https://cmsimpact.org/report/state-documentary-field-2018-study-documentary-professionals/.

61. Borum Chattoo and Harder, *The State of the Documentary Field*.

62. Peter Dahlgren, *Media and Political Engagement: Citizens, Communication, and Democracy* (New York: Cambridge University Press, 2009), 58.

63. Cara Mertes, in-person interview with author, June 18, 2018.

64. Marcia Smith, in-person interview with author, June 11, 2018.

65. Katie Galloway, phone interview with author, May 2, 2019.

66. John Corner, "Performing the Real: Documentary Diversions," *Television & New Media* 3, no. 3 (August 2002): 255–269, doi:10.1177/152747640200300302.

67. Corner, "Performing the Real," 262.

68. Sheila Nevins, in-person interview with author, August 22, 2018.

69. Corner, "Performing the Real," 264.

70. Jeffrey Jones, *Entertaining Politics: Satiric Television and Political Engagement* (Lanham, MD: Rowman and Littlefield, 2010).

71. James W. Carey, *Communication as Culture*, rev. ed. (New York: Routledge, 2008).

72. Henry Jenkins, Sangita Shresthova, Liana Gamber-Thompson, Neta Kligler-Vilenchik, and Arely M. Zimmerman *By Any Media Necessary: The New Youth Activism* (New York: New York University Press, 2016), 17.

73. Sonya Childress, phone interview with author, June 11, 2018.

74. For rich discussions, deliberations, and historical references to documentary tradition, evolution, and theory, please see the many works cited here, including books by Patricia Aufderheide, Erik Barnouw, Michael Chanan, John Corner, Michael Curtin, Joshua Glick, Jonathan Kahana, Betsy McLane, Kate Nash, Bill Nichols, Michael Renov, William Stott, Thomas Waugh, Brian Winston, and Patricia Zimmermann.

75. James McEnteer, *Shooting the Truth: The Rise of American Political Documentaries* (Westport, CT: Praeger, 2006); and Thomas W. Benson et al. (eds.), *The Rhetoric of the New Political Documentary* (Carbondale: Southern Illinois University Press, 2008).

76. Caty Borum Chattoo, Patricia Aufderheide, Michele Alexander, and Chandler Green, "American Realities on Public Television: Analysis of the Independent Television Service's Documentaries, 2007–2016," *International Journal of Communication* 12 (2018): 1541–1568, http://ijoc.org/index.php/ijoc/article/view/7826/2314, 1544.

77. Borum Chattoo et al., "American Realities on Public Television," 1545.

Chapter 2

1. Marc Weiss, in-person interview with author, July 17, 2018.

2. Judy Klemesrud, "Coal Miners Started the Strike—Then Their Women Took Over," *New York Times*, May 15, 1974, https://www.nytimes.com/1974/05/15/archives/coal-miners-started-the-strikethen-their-women-took-over-large.html?url=http://timesmachine.nytimes.com/timesmachine/1974/05/15/119460404.html.

3. *Harlan County USA*, prod. Barbara Kopple, dir. Barbara Kopple (United States: Cinema Five, 1976).

4. Robert Hatch, "Harlan County, USA," *The Nation*, January 23, 2009, https://www.thenation.com/article/harlan-county-usa/.

5. "Back to 'Harlan County, USA,'" review, *The Attic* (blog), February 23, 2018, https://www.theattic.space/home-page-blogs/2018/2/23/back-to-harlan-county-usa?rq=back%20to%20harlan%20county,%20usa.

6. Steven Gaydon, "Barbara Kopple Reflects on Joys and Dangers of Filming 'Harlan County, USA,'" *Variety*, July 24, 2015, https://variety.com/2015/film/features/barbara-kopple-reflects-on-harlan-county-usa-documentary-1201547157/

7. Patricia Aufderheide, "Barbara Kopple's Work within the Changing Documentary Business Ecology," 178-192, in *ReFocus: The Films of Barbara Kopple*, eds. Jeff Jaeckle and Susan Ryan (Edinburgh: Edinburgh University Press, 2019), 178.

8. Aufderheide, "Barbara Kopple's Work," 180.

9. Communications Act of 1934, 47 U.S.C. § 4 (1934).

10. F. Andrew Hanssen, "Vertical Integration during the Hollywood Studio Era," *The Journal of Law & Economics* 53, no. 3 (August 2010): 519–543, 10.1086/605567, 523, 519.

11. Amanda D. Lotz, *The Television Will Be Revolutionized*, Second *Edition* (New York: New York University Press, 2014), 24.

12. Michael Curtin, *Redeeming the Wasteland: Television Documentary and Cold War Politics* (New Brunswick, NJ: Rutgers University Press, 1995), 8–9.

13. Curtin, *Redeeming the Wasteland*, 19, 27.

14. Curtin, *Redeeming the Wasteland*, 23–24.

15. Curtin, *Redeeming the Wasteland*.

16. Chad Raphael, "Broadcast Network Documentaries," in *Encyclopedia of Journalism*, ed. Christopher H. Sterling and C. Whitney (Beverly Hills: Sage, 2009), 458–463.

17. Curtin, *Redeeming the Wasteland*, 168.

18. Curtin, *Redeeming the Wasteland*, 9.

19. Raphael, "Broadcast Network Documentaries," 458–463.

20. Patricia Aufderheide, phone interview with author, June 7, 2019.

21. Curtin, *Redeeming the Wasteland*, 252.

22. "National Educational Television," American Archive of Public Broadcasting, https://americanarchive.org/special_collections/net-catalog.

23. "National Education Television Center," Carolyn N. Brooks, Museum of Broadcast Communications, http://www.museum.tv/eotv/nationaleduc.htm.

24. "About CPB," Corporation for Public Broadcasting, https://www.cpb.org/aboutcpb.

25. Joshua Glick, *Los Angeles Documentary and the Production of Public History, 1958–1977* (Oakland: University of California Press, 2018), 75; "Carnegie I: Carnegie Commission on Educational Television, 1967," *Current*, https://current.org/1967/01/carnegie-i/.

26. Patricia Aufderheide, *The Daily Planet: A Critic on the Capitalist Culture Beat* (Minneapolis: University of Minnesota Press, 2000), 88.

27. "About PBS: Mission," PBS, http://about.lunchbox.pbs.org/about/about-pbs/mission-\statement/

28. Glick, *Los Angeles Documentary*, 84.

29. Eugenia Williamson, "PBS Self-Destructs: And What It Means for Viewers Like You," *Harpers*, October 2014, https://harpers.org/archive/2014/10/pbs-self-destructs/6/

30. Patricia Aufderheide, email correspondence with author, June 26, 2019.

31. Marc Weiss, in-person interview with author, July 17, 2018.

32. Marc Weiss, in-person interview with author, July 17, 2018.

33. DeeDee Halleck, *Hand-Held Visions: The Impossible Possibilities of Community Media* (New York: Fordham University Press, 2002).

34. "The Mission and History of Scribe," Scribe, http://scribe.org/mission-and-history-scribe.

35. Louis Massiah, phone interview with author, June 7, 2019.

36. Kathy Im, email correspondence with author, June 28, 2019.

37. Aufderheide, *The Daily Planet,* 112; Halleck, *Hand-Held Visions,* 237.

38. Caty Borum Chattoo, Patricia Aufderheide, Michele Alexander, and Chandler Green, "American Realities on Public Television: Analysis of the Independent Television Service's Documentaries, 2007–2016," *International Journal of Communication* 12 (2018): 1541–1568, http://ijoc.org/index.php/ijoc/article/view/7826/2314.

39. Aufderheide, *The Daily Planet,* 114.

40. POV, "How It All Began: POV Founder Marc Weiss Talks About The Series' Beginning," December 14, 2017, http://archive.pov.org/blog/news/2017/12/30marathon-marc-weiss-letter/

41. William Stott, *Documentary Expression in 1930s America* (Chicago: University of Chicago Press, 1973), 68.

42. Erik Barnouw, *A Tower of Babel: A History of Broadcasting in the United States,* vol. 1: *To 1933* (New York: Oxford University Press, 1966), 17.

43. Stott, *Documentary Expression in 1930s America,* 21.

44. Stott, *Documentary Expression in 1930s America,* 23.

45. Stott, *Documentary Expression in 1930s America,* 23.

46. Stott, *Documentary Expression in 1930s America,* 22.

47. Bill Nichols, *Introduction to Documentary,* 2nd ed. (Bloomington: Indiana University Press, 2010), 156.

48. Patricia R. Zimmermann and Helen De Michiel, *Open Space New Media Documentary: A Toolkit for Theory and Practice* (New York: Routledge, 2018), xiii.

49. Dave Saunders, *Direct Cinema: Observational Documentary and the Politics of the Sixties* (London: Wallflower Press, 2007), 1.

50. Patricia Aufderheide, *Documentary: A Very Short Introduction* (New York: Oxford University Press, 2007), 44.

51. Gordon Quinn, phone interview with author, June 30, 2018.

52. Glick, *Los Angeles Documentary,* 78–79.

53. Bill Nichols, "Newsreel: Film and Revolution," *Cinéaste* 5, no. 4 (1973): 7–13, https://www.jstor.org/stable/41685696

54. Marc Weiss, in-person interview with author, July 17, 2018.

55. Nichols, "Newsreel: Film and Revolution"; Zimmerman and De Michiel, *Open Space New Media Documentary,* xiii; Glick, *Los Angeles Documentary,* 80.

56. Formally, the Challenge for Change program was operational from 1967 to 1980.

57. Ezra Winton and Naomi Klein, "Putting Ideas into the World: A Conversation with Naomi Klein about Starting Conversations with Film, Foreword," xv–xxiv, in *Challenge for Change: Activist Documentary at the National Film Board of Canada,* ed. Thomas Waugh, Michael Brendan Baker, and Ezra Winton (Montreal: McGill-Queen's University Press, 2010), xix–xx.

58. Peter K. Wiesner, "Media for the People: The Canadian Experiments with Film and Video in Community Development," 73–102, in *Challenge for Change: Activist Documentary at the National Film Board of Canada,* ed. Thomas Waugh, Michael Brendan Baker, and Ezra Winton (Montreal: McGill-Queen's University Press, 2010), 96.

59. Kevin Howley, *Community Media: People, Place, and Communication Technologies* (Cambridge, UK: Cambridge University Press, 2005), 54.

60. Howley, *Community Media,* 55.

61. Cara Mertes, in-person interview with author, July 18, 2018.

62. "Homepage," Appalshop, accessed March 1, 2019, https://www.appalshop.org/.

63. Aufderheide, "Barbara Kopple's Work," 179.

64. Howley, *Community Media*, 146.

65. Howley, *Community Media*, 149–150.

66. Glick, *Los Angeles Documentary,* 71.

67. "From the 1980 Annual Meeting," New Day Films, How New Day Began, accessed March 1, 2019, https://www.newday.com/content/how-new-day-began.

68. "From the 1980 Annual Meeting," New Day Films.

69. "General Information," Women Make Movies, accessed March 1, 2019, http://www.wmm.com/about/general_info.shtml#history.

70. Cara Mertes, in-person interview with author, July 18, 2018.

71. Shirley Sneve, phone interview with author, May 10, 2019; "Vision Maker Media Documentaries," American Archive of Public Broadcasting, accessed March 1, 2019, http://americanarchive.org/special_collections/vision-maker-media.

72. Vincent Schilling, "Native American Public Telecommunications Rebrands Itself as Vision Maker Media," *Indian Country Today*, January 9, 2013, https://newsmaven.io/indiancountrytoday/archive/native-american-public-telecommunications-rebrands-itself-as-vision-maker-media-KUPV6f0UpEyE3ZTC3Ftq6g/.

73. Black Public Media, "About," accessed May 1, 2019, https://blackpublicmedia.org/about/; Sandie Viquez Pedlow, phone interview with author, June 4, 2019.

74. Stephen Gong, phone interview with author, May 24, 2019; "About CAAM," Center for Asian American Media, accessed March 1, 2019, https://caamedia.org/about-caam/.

75. Stephen Gong, phone interview with author, May 24, 2019; "History and Mission," Pacific Islanders in Communications, accessed March 1, 2019, https://www.piccom.org/pages/history-mission.

76. Stephen Gong, phone interview with author, May 24, 2019.

77. Stanley Nelson, phone interview with author, May 16, 2019.

78. "About Visual Communications," Visual Communications, accessed March 1, 2019, https://vcmedia.org/mission-history.

79. Glick, *Los Angeles Documentary*, 98.

80. Glick, *Los Angeles Documentary*, 101.

81. Stanley Nelson, phone interview with author, May 16, 2019.

82. Jill Nelson, "Two Dollars and a Dream," *Washington Post*, February 21, 1988, https://www.washingtonpost.com/archive/lifestyle/tv/1988/02/21/two-dollars-and-a-dream/a3d2f2d6-1877-495f-bdd2-e0fbc4277f44/?noredirect=on&utm_term=.2d30a007af52.

83. Denise Marie Glover, *Voices of the Spirit: Sources for Interpreting the African American Experience* (Chicago: American Library Association, 1995), 156.

84. "Sam Pollard," NYU Tisch School of the Arts, accessed March 1, 2019, https://tisch.nyu.edu/about/directory/film-tvs/3535147.

85. Renee Tajima-Peña, "#DocsSoWhite: A Personal Reflection," *Documentary* Magazine, August 30, 2016, https://www.documentary.org/feature/docssowhite-personal-reflection.

86. "About Us," National Multicultural Alliance, accessed June 15, 2019, https://nmcalliance.org/about/.

87. Shirley Sneve, phone interview with author, May 10, 2019.

88. Aufderheide, *Documentary: A Very Short Introduction,* 46; Patricia Aufderheide, phone interview with author, May 7, 2019.

89. Patricia Aufderheide, phone interview with author, May 7, 2019.

90. Michael Chanan, *The Politics of Documentary* (London: British Film Institute, 2007), 166.

91. Aufderheide, *Documentary: A Very Short Introduction,* 46.

92. Betsy A. McLane, *A New History of Documentary Film*, 2nd ed. (New York: Bloomsbury Academic, 2012), 224.

93. Halleck, *Hand-Held Visions,* 439.

94. Dave Saunders, *Direct Cinema: Observational Documentary and the Politics of the Sixties* (London: Wallflower Press, 2007), 145–146.

95. Cara Mertes, in-person interview with author, July 18, 2018.

96. Betsy A. McLane, *A New History of Documentary Film*, 195.

97. Janine Marchessault, "Amateur Video and the Challenge for Change," 354–365, in *Challenge for Change: Activist Documentary at the National Film Board of Canada*, ed. Thomas Waugh, Michael Brendan Baker, and Ezra Winton (Montreal: McGill-Queen's University Press, 2010), 359.

98. Gordon Quinn, phone interview with author, June 30, 2018.

99. Brian Winston, *The Documentary Film Book* (London: British Film Institute, 2013), 13–14.

100. Nichols, *Introduction to Documentary*, 160.

101. Nichols, *Introduction to Documentary,* 32.

102. Nichols, *Introduction to Documentary,* 182–183.

103. Amanda D. Lotz, *The Television Will Be Revolutionized*, 2nd ed. (New York: New York University Press, 2014), 8.

104. Howley, *Community Media*, 175.

105. Susan Murray, "America Undercover," 262-273, in Gary R. Edgerton and Jeffrey P. Jones, eds., *The Essential HBO Reader* (Lexington: University Press of Kentucky, 2008), 264, 262–273.

106. Sheila Nevins, in-person interview with author, August 22, 2018.

107. Howley, *Community Media*, 175.

108. Aufderheide, "Barbara Kopple's Work," 185; "Documentary," Box Office Mojo, accessed March 1, 2019, https://www.boxofficemojo.com/genres/chart/?id=documentary.htm.

109. "Documentary," Box Office Mojo.

110. "Sundance Film Festival," Sundance Institute, accessed March 1, 2019, https://www.sundance.org/timeline.

111. "Hoop Dreams," Kartemquin Films, accessed March 1, 2019, https://kartemquin.com/films/hoop-dreams.

112. Gabriel Baumgaertner, "Hoop Dreams: Where Are the Main Figures Now?," *The Guardian*, February 18, 2015, https://www.theguardian.com/sport/2015/feb/18/hoop-dreams-where-are-the-main-figures-now.

113. Gordon Quinn, phone interview with author, June 30, 2018.

114. "Hoop Dreams," Box Office Mojo, https://www.boxofficemojo.com/movies/?id=hoop-dreams.htm.

115. "Documentary," Box Office Mojo.

116. Chanan, *The Politics of Documentary,* 9.

117. Andrew R. Chow, "It's Been 25 Years Since Hoop Dreams Debuted. Here's How It Changed the Game for Documentaries," *Time*, April 9, 2019, http://time.com/5562158/hoop-dreams-documentary-25-years/.

118. Paul Arthur, "Extreme Makeover: The Changing Face of Documentary," *Cinéaste* 30, no. 3 (2005): 18–23, https://www.jstor.org/stable/41689868, 19.

119. "Documentary," Box Office Mojo.

120. "Documentary," Box Office Mojo.
121. "Video Camera," Sony, Corporate Info, accessed March 1, 2019, https://www.sony.net/SonyInfo/CorporateInfo/History/sonyhistory-f.html.
122. International Electrotechnical Commission, *Recording—Helical-Scan Digital Video Cassette Recording System Using 6,35 mm Magnetic Tape for Consumer Use (525-60, 625-50, 1125-60 and 1250-50 Systems)* (Geneva: International Electrotechnical Commission, 1998).
123. "Video Camera," Sony.
124. "Apple's Final Cut Pro Wins Emmy Award," Apple, Newsroom, last updated August 20, 2002, https://www.apple.com/newsroom/2002/08/20Apples-Final-Cut-Pro-Wins-Emmy-Award/.
125. Lotz, *The Television Will Be Revolutionized*, 8.
126. Matthew Crick, *Power, Surveillance, and Culture in YouTube™'s Digital Sphere* (Hershey: Information Science Reference, 2016), 37.
127. "About Netflix," Netflix, accessed March 1, 2019, https://media.netflix.com/en/about-netflix.
128. Cynthia Littleton and Janko Roettgers, "Ted Sarandos on How Netflix Predicted the Future of TV," *Variety*, August 21, 2018, https://variety.com/2018/digital/news/netflix-streaming-dvds-original-programming-1202910483/.
129. Lotz, *The Television Will Be Revolutionized*, 70, 72.
130. Alison Willmore, "Netflix Acquires Its First Original Documentary: 'The Square,'" *IndieWire*, November 4, 2013, https://www.indiewire.com/2013/11/netflix-acquires-its-first-original-documentary-the-square-33332/.
131. Julia Greenberg, "Netflix Wants to Usher in a New Golden Age of Nonfiction TV," *Wired*, May 25, 2015, https://www.wired.com/2015/05/netflix-original-documentaries/.
132. Paula Bernstein, "What Does Netflix's Investment in Documentaries Mean for Filmmakes?," *IndieWire*, March 9, 2015, https://www.indiewire.com/2015/03/what-does-netflixs-investment-in-documentaries-mean-for-filmmakers-64347/.
133. "Oscar Nominees," Oscars, accessed March 1, 2019, http://oscar.go.com/nominees.
134. "Press Release: New Roster of Independent Non-Fiction Films Join PBS Primetime Lineup in 2003," PBS, Independent Television Service, last update July 26, 2002, https://web.archive.org/web/20020803102104/http:/www.itvs.org/pressroom/pressRelease.htm?pressId=143.
135. POV, "Why Did CNN, Time, Al Jazeera and Netflix Start Documentary Units?," *POV's Documentary Blog*, August 22, 2013, http://www.pbs.org/pov/blog/news/2013/08/why-did-cnn-time-al-jazeera-and-netflix-start-documentary-units/.
136. Ezra Winton and Jason Garrison, "If a Revolution Is Screened and No One Is There to See it, Does It Make a Sound?," 404-424, in *Challenge for Change: Activist Documentary at the National Film Board of Canada*, ed. Thomas Waugh, Michael Brendan Baker, and Ezra Winton (Montreal: McGill-Queen's University Press, 2010), 404.
137. Reuters, "Comcast Completes NBC Universal Merger," *Reuters Business News*, January 29, 2011, https://www.reuters.com/article/us-comcast-nbc/comcast-completes-nbc-universal-merger-idUSTRE70S2WZ20110129.
138. James B. Stewart, "How the Government Could Win the AT&T-Time Warner Case," *New York Times*, May 31, 2018, https://www.nytimes.com/2018/05/31/business/att-time-warner-antitrust-stewart.html.

139. "Consolidation in the Internet Economy: Executive Summary," The Internet Society, https://future.internetsociety.org/2019/introduction/executive-summary/, 8.

140. Ben H. Bagdikian, *The New Media Monopoly* (Boston: Beacon Press, 2004), 9.

141. Manuel Castells, *Networks of Outrage and Hope: Social Movements in the Internet Age* (Cambridge: Polity Press, 2012).

142. Zeynep Tufekci, *Twitter and Tear Gas: The Power and Fragility of Networked Protest* (New Haven, CT: Yale University Press, 2017).

Chapter 3

1. Sally Fifer, phone interview with author, July 25, 2018.

2. Time Photo, "When One Mother Defied America: The Photo That Changed the Civil Rights Movement," *Time*, July 10, 2016, http://time.com/4399793/emmett-till-civil-rights-photography/.

3. "The Trial of J. W. Milam and Roy Bryant," PBS, accessed February 1, 2019, https://www.pbs.org/wgbh/americanexperience/features/emmett-trial-jw-milam-and-roy-bryant/.

4. "The Trial of J. W. Milam and Roy Bryant," PBS.

5. "American Experience: The Murder of Emmett Till," Peabody Awards, accessed February 1, 2019, http://www.peabodyawards.com/award-profile/american-experience-the-murder-of-emmett-till.

6. James R. Ralph Jr., "The Murder of Emmett Till. Prod. by Stanley Nelson. Firelight Media Production for American Experience, 2003. 60 Mins.," *Journal of American History* 90, no. 3 (December 1, 2003), doi:10.2307/3661057.

7. Marcia Smith, in-person interview with author, June 11, 2018.

8. Marcia Smith, in-person interview with author, June 11, 2018.

9. Monica Davey and Gretchen Ruethling, "After 50 Years, Emmett Till's Body Is Exhumed," *New York Times*, June 2, 2005, https://www.nytimes.com/2005/06/02/us/after-50-years-emmett-tills-body-is-exhumed.html.

10. Stanley Nelson, phone interview with author, May 10, 2019.

11. Sonya Childress, email correspondence with author, September 6, 2019.

12. Kurt Andersen, "The Protester," *Time*, December 14, 2011, http://content.time.com/time/specials/packages/article/0,28804,2101745_2102132,00.html.

13. "Person of the Year 2011," *Time*, December 16, 2011, http://content.time.com/time/person-of-the-year/2011/.

14. "Social Media Fact Sheet," Pew Research Center, February 5, 2018, http://www.pewinternet.org/fact-sheet/social-media/.

15. *Topline Questionnaire: January 2018 Core Trends Survey*. PDF. Washington: Pew Research Center, February 14, 2018, https://www.pewinternet.org/dataset/jan-3-10-2018-core-trends-survey/.

16. Sara Salinas, "PEAK SOCIAL? The Major Social Platforms Are Showing a Significant Slowdown in Users," CNBC, August 8, 2018, https://www.cnbc.com/2018/08/08/social-media-active-users-around-the-world.html.

17. *Topline Questionnaire: January 2018 Core Trends Survey*.

18. Zeynep Tufekci, *TWITTER AND TEAR GAS: The Power and Fragility of Networked Protest* (New Haven, CT: Yale University Press, 2018), 22.

19. Tufekci, *TWITTER AND TEAR GAS*, 118.

20. Tufekci, *TWITTER AND TEAR GAS*, 119.

21. Tufekci, *TWITTER AND TEAR GAS*, 119.

22. Manuel Castells, *Networks of Outrage and Hope: Social Movements in the Internet Age* (Cambridge, UK: Polity Press, 2012), 21.

23. Jelani Cobb, "Where Is Black Lives Matter Headed," *New Yorker*, March 14, 2016, https://www.newyorker.com/magazine/2016/03/14/where-is-black-lives-matter-headed.

24. Cobb, "Where Is Black Lives Matter Headed."

25. Deen Freelon, Charlton Mcilwain, and Meredith Clark, "Quantifying the Power and Consequences of Social Media Protest," *New Media & Society* 20, no. 3 (November 15, 2016): 990-1011,doi:10.1177/1461444816676646, 990.

26. Tarana Burke, "Me Too. Movement," Me Too, accessed February 1, 2019, https://metoomvmt.org/.

27. Stephanie Zacharek, Eliana Dockterman, and Haley Sweetland Edwards, "Person of the Year 2017: The Silence Breakers," *Time*, December 18, 2017, http://time.com/time-person-of-the-year-2017-silence-breakers/.

28. Sarah Almukhtar, Michael Gold, and Larry Buchanan, "After Weinstein: 71 Men Accused of Sexual Misconduct and Their Fall from Power," *New York Times*, November 10, 2017, https://www.nytimes.com/interactive/2017/11/10/us/men-accused-sexual-misconduct-weinstein.html.

29. Zacharek et al., "Person of the Year 2017."

30. Castells, *Networks of Outrage and Hope,* 221–228.

31. Castells, *Networks of Outrage and Hope,* 224.

32. Castells, *Networks of Outrage and Hope,* 221.

33. Castells, *Networks of Outrage and Hope,* 2.

34. Castells, *Networks of Outrage and Hope,* 225.

35. Zeynep Tufekci, "'Not This One': Social Movements, the Attention Economy, and Microcelebrity Networked Activism," *American Behavioral Scientist* 57, no. 7 (March 26, 2013): 848–870, doi:10.1177/0002764213479369.

36. Laura DeNardis, *The Internet in Everything: Freedom and Security in a World with No Off Switch* (New Haven, CT: Yale University Press, 2020), 180.

37. DeNardis, *The Internet in Everything.*

38. Castells, *Networks of Outrage and Hope,* 2.

39. "Consolidation in the Internet Economy: Executive Summary," Internet Society, https://future.internetsociety.org/2019/introduction/executive-summary/, 8.

40. Paul Bernal, "Data Gathering, Surveillance and Human Rights: Recasting the Debate," *Journal of Cyber Policy* 1, no. 2 (September 16, 2016): 243–264, doi:10.1080/23738871.2016.1228990.

41. Jeffrey P. Jones, *Entertaining Politics: Satiric Television and Political Engagement* (Lanham, MD: Rowman & Littlefield, 2010), 38.

42. Peter Dahlgren, "The Internet, Public Spheres, and Political Communication: Dispersion and Deliberation," *Political Communication* 22, no. 2 (August 21, 2006): 147-162, doi:10.1080/10584600590933160, 148.

43. Silvio Waisbord, "Why Populism Is Troubling for Democratic Communication," *Communication, Culture, & Critique* 11 (2018): 21-34, https://doi.org/10.1093/ccc/tcx005, 21.

44. Peter Dahlgren, *Media and Political Engagement: Citizen, Communication, and Democracy* (New York: Cambridge University Press, 2009), 58.

45. Dahlgren, *Media and Political Engagement*, 58.

46. Peter Dahlgren, *Television and the Public Sphere* (London: Sage, 1995), 19, 21.

47. Nick Couldry, Sonia M. Livingstone, and Tim Markham, *Media Consumption and Public Engagement: Beyond the Presumption of Attention* (London: Palgrave Macmillan, 2010), 31.

48. Henry Jenkins, Sam Ford, and Joshua Green, *Spreadable Media: Creating Value and Meaning in a Networked Culture (Postmillennial Pop)* (New York: New York University Press, 2013), 166.

49. Michael Edwards, *Civil Society*, 3rd ed. (Cambridge, UK: Polity Press, 2014), 14.

50. W. Lance Bennett and Alexandra Segerberg, "The Logic of Connective Action," *Information, Communication & Society* 15, no. 5 (April 10, 2012): 739-768, doi:10.1080/1369118X.2012.670661, 752.

51. Jenkins, Ford, and Green, *Spreadable Media*, 1-3.

52. Jenkins, Ford, and Green, *Spreadable Media*, 21.

53. Raymond Williams, "Culture," in *Keywords: A Vocabulary of Culture and Society* (Oxford: Oxford University Press, 1985), 35–41, quoted in Stephen Duncombe, *Cultural Resistance Reader* (London: Verso, 2002), 35.

54. Craig Calhoun, *Habermas and the Public Sphere* (Cambridge, MA: MIT Press, 1992), 17.

55. Nicholas Garnham, "The Media and the Public Sphere," in *Habermas and the Public Sphere* (Cambridge, MA: MIT Press, 1992), 365.

56. Stephen Duncombe, *Dream: Re-imagining Progressive Politics in an Age of Fantasy* (New York: New Press, 2007), 20.

57. Henry Jenkins et al., *By Any Media Necessary: The New Youth Activism (Connected Youth and Digital Futures)* (New York: New York University Press, 2016), 29.

58. Dahlgren, *Television and the Public Sphere*, 12.

59. Dahlgren, "The Internet, Public Spheres, and Political Communication," 147–62.

60. Henry Jenkins et al., *By Any Media Necessary*, 29.

61. John Corner, "Performing the Real: Documentary Diversions," *Television & New Media* 3, no. 3 (August 2002): 255–269. doi:10.1177/152747640200300302, 258–59.

62. Couldry et al., *Media Consumption and Public Engagement*, 38.

63. Matt Sheehan and Annie Neimand, "Science of Story Building: Master and Counter Narratives," *Medium*, May 10, 2018, https://medium.com/science-of-story-building/science-of-story-building-master-counter-narratives-1992bec6b8f.

64. Daniel G. Solórzano and Tara J. Yosso, "Critical Race Methodology: Counter-Storytelling as an Analytical Framework for Education Research," *Qualitative Inquiry* 8, no. 1 (February 01, 2002): 23-44, doi:10.1177/107780040200800103, 32.

65. Loira Limbal, phone interview with author, May 24, 2019.

66. POV Staff, "Whose Streets?" *PBS*, July 30, 2018, http://www.pbs.org/pov/whosestreets/.

67. Matt Zoller Seitz, "Whose Streets? (2017) Movie Review," review of *Whose Streets? (2017)*, *Roger Ebert.com*, August 11, 2017, https://www.rogerebert.com/reviews/whose-streets-2017.

68. Jason DaSilva, "AXS MAP—When I Walk," When I Walk, https://www.wheniwalk.com/axs-map/.

69. Harold D. Lasswell, "The Structure and Function of Communication in Society," in *The Communication of Ideas* (New York: Harper and Row, 1948).

70. Clifford G. Christians and Theodore L. Glasser, *Normative Theories of the Media: Journalism in Democratic Societies* (Urbana: University of Illinois Press, 2009).

71. Thomas Hanitzsch and Tim P. Vos, "Journalism beyond Democracy: A New Look into Journalistic Roles in Political and Everyday Life," *Journalism: Theory, Practice & Criticism* 19, no. 2 (November 11, 2016): 146–164, doi:10.1177/1464884916673386.

72. Reuters in Boston, "Gasland: HBO Documentary Key Driver of Opposition to Fracking, Study Finds," *The Guardian*, September 2, 2015, https://www.theguardian.com/environment/2015/sep/02/gasland-hbo-documentary-fracking-opposition.

73. Mark Jenkins, "'Invisible War' Documentary Examines Rape in the Military," *Washington Post*, June 21, 2012, https://www.washingtonpost.com/entertainment/movies/invisible-war-documentary-examines-rape-in-the-military/2012/06/21/gJQAcGqhtV_story.html?noredirect=on&utm_term=.686738c818f0.

74. Ted Johnson, "PopPolitics: Did Netflix's 'The Bleeding Edge' Force a Medical Device Off the Market? (Listen)," *Variety*, July 29, 2018, https://variety.com/2018/politics/news/bleeding-edge-kirby-dick-amy-ziering-1202889418/.

75. Holly Gordon, in-person interview with author, April 9, 2019.

76. Rush Holt, "Trying to Get Us to Change Course," *Science* 317, no. 5835 (July 13, 2007): 198–199, doi: 10.1126/science.1142810, 198.

77. Sally Fifer, phone interview with author, July 25, 2018.

78. "Women & Girls Lead Global," Women & Girls Lead Global, accessed February 1, 2019, http://www.womenandgirlslead.org/.

79. Cara Mertes, in-person interview with author, June 18, 2018.

80. Lars Willnat, David H. Weaver, and G. Cleveland Wilhoit, "The American Journalist in the Digital Age," *Journalism Studies* 20, no. 3 (October 26, 2017): 423–441, doi:10.1080/1461670X.2017.1387071, 430,.

81. Brenda Coughlin, in-person interview with author, June 12, 2018.

82. Holly Gordon, in-person interview with author, April 9, 2019.

83. Richard Brody, "'Minding the Gap,' Reviewed: A Self-Questioning Documentary about What Happened to a Group of Young Skaters," *New Yorker*, August 17, 2018, https://www.newyorker.com/culture/the-front-row/minding-the-gap-reviewed-a-self-questioning-documentary-about-what-happened-to-a-group-of-young-skaters.

84. Owen Gleiberman, "Sundance Film Review: 'Strong Island,'" *Variety*, February 4, 2017, https://variety.com/2017/film/reviews/strong-island-review-sundance-1201976864/.

85. Tabitha Jackson, phone interview with author, May 20, 2019.

86. Marcia Smith, in-person interview with author, June 11, 2018.

87. Sally Fifer, phone interview with author, July 25, 2018.

88. David H. Weaver et al., *The American Journalist in the 21st Century: U.S. News People at the Dawn of a New Millennium* (London: Routledge, 2006).

89. Scott MacKenzie, "Societe Nouvelle: The Challenge for Change in the Alternative Public Sphere," 136-148, in *Challenge for Change: Activist Documentary at the National Film Board of Canada* (Montreal: McGill-Queen's University Press, 2010).

90. *Bag It: The Impact Field Guide & Toolkit*, London: Doc Society, accessed February 1, 2019, https://impactguide.org/introduction/analysing-the-story-environment/.

91. Ben Sisario, "R. Kelly Dropped by RCA Records after Documentary Furor," *New York Times*, January 18, 2019, https://www.nytimes.com/2019/01/18/arts/music/r-kelly-rca-sony.html.

92. Joe Coscarelli, "Investigators Looking into Accusations from R. Kelly Documentary," *New York Times*, January 8, 2019, https://www.nytimes.com/2019/01/08/arts/music/r-kelly-criminal-investigation.html.

93. Abigail Disney, in-person interview with author, August 29, 2018.

94. Sonya Childress, phone interview with author, October 29, 2018.

95. Michael Edwards, *Civil Society*, 3rd ed. (Cambridge, UK: Polity Press, 2014), 14–15.

96. "About," Next Foundation, accessed February 1, 2019, https://www.nestfoundation.org/about.

97. "Girl Rising," Girl Rising, accessed February 1, 2019, https://girlrising.org/

98. "About #MEAction," #MEAction, accessed May 15, 2019, https://www.meaction.net/about/.

99. "What We Do," Just Vision, accessed May 15, 2019, https://www.justvision.org/about.

100. "Projects," Doc Society, accessed May 15, 2019, https://docsociety.org/projects/.

101. Beadie Finzi, phone interview with author, June 12, 2018.

102. "About," Good Pitch, accessed February 1, 2019, https://goodpitch.org/about.

103. "Impact Producer Fellowship," Firelight Media, accessed May 15, 2019, http://www.firelightmedia.tv/impact-producer-lab.

104. "8 Organizations Selected to Put Films to Work," Working Films, accessed June 1, 2019, http://www.workingfilms.org/8-organizations-selected-to-put-films-to-work/.

105. Molly Murphy, phone interview with author, October 19, 2018.

106. John Valverde, phone interview with author, April 23, 2019.

107. "The Pushouts," Good Pitch, accessed May 15, 2019, https://goodpitch.org/films/the-pushouts.

108. Katie Galloway, phone interview with author, May 2, 2019.

109. Richard Ray Perez, in-person interview with author, April 12, 2019.

110. John Valverde, phone interview with author, April 23, 2019.

111. Katie Galloway, phone interview with author, May 2, 2019.

Chapter 4

1. Sonya Childress, phone interview with author, October 26, 2018, and email correspondence with author, August 27, 2019.

2. Lee Hirsch, phone interview with original report ("When Movies Go to Washington," 2017, Center for Media & Social Impact, American University) authors (Caty Borum Chattoo and Will Jenkins), December 14, 2015.

3. Louis Jordan, "The Bully Project Director Talks about Documenting Bullying in American Schools," *Daily Beast*, April 30, 2011, http://www.thedailybeast.com/articles/2011/04/30/the-bully-project-director-talks-about-documenting-bullying-in-american-schools.html.

4. Jordan, "The Bully Project Director Talks;" "It Gets Better Project," It Gets Better, accessed February 13, 2020, https://itgetsbetter.org/about/

5. "A Collection of It Gets Better Videos," It Gets Better Project, accessed June 29, 2019, https://itgetsbetter.org/blog/lesson/finding-pride-1/.

6. "About Bully," The Bully Project, accessed March 1, 2019, http://www.thebullyproject.com/about_film.

7. Lee Hirsch, email with author, May 10, 2019.

8. "Bully," Independent Lens," accessed March 1, 2019, http://www.pbs.org/independentlens/films/bully/.

9. Lee Hirsch, phone interview with original report authors (Borum Chattoo and Jenkins), December 14, 2015.

10. Lee Hirsch, phone interview with original report authors (Borum Chattoo and Jenkins), December 14, 2015.

11. Lee Hirsch, phone interview with original report authors (Borum Chattoo and Jenkins), December 14, 2015.

12. "About The Bully Project," The Bully Project, accessed March 1, 2019, http://www.thebullyproject.com/about_the_bully_project.

13. "Help 1 Million Students See the New Film, Bully!," DonorsChoose.org, accessed March 1, 2019, https://www.donorschoose.org/giving/help-1-million-students-see-the-new-fil/233494/?historical=true.

14. "A Guide to the Film BULLY: Fostering Empathy and Action in Schools," Facing History and Ourselves, accessed March 1, 2019, https://www.facinghistory.org/books-borrowing/guide-film-bully-fostering-empathy-and-action-schools.

15. "Tools for Educators," The Bully Project, accessed March 1, 2019, http://www.thebullyproject.com/tools_educators.

16. "Take the Pledge, Join the Movement," The Bully Project, accessed March 1, 2019, http://www.thebullyproject.com/; "Tools for Educators," The Bully Project, accessed March 1, 2019, http://www.thebullyproject.com/tools_educators.

17. Aaron Couch, "'Bully' Director, U.S. Mayors Teaming for Anti-Bullying Program (Exclusive)," Hollywood Reporter, June 20, 2014, https://www.hollywoodreporter.com/news/bully-director-us-mayors-teaming-713760.

18. Erin Reiney, Lee Hirsch, and Tom Cochran, "Take Action Today: Mayors Bringing the Community Together to Stop Bullying," StopBullying.gov, US Department of Health and Human Services, October 15, 2014, https://www.stopbullying.gov/blog/2014/10/15/take-action-today-mayors-bringing-community-together-stop-bullying.html.

19. Lee Hirsch, phone interview with original report authors (Borum Chattoo and Jenkins), December 14, 2015.

20. Etienne Wenger-Trayner and Beverly Wenger-Trayner, "Introduction to Communities of Practice: A Brief Overview of the Concept and Its Uses," Wenger-Trayner.com, 2015, https://wenger-trayner.com/introduction-to-communities-of-practice/.

21. Cara Mertes, "Celebrating Five Years of JustFilms," Equals Change Blog (blog), December 10, 2015, https://www.fordfoundation.org/ideas/equals-change-blog/posts/celebrating-five-years-of-justfilms/.

22. "JustFilms," Ford Foundation, April 6, 2018, https://www.fordfoundation.org/work/our-grants/justfilms/.

23. Cara Mertes, email correspondence with author, August 13, 2019.

24. Cara Mertes, in-person interview with author, June 18, 2018.

25. Kathy Im, email correspondence with author, June 28, 2019.

26. Lauren Pabst, "Why We're Strengthening a National Network to Support Nonfiction Multimedia Makers," MacArthur Foundation, August 15, 2017, https://www.macfound.org/press/perspectives/why-were-strengthening-national-network-support-nonfiction-multimedia-makers/.

27. Nishant Lalwani, "Stories for Stronger Societies," Luminate (blog), January 15, 2019, https://luminategroup.com/posts/blog/stories-for-stronger-societies.

28. Sandy Herz and Zachary Slobig, "A Decade of Stories of Change: How a Partnership with Sundance Institute Harnessed Storytelling for Social Impact," Skoll Foundation, January 26, 2018, http://skoll.org/2018/01/26/stories-of-change-sundance-impact-storytelling/.

29. Rick Perez, in-person interview with author, April 9, 2019.

30. "The Fledgling Fund," The Fledgling Fund, accessed March 1, 2019, http://www.thefledglingfund.org/.

31. "Who We Are," The Fledgling Fund, accessed March 1, 2019, http://www.thefledglingfund.org/who-we-are/.

32. Sheila Leddy, phone interview with author, October 19, 2018.

33. Lindsay Lavine, "How Participant Media Gets You to Care about Making the World a Better Place," *Fast Company*, April 8, 2014, https://www.fastcompany.com/3028760/how-participant-media-gets-you-to-care-about-making-the-world-a-better-place.

34. "Diane Weyermann," Participant Media, accessed September 26, 2019, https://participant.com/about-us/diane-weyermann; "Open Society Institute Awards $5 Million to Support Sundance Institute and Documentary Films," Open Society Foundations, July 15, 2009, https://www.opensocietyfoundations.org/newsroom/open-society-institute-awards-5-million-support-sundance-institute-and-documentary.

35. Dov Kornits, "Diane Weyermann: Passion Goes a Long Way at Participant," FilmInk, April 14, 2019, https://www.filmink.com.au/diane-weyermann-passion-goes-long-way-participant/.

36. Holly Gordon, in-person interview with author, April 9, 2019.

37. "Allen's Film Production Company Takes Vulcan Name," *Puget Sound Business Journal*, August 27, 2002, https://www.bizjournals.com/seattle/stories/2002/08/26/daily13.html.

38. "Vulcan Productions," Vulcan Productions, accessed March 1, 2019, https://www.vulcanproductions.com/.

39. Dan Cogan, in-person interview with author, July 17, 2018.

40. Skadi Loist, "The Film Festival Circuit: Networks, Hierarchies, and Circulation," 49–64, in *Film Festivals: History, Theory, Method, Practice*, ed. Marijke de Valck, Brendan Kredell, and Skadi Loist (New York: Routledge, 2016), 59.

41. "Industry Meetup: The Global Impact Producers Assembly | Hosted by Doc Society," International Documentary Festival Amsterdam, accessed March 1, 2019, https://www.idfa.nl/en/shows/af9933fe-49d1-4fa7-804d-972944226add/industry-meetup-the-global-impact-producers-assembly-hosted-by-doc-society.

42. "AFI DOCS IMPACT LAB," AFI DOCS Film Festival, accessed March 1, 2019, https://www.afi.com/afidocs/impact_lab.aspx.

43. "Getting Real '18," International Documentary Association, accessed March 1, 2019, https://www.documentary.org/gettingreal18; "Impact Producers Convening," International Documentary Association Getting Real '18, accessed February 19, 2019, https://sites.grenadine.co/sites/documentary/en/gettingreal18/items/462.

44. "Moving Docs," Moving Docs, accessed March 1, 2019, https://www.movingdocs.org/.

45. "Meet the Impact Producer," The Impact Field Guide & Toolkit, accessed February 1, 2019, https://impactguide.org/impact-in-action/meet-the-impact-producer/.

46. Jennifer MacArthur, "What's in a Name: Impact Producer," *POV's Documentary Blog* (blog), November 15, 2013, http://archive.pov.org/blog/news/2013/11/whats-in-a-name-impact-producer/.

47. POV Staff, "Silverlake Life," POV, accessed March 1, 2019, https://www.pbs.org/pov/silverlakelife/.

48. Ellen Schneider, phone interview with author, June 29, 2018.

49. Ellen Schneider, phone interview with author, June 29, 2018.

50. POV Staff, "The Uprising of '34," POV, accessed March 1, 2019, https://www.pbs.org/pov/uprisingof34/.

51. Judith Helfand, phone interview with author, June 22, 2018.

52. Judith Helfand, phone interview with author, June 22, 2018.

53. "About," Working Films, accessed March 1, 2019, http://www.workingfilms.org/about/.

54. Molly Murphy, phone interview with author, October 19, 2018.

55. Molly Murphy, phone interview with author, October 19, 2018.

56. "Fracking Stories," Working Films, accessed May 1, 2019, http://www.workingfilms.org/projects/fracking-stories/.

57. "Portfolio," Film Sprout, accessed February 19, 2019, http://www.filmsprout.org/#portfolio; "Campaigns," Picture Motion, accessed February 20, 2019, https://picturemotion.com/campaigns.

58. Caitlin Boyle, phone interview with author, October 19, 2018.

59. Ted Johnson, "PopPolitics: Did Netflix's 'The Bleeding Edge' Force a Medical Device Off the Market? (Listen)," *Variety*, July 29, 2018, https://variety.com/2018/politics/news/bleeding-edge-kirby-dick-amy-ziering-1202889418/.

60. Jamie Dobie, in-person interview with author, June 11, 2018.

61. "Documentary Lab," Firelight Media, accessed March 1, 2019, http://www.firelightmedia.tv/documentary-lab/; "Impact Producer Fellowship," Firelight Media, accessed March 1, 2019, http://www.firelightmedia.tv/impact-producer-lab/.

62. Sonya Childress, email correspondence with author, August 27, 2019.

63. Sonya Childress, email correspondence with author, August 27, 2019.

64. Sonya Childress, phone interview with author, October 26, 2018.

65. Sonya Childress, phone interview with author, October 26, 2018.

66. Justine Nagan, in-person interview with author, June 12, 2018.

67. Caty Borum Chattoo, Patricia Aufderheide, Michele Alexander, and Chandler Green, "American Realities on Public Television: Analysis of Independent Television Service's Independent Documentaries, 2007–2016," *International Journal of Communication* 12 (March 2018): 1541–1568, https://ijoc.org/index.php/ijoc/article/view/7826, 1544.

68. Molly Murphy, email correspondence with author, June 19, 2019.

69. Patricia Aufderheide, "Ethical Challenges for Documentarians," 239–240, in *New Documentary Ecologies*, ed. Kate Nash, Craig Hight, and Catherine Summerhayes (London: Palgrave Macmillan, 2014).

70. Bill Nichols, *Speaking Truths with Film* (Oakland: University of California Press, 2016), 224.

71. Nichols, *Speaking Truths with Film*, 227.

Chapter 5

1. Gabriela Cowperthwaite, phone interview with author, May 3, 2019.

2. Jeffrey Ventre, "Blackfish Premiere at Sundance: The 1st Public Introduction of the Film," YouTube, February 10, 2013, https://www.youtube.com/watch?v=fOkosCeyGqE.

3. United States of America, Department of Commerce, National Oceanic and Atmospheric Administration, *Recovery Plan for Southern Resident Killer Whales (Orcinus Orca)*, by National Marine Fisheries Service Northwest Regional Office (2008), 38, https://www.

westcoast.fisheries.noaa.gov/publications/protected_species/marine_mammals/killer_whales/esa_status/srkw-recov-plan.pdf.

4. "Synopsis," Blackfish, accessed January 15, 2019, http://www.blackfishmovie.com/about.

5. Jeannette Catsoulis, "Do Six-Ton Captives Dream of Freedom?" review of *Blackfish, New York Times*, July 18, 2013, https://www.nytimes.com/2013/07/19/movies/blackfish-a-documentary-looks-critically-at-seaworld.html; "*Blackfish* Transcript," CNN Transcripts, November 2, 2013, http://transcripts.cnn.com/TRANSCRIPTS/1311/02/se.02.html.

6. Gabriela Cowperthwaite, "Filmmaker: Why I Made 'Blackfish,'" CNN, October 28, 2013, https://www.cnn.com/2013/10/23/opinion/blackfish-filmmaker-statement/index.

7. Cowperthwaite, "Filmmaker: Why I Made 'Blackfish.'"

8. Gabriela Cowperthwaite, phone interview with author, May 3, 2019.

9. David Rooney, "Blackfish: Sundance Review," *Hollywood Reporter*, January 21, 2013, https://www.hollywoodreporter.com/review/blackfish-sundance-review-414203.

10. Alan Duke, "Martina McBride, 38 Special, Cancel SeaWorld Gig over 'Blackfish,'" CNN, December 16, 2013, https://www.cnn.com/2013/12/16/showbiz/seaworld-martina-mcbride-cancels/index.html.

11. Paul Janes, "California Bill Would Ban SeaWorld Orca Shows," *USA Today*, March 7, 2014, https://www.usatoday.com/story/news/nation-now/2014/03/07/san-diego-seaworld-orca-shows/6162331/.

12. Roberto A. Ferdman, "Chart: What the Documentary 'Blackfish' Has Done to SeaWorld," *Washington Post,* December 12, 2014, www.washingtonpost.com/news/wonk/wp/2014/12/12/chart-what-the-documentary-blackfish-has-done-to-seaworld/.

13. Hugo Martin, "Bad Weather Blamed as SeaWorld Attendance Falls 4 percent," *Los Angeles Times*, June 3, 2014, https://www.latimes.com/business/la-fi-theme-park-attendance-20140604-story.html.

14. Associated Press in Orlando, "Southwest Ends SeaWorld Partnership after Animal Rights Complaints," *The Guardian*, July 31, 2014, https://www.theguardian.com/world/2014/jul/31/southwest-seaworld-end-partnership; Letitia Stein, "Southwest Airlines, SeaWorld to End Marketing Partnership," Reuters, July 31, 2014, https://www.reuters.com/article/us-usa-southwest-seaworld-entrnmt-idUSKBN0G02GJ20140731; Sandra Pedicini, "Virgin America Drops SeaWorld from Program," *Orlando Sentinel*, October 14, 2014, https://www.orlandosentinel.com/business/os-seaworld-virgin-america-20141014-20-story.html.

15. Maya Rhodan, "Seaworld's Profits Drop 84 percent after Blackfish Documentary," *Time*, August 6, 2015, http://time.com/3987998/seaworlds-profits-drop-84-after-blackfish-documentary/.

16. Joel Manby, "SeaWorld CEO: We're Ending Our Orca Breeding Program. Here's Why," *Los Angeles Times*, March 17, 2016, https://www.latimes.com/opinion/op-ed/la-oe-0317-manby-sea-world-orca-breeding-20160317-story.html.

17. Wayne Pacelle, "More Impressions on 'Massive' SeaWorld-HSUS Announcement, including from 'Blackfish' Director," *A Humane World: Kitty Block's Blog* (blog), March 18, 2016, https://blog.humanesociety.org/2016/03/reactions-to-hsus-seaworld-news.html.

18. Kate Briquelet, "Lawsuit: SeaWorld Tried to Spin 'Blackfish' as Good for Business," *Daily Beast*, December 10, 2017, https://www.thedailybeast.com/lawsuit-seaworld-tried-to-spin-blackfish-as-good-for-business; Caitlyn Burford and Julie "Madrone" Kalil Schutten, "Internatural Activists and the 'Blackfish Effect': Contemplating Captive Orcas' Protest Rhetoric through a Coherence Frame," *Frontiers in Communication* 1 (2017): 1–11, doi:10.3389/fcomm.2016.00016.

19. *Blackfish*, dir. Gabriela Cowperthwaite, prod. Manuel Oteyza (USA: CNN, Magnolia Pictures, 2013), film.

20. *Blackfish*, dir. Gabriela Cowperthwaite, prod. Manuel Oteyza; "*Blackfish* Transcript," CNN Transcripts, November 2, 2013, http://transcripts.cnn.com/TRANSCRIPTS/1311/02/se.02.html.

21. Francesca Polletta, *It Was Like a Fever: Storytelling in Protest and Politics* (Chicago: University of Chicago Press, 2006), 9.

22. Polletta, *It Was Like a Fever,* 13.

23. Melanie C. Green and Timothy C. Brock, "The Role of Transportation in the Persuasiveness of Public Narratives," Journal of Personality and Social Psychology 79, no. 5 (2000): 701–721, doi:10.1037//0022-3514.79.5.701.

24. M. D. Slater, "Entertainment-Education and Elaboration Likelihood: Understanding the Processing of Narrative Persuasion," *Communication Theory* 12, no. 2 (2002): 173–191, doi:10.1093/ct/12.2.173.

25. Sheila T. Murphy et al., "Narrative versus Nonnarrative: The Role of Identification, Transportation, and Emotion in Reducing Health Disparities," *Journal of Communication* 63, no. 1 (2013): 116–137, doi:10.1111/jcom.12007; Green and Brock, "The Role of Transportation."

26. Nurit Tal-Or and Jonathan Cohen, "Understanding Audience Involvement: Conceptualizing and Manipulating Identification and Transportation," *Poetics* 38, no. 4 (2010): 402–418, doi:10.1016/j.poetic.2010.05.004.

27. Caty Borum Chattoo and Lauren Feldman, "Storytelling for Social Change: Leveraging Documentary and Comedy for Public Engagement in Global Poverty," *Journal of Communication* 67, no. 5 (2017): 678–701, doi:10.1111/jcom.12318.

28. Heather L. Lamarre and Kristen D. Landreville, "When Is Fiction as Good as Fact? Comparing the Influence of Documentary and Historical Reenactment Films on Engagement, Affect, Issue Interest, and Learning," *Mass Communication and Society* 12, no. 4 (2009): 537–555, doi:10.1080/15205430903237915.

29. Borum Chattoo and Feldman, "Storytelling for Social Change"; Frank M. Schneider et al., "Learning from Entertaining Online Video Clips? Enjoyment and Appreciation and Their Differential Relationships with Knowledge and Behavioral Intentions," *Computers in Human Behavior* 54 (2016): 475–82, doi:10.1016/j.chb.2015.08.028.

30. Paul Slovic, "Psychic Numbing and Genocide," *Psychological Science Agenda* 21, no. 10 (2007), http://www.apa.org/science/about/psa/2007/11/slovic.aspx.

31. Witness, "The Blackfish Effect—How Film Can Impact Big Business," *Witness* (blog), December 2014, http://blog.witness.org/2014/12/blackfish-effect-film-can-impact-big-business/.

32. Gabriela Cowperthwaite, phone interview with author, May 3, 2019.

33. Gabriela Cowperthwaite, phone interview with author, May 3, 2019.

34. Slovic, "Psychic Numbing and Genocide."

35. Slovic, "Psychic Numbing and Genocide."

36. Clay Shirky, *Here Comes Everybody: The Power of Organizing Without Organizations* (London: Penguin, 2008), 161.

37. Manuel Castells, *Networks of Outrage and Hope: Social Movements in the Internet Age* (Cambridge, UK: Polity Press, 2013), 221.

38. John Paul Titlow, "SeaWorld Is Spending $10 Million To Make You Forget about 'Blackfish,'" *Fast Company*, August 4, 2015, https://www.fastcompany.com/3046342/seaworld-is-spending-10-million-to-make-you-forget-about-blackfish; Smfrogers, "The #Blackfish Phenomenon: A

Whale of a Tale Takes over Twitter," *Twitter Blog* (blog), November 6, 2013, https://blog.twitter.com/en_us/a/2013/the-blackfish-phenomenon-a-whale-of-a-tale-takes-over-twitter.html.

39. Gabriela Cowperthwaite, phone interview with author, May 3, 2019.
40. W. Lance Bennett and Alexandra Segerberg, "The Logic of Connective Action: Digital Media and the Personalization of Contentious Politics," *Information, Communication & Society* 15, no. 5 (2012): 739–768, https://doi.org/10.1080/1369118X.2012.670661, 742.
41. Richard Horgan, "Makers of The Cove Respond to SeaWorld Newspaper Ad," *Adweek*, December 24, 2013, https://www.adweek.com/digital/seaworld-blackfish-cove-oceanic-preservation-society-response/.
42. Horgan, "Makers of The Cove Respond."
43. Wayne Pacelle, "'Blackfish' Is a Must-See Film for Summer," *A Humane World: Kitty Block's Blog*, July 15, 2013, https://blog.humanesociety.org/2013/07/blackfish-is-a-must-see-film-for-summer.html.
44. Hugo Martin, "PETA Rakes in More Donations as It Denounces SeaWorld," *Los Angeles Times*, February 16, 2016, https://www.latimes.com/business/la-fi-peta-donations-20160216-story.html.
45. Bonnie McEwan, "PETA vs. SeaWorld: The Creative Tactics and Tech That Drive PETA's SeaWorld Campaign," *Nonprofit Quarterly*, June 3, 2014, https://nonprofitquarterly.org/2014/06/03/peta-vs-seaworld-the-creative-tactics-and-tech-that-drive-peta-s-seaworld-campaign/.
46. Smfrogers, "The #Blackfish Phenomenon: A Whale of a Tale Takes over Twitter."
47. Martin, "PETA Rakes in More Donations."
48. Martin, "PETA Rakes in More Donations"; "PETA Takes Dramatic Stand against SeaWorld's Rose Parade Float, Leading to 19 Arrests," *Huffington Post*, January 2, 2014, https://www.huffingtonpost.com/2014/01/02/peta-seaworld-rose-parade_n_4532159.html.
49. Martin, "PETA Rakes in More Donations."
50. Ashli Stokes, "Raining on SeaWorld's Parade: PETA's Direct Action and Public Interest Communications," *Journal of Public Interest Communications* 3, no. 1 (2019): 109, doi: 10.32473/jpic.v3.i1.p9.
51. Jordan Zakarin, "The Documentary 'Blackfish' Is Causing More Major Problems for SeaWorld," Buzzfeed, January 3, 2014, https://www.buzzfeed.com/jordanzakarin/the-documentary-blackfish-problems-for-seaworld.
52. Briquelet, "Lawsuit: SeaWorld Tried to Spin 'Blackfish' as Good for Business."
53. Maxwell E. Mccombs and Donald L. Shaw, "The Agenda-Setting Function of Mass Media," *Public Opinion Quarterly* 36, no. 2 (1972): 176–187, doi:10.1086/267990.
54. Maxwell McCombs, *The Agenda-Setting Role of the Mass Media in the Shaping of Public Opinion*, report, University of Texas at Austin, 2002, https://www.infoamerica.org/documentos_pdf/mccombc s01.pdf.
55. Gabriela Cowperthwaite, phone interview with author, May 3, 2019.
56. Dietram A. Scheufele, "Agenda-Setting, Priming, and Framing Revisited: Another Look at Cognitive Effects of Political Communication," *Mass Communication and Society* 3, no. 2 (2000): 297–316, https://doi.org/10.1207/S15327825MCS0323_07.
57. W. A. Gamson and A. Modigliani, "The Changing Culture of Affirmative Action," 137–177, in *Research in Political Sociology*, vol. 3 (Greenwich, CT: JAI Press, 1986), 143.
58. Bryce J. Renninger, "SeaWorld Unleashes 8 Assertions about 'Blackfish' and Filmmakers Respond," *IndieWire*, July 15, 2013, https://www.indiewire.com/2013/07/seaworld-unleashes-8-assertions-about-blackfish-and-filmmakers-respond-36897/.

Author Note: I wrote earlier drafts of this chapter in late 2015 and early 2016, and since that time, SeaWorld has deleted its various webpages that criticized *Blackfish* with pointed rebuttals; original web links for the SeaWorld content are no longer operational. However, the existence of the SeaWorld public response is preserved through news coverage about SeaWorld's various tactics, along with the responses of the filmmakers, offered throughout this chapter as cited sources. Additionally, SeaWorld's open letter ad (December 2013) and "Truth about Blackfish" web copy (early 2014) have been preserved as Appendix 2 (p. 10) and Appendix 3 (p. 11), respectively, in Amy Newman, "SeaWorld's Response to the Movie Blackfish" (2014), retrieved from https://www.bizcominthenews.com/files/seaworlds-response-to-blackfish.pdf.

59. Michael Cieply, "SeaWorld's Unusual Retort to a Critical Documentary," *New York Times*, July 19, 2013, https://www.nytimes.com/2013/07/19/business/media/seaworlds-unusual-retort-to-a-critical-documentary.html?pagewanted=1&_r=1; Renninger, "SeaWorld Unleashes 8 Assertions"; Michael O'Sullivan, "'Blackfish' Movie Review," *Washington Post*, July 25, 2013, https://www.washingtonpost.com/goingoutguide/movies/blackfish-movie-review/2013/07/24/63e20c48-f0b8-11e2-a1f9-ea873b7e0424_story.html?noredirect=on&utm_term=.eb7c01c32b76; Bilge Ebiri, "SeaWorld Fights Back at the Critical Documentary 'Blackfish,'" *Bloomberg*, July 19, 2013, https://www.bloomberg.com/news/articles/2013-07-19/seaworld-fights-back-at-the-critical-documentary-blackfish.

60. Cieply, "SeaWorld's Unusual Retort."

61. Cieply, "SeaWorld's Unusual Retort."

62. Cieply, "SeaWorld's Unusual Retort."

63. Michael O'Sullivan, "'Blackfish' Movie Review."

64. "SeaWorld Responds to Questions about Captive Orcas, 'Blackfish' Film," CNN, October 28, 2013, https://www.cnn.com/2013/10/21/us/seaworld-blackfish-qa.

65. Associated Press, "SeaWorld Runs Ads after 'Blackfish' Doc Spurs Performers to Cancel," *Hollywood Reporter*, December 21, 2013, https://www.hollywoodreporter.com/news/seaworld-runs-ads-blackfish-doc-667391.

66. Sam Mattera, "After You Watch This on Netflix, You'll Never Go to SeaWorld Again," Motley Fool, December 22, 2013, https://www.fool.com/investing/general/2013/12/22/after-you-watch-this-on-netflix-youll-never-go-to.aspx.

67. Lisa Halverstadt, "Takeaways from SeaWorld's Big Anti-'Blackfish' Campaign," Voice of San Diego, March 4, 2014, https://www.voiceofsandiego.org/topics/economy/takeaways-from-seaworlds-big-anti-blackfish-campaign/.

68. Michael Cieply, "SeaWorld's Unusual Retort."

69. Ezra Winston and Jason Garrison, "'If a Revolution Is Screened and No One Is There to See It, Does It Make a Sound?': The Politics of Distribution and Counterpublics," 404–424, in *Challenge for Change: Activist Documentary at the National Film Board of Canada* (Montreal: McGill-Queen's University Press, 2010), 404.

70. Winston and Garrison, "'If a Revolution Is Screened and No One Is There to See It,'" 405.

71. Patricia Aufderheide, *What Keeps Social Documentaries from Audiences—And How to Fix It*, report, Center for Media & Social Impact, American University, January 2004, http://cmsimpact.org/wp-content/uploads/2016/02/what_keeps-1.pdf, 11.

72. IDA Editorial Staff, "Independent Documentary Distribution in Turbulent Times," *International Documentary Association*, January 17, 2017, https://www.documentary.org/feature/independent-documentary-distribution-turbulent-times.

73. Lene Bech Sillesen, "Do Documentary Filmmakers Need Data about Their Audiences?" *Columbia Journalism Review*, August 8, 2014, https://archives.cjr.org/behind_the_news/do_documentary_filmmakers_need_audience_data.php#.

74. Sean Fennessey, "We Are Living through a Documentary Boom," The Ringer, July 24, 2018, https://www.theringer.com/movies/2018/7/24/17607044/documentaries-box-office-three-identical-strangers-rbg-wont-you-be-my-neighbor-mister-rogers-cnn.

75. Aufderheide, *What Keeps Social Documentaries from Audiences*, 10.

76. Vivienne Chow, "FilMart: Booming Documentaries Still Need Support, Careful Positioning," *Variety*, March 20, 2018, https://variety.com/2018/film/asia/booming-documentaries-still-need-support-positioning-1202731366/.

77. Mike Fleming Jr., "Sundance: Magnolia Pictures and CNN Films Reel in 'Blackfish,'" *Deadline Hollywood*, January 22, 2013, https://deadline.com/2013/01/sundance-magnolia-reeling-in-blackfish-409955/.

78. IDA Editorial Staff, "Independent Documentary Distribution in Turbulent Times."

79. Aufderheide, *What Keeps Social Documentaries from Audiences*, 9.

80. Pew Research Center, "Demographics and Political Views of News Audiences," *Pew Research Center: U.S. Politics & Policy*, September 18, 2018, http://www.people-press.org/2012/09/27/section-4-demographics-and-political-views-of-news-audiences/.

81. Fennessey, "We Are Living through a Documentary Boom."

82. "Internatural Activists and the "Blackfish Effect," interview by Kate Bolduan, CNN, July 29, 2013, https://www.cnn.com/videos/bestoftv/2013/07/29/exp-newday-bolduan-seaworldtrainer.cnn.

83. Renninger, "SeaWorld Unleashes 8 Assertions"; "SeaWorld Responds to Questions about Captive Orcas."

84. Bill Carter, "CNN Jolts Ratings Race with 'Blackfish,'" *New York Times*, October 26, 2013, https://www.nytimes.com/2013/10/27/business/media/cnn-jolts-ratings-race-with-blackfish.html?_r=1&.

85. Smfrogers, "The #Blackfish Phenomenon: A Whale of a Tale Takes over Twitter.".

86. "SeaWorld Trainer on Recent Controversy," interview by Kate Bolduan.

87. Marilee Menard, "What 'Blackfish' Documentary Left on the Cutting Room Floor," CNN, February 9, 2014, http://www.cnn.com/2014/02/09/opinion/marilee-menard-blackfish-marine-parks/.

88. Jeff Dunn, "Here's How Huge Netflix Has Gotten in the past Decade," Business Insider, January 19, 2017, https://www.businessinsider.com/netflix-subscribers-chart-2017-1.

89. "'Blackfish': The Documentary That Exposes SeaWorld," SeaWorld of Hurt, https://www.seaworldofhurt.com/features/blackfish-documentary-exposes-seaworld/.

90. Arvind Singhal and Everett Mitchell Rogers, *Entertainment-Education: A Communication Strategy for Social Change* (Mahwah, NJ: Lawrence Erlbaum, 1999).

91. Singhal and Rogers, *Entertainment-Education*, 37.

92. Singhal and Rogers, *Entertainment-Education*, 54.

93. W. A. Smith, "Social Marketing: An Overview of Approach and Effects," *Injury Prevention* 12, no. Suppl_1 (2006): i38–i43, doi:10.1136/ip.2006.012864.

94. Diana Barrett and Sheila Leddy, "Assessing Creative Media's Social Impact," Fledgling Fund, 2008, http://www.thefledglingfund.org/resources/impact, 4, 11-12.

95. Barrett and Leddy, "Assessing Creative Media's Social Impact," 5.

96. Eric Kohn, "Sundance Interview: 'Blackfish' Director Gabriela Cowperthwaite Discusses Suffering Orcas, Trainer Death, and Why SeaWorld Hasn't Seen the Movie," IndieWire,

January 26, 2013, http://www.indiewire.com/article/sundance-interview-blackfish-director-gabriela-cowperthwaite-discusses-suffering-orcas-trainer-death-and-why-seaworld-hasnt-seen-the-movie?page=2.

97. Burford and "Madrone" Kalil Schutten, "Internatural Activists and the 'Blackfish Effect.'"

98. Colby Itkowitz, "After 'Blackfish,' SeaWorld Hurt Financially but Keeps Up Political Spending," *Washington Post*, August 19, 2014, https://www.washingtonpost.com/blogs/in-the-loop/wp/2014/08/19/after-blackfish-seaworld-hurt-financially-but-keeps-up-political-spending/?utm_term=.39e196cf31e2.

99. Roberto A. Ferdman, "Chart: What the Documentary 'Blackfish' Has Done to SeaWorld," *Washington Post,* December 12, 2014, www.washingtonpost.com/news/wonk/wp/2014/12/12/chart-what-the-documentary-blackfish-has-done-to-seaworld/.

100. Andy Grimm, "Family of SeaWorld Trainer Killed by Whale Distances Itself from Critical Documentary," *Chicago Tribune*, January 21, 2014, https://www.chicagotribune.com/news/ct-xpm-2014-01-21-chi-sea-world-blackfish-statment-20140121-story.html.

101. Kolten Parker, "Ex-SeaWorld Trainers Dispute 'Blackfish,' Say Phase Out Whale Show," *San Antonio Express-News*, January 16, 2014, https://www.mysanantonio.com/news/local/article/Ex-SeaWorld-trainers-dispute-Blackfish-say-5145648.php.

102. Cieply, "SeaWorld's Unusual Retort."

103. John Paul Titlow, "SeaWorld Is Spending $10 Million to Make You Forget about 'Blackfish,'" *Fast Company*, August 4, 2015, https://www.fastcompany.com/3046342/seaworld-is-spending-10-million-to-make-you-forget-about-blackfish.

104. Anita Varma, "When Empathy Is Not Enough," *Journalism Practice* 13, no. 1 (2019): 105–121, , doi: 10.1080/17512786.2017.1394210, 105.

Chapter 6

1. Elaine McMillion Sheldon, phone interview with the author, March 12, 2019.

2. Martin R. Huecker and William Smock, "Domestic Violence," National Center for Biotechnology Information, U.S. National Library of Medicine (October 27, 2019), https://www.ncbi.nlm.nih.gov/books/NBK499891/

3. David Zurawik, "HBO Stays on the Case of Intimate Violence after Others Move On," *Baltimore Sun*, October 20, 2014, https://www.baltimoresun.com/entertainment/tv/z-on-tv-blog/bs-ae-zontv-violence-20141016-story.html.

4. NFL.com, "The NFL's Response to Domestic Violence and Sexual Assault," NFL, August 12, 2015, http://www.nfl.com/news/story/0ap3000000439286/article/the-nfls-response-to-domestic-violence-and-sexual-assault.

5. "NFL Players Say NO MORE to Domestic Violence & Sexual Assault," NO MORE, https://nomore.org/campaigns/public-service-announcements/nflplayerspsa/.

6. Kimberly A. Maxwell, John Huxford, Catherine Borum, and Bob Hornik, "Covering Domestic Violence: How the O. J. Simpson Case Shaped Reporting of Domestic Violence in the News Media," *Journalism & Mass Communication Quarterly* 77, no. 2 (2000): 258–272, doi:10.1177/107769900007700203, 259.

7. Maxwell et al., "Covering Domestic Violence." 260.

8. Cynthia Hill, phone interview with author, May 1, 2019.

9. Cynthia Hill, phone interview with author, May 1, 2019.

10. Marian Meyers, "News of Battering," *Journal of Communication* 44, no. 2 (1994): 47–63, doi:10.1111/j.1460-2466.1994.tb00676.x.; Mia Consalvo, "'3 Shot Dead in Courthouse':

Examining News Coverage of Domestic Violence and Mail-order Brides," *Women's Studies in Communication* 21, no. 2 (1998): 188–211, doi:10.1080/07491409.1998.10162556; Marian Meyers, *News Coverage of Violence against Women: Engendering Blame* (Thousand Oaks, CA: Sage, 1997), 148; Sharon Lamb, "Acts without Agents: An Analysis of Linguistic Avoidance in Journal Articles on Men Who Batter Women," *American Journal of Orthopsychiatry* 61, no. 2 (1991): 250–257, doi:10.1037/h0079243.

11. David Zurawik, "HBO Stays on the Case of Intimate Violence after Others Move On," *Baltimore Sun*, October 20, 2014, https://www.baltimoresun.com/entertainment/tv/z-on-tv-blog/bs-ae-zontv-violence-20141016-story.html.

12. Zurawik, "HBO Stays on the Case of Intimate Violence."

13. "Impact Story: Private Violence," Fledgling Fund, accessed April 1, 2019, http://www.thefledglingfund.org/impact-resources/private-violence/.

14. Matthew Barnidge, "Social Affect and Political Disagreement on Social Media," *Social Media Society* 4, no. 3 (2018): , doi:10.1177/2056305118797721, 7.

15. David Karpf, *The MoveOn Effect: The Unexpected Transformation of American Political Advocacy* (New York: Oxford University Press, 2012), 9.

16. Jennifer Lynn McCoy, "Extreme Political Polarization Weakens Democracy—Can the US Avoid That Fate?" *The Conversation*, November 2, 2018, http://theconversation.com/extreme-political-polarization-weakens-democracy-can-the-us-avoid-that-fate-105540; Jennifer Mccoy, Tahmina Rahman, and Murat Somer, "Polarization and the Global Crisis of Democracy: Common Patterns, Dynamics, and Pernicious Consequences for Democratic Polities," *American Behavioral Scientist* 62, no. 1 (2018): 16–42, doi:10.1177/0002764218759576.

17. Pew Research Center, "More Now Say It's 'Stressful' to Discuss Politics With People They Disagree With," Pew Research Center for the People and the Press, November 14, 2018, https://www.people-press.org/2018/11/05/more-now-say-its-stressful-to-discuss-politics-with-people-they-disagree-with/.

18. Gallup, "Most Important Problem," Gallup, Inc., https://news.gallup.com/poll/1675/most-important-problem.aspx.

19. Lars Willnat, David H. Weaver, and G. Cleveland Wilhoit, "The American Journalist in the Digital Age," *Journalism Studies*, October 26, 2017, 3, doi:10.1080/1461670X.2017.1387071.

20. Richard Gehr, "Why Movies Make the Best Journalism," *Columbia Journalism Review*, May 27, 2015, https://www.cjr.org/analysis/documentary_journalism.php.

21. Kathy Im, email correspondence with author, June 28, 2019.

22. Martha Nussbaum, "Chapter 10: Democratic Citizenship and the Narrative Imagination," *Yearbook of the National Society for the Study of Education*, 107 (2008): 143–157, doi:10.1111/j.1744-7984.2008.00138.x, 148.

23. Roy Walmsley, *World Prison Population List*, PDF, World Prison Brief, Institute for Criminal Policy Research, September 2018.

24. Walter Enders, Paul Pecorino, and Anne-Charlotte Souto, "Racial Disparity in U.S. Imprisonment across States and over Time," *Journal of Quantitative Criminology* (August 9, 2018): 1–28, https://doi.org/10.1007/s10940-018-9389-6; Alfred Blumstein and Allen J. Beck, "Population Growth in U.S. Prisons, 1980–1996," *Crime and Justice* 26 (1999): 17–61, doi:10.1086/449294; Lawrence D. Bobo and Victor Thompson, "Racialized Mass

Incarceration: Poverty, Prejudice, and Punishment," in *Doing Race: 21 Essays for the 21st Century* (New York: W. W. Norton, 2010), 324–325.

25. Enders et al., "Racial Disparity in U.S. Imprisonment."

26. James Cullen, "The History of Mass Incarceration," *Brennan Center for Justice*, July 20, 2018, https://www.brennancenter.org/blog/history-mass-incarceration; Bobo and Thompson, "Racialized Mass Incarceration."

27. Enders et al., "Racial Disparity in U.S. Imprisonment," 3.

28. Office of the Inspector General Evaluation and Inspections Division, *Review of the Federal Bureau of Prisons' Monitoring of Contract Prisons*, PDF, Washington, DC: US Department of Justice, August 2016, https://oig.justice.gov/reports/2016/e1606.pdf.

29. Blumstein and Beck, "Population Growth in U.S. Prisons," 22.

30. The Sentencing Project, *Fact Sheet: Trends in U.S. Corrections*, PDF, Washington, DC: The Sentencing Project, June 2018, 5, https://sentencingproject.org/wp-content/uploads/2016/01/Trends-in-US-Corrections.pdf.

31. Bobo and Thompson, "Racialized Mass Incarceration," 327.

32. Bobo and Thompson, "Racialized Mass Incarceration," 339–340, 330–331.

33. Justin T. Pickett, "Reintegrative Populism? Public Opinion and the Criminology of Downsizing," *Criminology & Public Policy* 15, no. 1 (2016): 131–135, doi:10.1111/1745-9133.12191; Peter K. Enns, "The Public's Increasing Punitiveness and Its Influence on Mass Incarceration in the United States," *American Journal of Political Science* 58, no. 4 (October 05, 2014): 859, doi:10.1111/ajps.12098.

34. Marie Gottschalk, *The Prison and the Gallows: The Politics of Mass Incarceration in America* (New York: Cambridge University Press, 2006), 12.

35. Enns, "The Public's Increasing Punitiveness," 859.

36. Bobo and Thompson, "Racialized Mass Incarceration," 339–340.

37. Ray Surette, *Media, Crime, and Criminal Justice: Images and Realities*, 2nd ed. (New York: Wadsworth, 1998).

38. George Gerbner and Larry Gross, "Living with Television: The Violence Profile," *Journal of Communication* 26, no. 2 (1976): 173–199, doi:10.1111/j.1460-2466.1976.tb01397.x.

39. Lisa A. Kort-Butler and Kelley J. Sittner Hartshorn, "Watching the Detectives: Crime Programming, Fear of Crime, and Attitudes about the Criminal Justice System," *Sociological Quarterly* 52, no. 1 (2011): 36–55, doi:10.1111/j.1533-8525.2010.01191.x; Mark D. Ramirez, "Punitive Sentiment," *Criminology* 51, no. 2 (2013): 329–364, doi:10.1111/1745-9125.12007.

40. Jenn M. Jackson, "Black Americans and the 'Crime Narrative': Comments on the Use of News Frames and Their Impacts on Public Opinion Formation," *Politics, Groups, and Identities* 7, no. 1 (2018): 231–241, doi:10.1080/21565503.2018.1553198, 236.

41. Mary Beth Oliver, "African American Men as 'Criminal and Dangerous': Implications of Media Portrayals of Crime on the 'Criminalization' of African American Men," *Journal of African American Studies* 7, no. 2 (September 2003): 3–18, doi:10.1007/s12111-003-1006-5, 4–5.

42. *13th*, dir. Ava DuVernay (USA: Kandoo Films, Forward Movement, 2016), film, 2016, https://www.netflix.com/watch/80091741?source=35; Kenneth Turan, "Ava DuVernay's Documentary '13th' Simmers with Anger and Burns with Eloquence," *Los Angeles Times*, October 6, 2016, https://www.latimes.com/entertainment/movies/la-et-mn-13th-review-20161001-snap-story.html.

43. Manohla Dargis, "Review: '13TH,' the Journey from Shackles to Prison Bars," *New York Times*, September 30, 2016, https://www.nytimes.com/2016/09/30/movies/13th-review-ava-duvernay.html.

44. "13th: Awards," IMDb, https://www.imdb.com/title/tt5895028/awards.

45. "13th Amendment to the U.S. Constitution: Abolition of Slavery," National Archives and Records Administration, accessed April 1, 2019, https://www.archives.gov/historical-docs/13th-amendment.

46. Dargis, "Review: '13TH.'"

47. Loïc Wacquant, "Deadly Symbiosis: When Ghetto and Prison Meet and Mesh," *Punishment & Society* 3, no. 1 (January 1, 2001): 95–133, https://doi.org/10.1177/14624740122228276.

48. Michelle Alexander, *The New Jim Crow: Mass Incarceration in the Age of Colorblindness* (New York: New Press, 2010); Dargis, "Review: '13TH.'"

49. Bob Verini, "Criminal Justice in America: 'For Storytellers, It's Fertile Ground,'" *Variety*, December 1, 2018, https://variety.com/2018/politics/features/ava-duvernay-criminal-justice-reform-in-america-1203071243/.

50. "Documentary '13TH' Argues Mass Incarceration Is an Extension of Slavery," interview, NPR (audio blog), December 17, 2016, https://www.npr.org/2016/12/17/505996792/documentary-13th-argues-mass-incarceration-is-an-extension-of-slavery.

51. Juleyka Lantigua-Williams, "Ava DuVernay's 13th Reframes American History," *The Atlantic*, October 6, 2016, https://www.theatlantic.com/entertainment/archive/2016/10/ava-duvernay-13th-netflix/503075/.

52. Lantigua-Williams, "Ava DuVernay's 13th Reframes."

53. John Gramlich, "U.S. Incarceration Rate Is at Its Lowest in 20 Years," *Pew Research Center*, May 2, 2018, https://www.pewresearch.org/fact-tank/2018/05/02/americas-incarceration-rate-is-at-a-two-decade-low/.

54. Greenberg Quinlan Rosner Research, *The Evolving Landscape of Crime and Incarceration*, PDF, Washington: Greenberg Quinlan Rosner Research, April 19, 2018.

55. Tim Lau, "Historic Criminal Justice Reform Legislation Signed into Law," *Brennan Center for Justice*, December 21, 2018, https://www.brennancenter.org/blog/historic-criminal-justice-reform-legislation-signed-law.

56. Nicholas Fandos, "Senate Passes Bipartisan Criminal Justice Bill," *New York Times*, December 18, 2018, https://www.nytimes.com/2018/12/18/us/politics/senate-criminal-justice-bill.html; Tim Lau, "Historic Criminal Justice Reform Legislation Signed into Law," *Brennan Center for Justice*, December 21, 2018, https://www.brennancenter.org/blog/historic-criminal-justice-reform-legislation-signed-law.

57. Justin T. Pickett, "Reintegrative Populism? Public Opinion and the Criminology of Downsizing," *Criminology & Public Policy* 15, no. 1 (2016): 131–135, doi:10.1111/1745-9133.12191, 131.

58. Lantigua-Williams, "Ava DuVernay's 13th Reframes."

59. USA, Department of Health and Human Services, Office of the Assistant Secretary for Planning and Evaluation, *ASPE Research Brief: The Opioid Crisis and Economic Opportunity: Geographic and Economic Trends*, by Robin Ghertner and Lincoln Groves, 3, September 11, 2018, https://aspe.hhs.gov/system/files/pdf/259261/ASPEEconomicOpportunityOpioidCrisis.pdf.

60. Michael R. Betz and Mark D. Partridge, "Country Road Take Me Home: Migration Patterns in Appalachian America and Place-Based Policy," *International Regional Science Review* 36, no. 3 (December 13, 2012): 267–295, doi:10.1177/0160017612467646, 268.

61. Richard A. Couto, "The Spatial Distribution of Wealth and Poverty in Appalachia," *Journal of Appalachian Studies* 1, no. 1 (Fall 1995): 99–120, https://www.jstor.org/stable/41446307?seq=1#page_scan_tab_contents, 107-108.

62. Eric Bowen et al., *An Overview of the Coal Economy in Appalachia*, PDF, Morgantown: West Virginia University, Appalachian Regional Commission, January 2018, 5.

63. Centers for Disease Control and Prevention, "Opioid Overdose: Drug Overdose Deaths," *Centers for Disease Control and Prevention*, December 19, 2018, https://www.cdc.gov/drugoverdose/data/statedeaths.html.

64. Centers for Disease Control and Prevention, "Opioid Overdose: Drug Overdose Deaths."

65. Centers for Disease Control and Prevention, "Opioid Overdose: Understanding the Epidemic," Centers for Disease Control and Prevention, December 19, 2018, https://www.cdc.gov/drugoverdose/epidemic/index.html.

66. USA, Department of Health and Human Services, Office of the Assistant Secretary for Planning and Evaluation, *ASPE Research Brief: The Opioid Crisis and Economic Opportunity*.

67. Nabarun Dasgupta, Leo Beletsky, and Daniel Ciccarone, "Opioid Crisis: No Easy Fix to Its Social and Economic Determinants," *American Journal of Public Health* 108, no. 2 (2018): 182–186, doi:10.2105/ajph.2017.304187, 182.

68. Richard D. Deshazo et al., "Backstories on the US Opioid Epidemic. Good Intentions Gone Bad, an Industry Gone Rogue, and Watch Dogs Gone to Sleep," *American Journal of Medicine* 131, no. 6 (2018): 595–601, doi:10.1016/j.amjmed.2017.12.045; Rummans et al., "How Good Intentions Contributed to Bad Outcomes," 344–350.

69. Deshazo et al., "Backstories on the US Opioid Epidemic," 596.

70. Deshazo et al., "Backstories on the US Opioid Epidemic," 596.

71. Rummans et al., "How Good Intentions Contributed to Bad Outcomes," 346–47.

72. Rummans et al., "How Good Intentions Contributed to Bad Outcomes," 346.

73. Rummans et al., "How Good Intentions Contributed to Bad Outcomes," 346.

74. Deshazo et al., "Backstories on the US Opioid Epidemic," 596.

75. Rummans et al., "How Good Intentions Contributed to Bad Outcomes," 346.

76. Associated Press, "Purdue Pharma, Execs to Pay $634.5 Million Fine in OxyContin Case," CNBC, August 5, 2010, https://www.cnbc.com/id/18591525.

77. Rummans et al., "How Good Intentions Contributed to Bad Outcomes," 346.

78. Scott E. Hadland et al., "Association of Pharmaceutical Industry Marketing of Opioid Products with Mortality from Opioid-Related Overdoses," *JAMA Network Open* 2, no. 1 (2019): 1–12, doi:10.1001/jamanetworkopen.2018.6007, 1.

79. Brian Mann, "Opioid Litigation Brings Company Secrets into the Public Eye," NPR (audio blog), March 13, 2019, https://www.npr.org/sections/health-shots/2019/03/13/702665619/opioid-litigation-brings-company-secrets-into-the-public-eye.

80. Jackie Fortier and Brian Mann, "Johnson & Johnson Ordered to Pay Oklahoma $572 Million in Opioid Trial," NPR, August 26, 2019, https://www.npr.org/sections/health-shots/2019/08/26/754481268/judge-in-opioid-trial-rules-johnson-johnson-must-pay-oklahoma-572-million.

81. Emma E. McGinty et al., "Criminal Activity or Treatable Health Condition? News Media Framing of Opioid Analgesic Abuse in the United States, 1998–2012," *Psychiatric Services* 67, no. 4 (2016): 405–411, doi:10.1176/appi.ps.201500065, 405.

82. McGinty et al., "Criminal Activity or Treatable Health Condition?," 405.

83. McGinty et al., "Criminal Activity or Treatable Health Condition?," 410.

84. John Dreyzehner and Nat Kendall-Taylor, "Reframing America's Opioid Epidemic to Find Solutions," *Stanford Social Innovation Review*, June 26, 2018, https://ssir.org/articles/entry/reframing_americas_opioid_epidemic_to_find_solutions.

85. Elaine McMillion Sheldon, phone interview with author, March 12, 2019.

86. Elaine McMillion Sheldon, phone interview with author, March 12, 2019.

87. *Heroin(e)*, dir. Elaine McMillion Sheldon (USA: Netflix, 2017), https://www.netflix.com/title/80192445.

88. Elaine McMillion Sheldon, phone interview with author, March 12, 2019.

89. Elaine McMillion Sheldon, phone interview with author, March 12, 2019.

90. Michael Malone, "Netflix to Premiere Documentary Shorts at Telluride," *Broadcasting & Cable*, August 31, 2017, https://www.broadcastingcable.com/news/netflix-premiere-documentary-shorts-telluride-168259.

91. Jenna Marotta, "Netflix's Oscar-Nominated 'Heroin(e)' Offers Hope for Addicts, One Recovery at a Time," *IndieWire*, February 27, 2018, https://www.indiewire.com/2018/02/netflix-oscar-nominated-heroine-hope-addicts-recovery-1201933164/.

92. Reveal Staff, "'Heroin(e)' Wins Emmy for Outstanding Short Documentary," *Reveal News*, October 2, 2018, https://www.revealnews.org/blog/herione-wins-the-emmy-for-outstanding-short-documentary/.

93. *Heroin(e)*, dir. Elaine McMillion Sheldon.

94. *Heroin(e)*, dir. Elaine McMillion Sheldon. .

95. Baylee DeMuth, "'Heroin(e)' Documentary Screening and Discussion Aim to Educate Audiences about Opioid Epidemic," *Post Athens*, January 27, 2019, https://www.thepostathens.com/article/2019/01/heroine-documentary-screening-free-athens.

96. Elaine McMillion Sheldon, phone interview with author, March 12, 2019.

97. Elaine McMillion Sheldon, phone interview with author, March 12, 2019.

98. Elaine McMillion Sheldon, phone interview with author, March 12, 2019.

99. Joe Manchin, "Most Influential People of 2018: Jen Rader," *TIME*, 2018, http://time.com/collection/most-influential-people-2018/5238151/jan-rader/.

100. Jan Rader, phone interview with author, March 13, 2019.

101. Jerome M. Adams, "Increasing Naloxone Awareness and Use: The Role of Health Care Practitioners," *Journal of the American Medical Association* 319, no. 20 (May 22, 2018): 2073, doi:10.1001/jama.2018.4867; Office of the Surgeon General, "Surgeon General's Advisory on Naloxone and Opioid Overdose," Surgeongeneral.gov, https://www.surgeongeneral.gov/priorities/opioid-overdose-prevention/naloxone-advisory.html; Robert B. Dunne, "Prescribing Naloxone for Opioid Overdose Intervention," *Pain Management* 8, no. 3 (2018): 197–208, doi:10.2217/pmt-2017-0065, 197.

102. Office of the Surgeon General, "Surgeon General's Advisory on Naloxone and Opioid Overdose," *Surgeongeneral.gov*, https://www.surgeongeneral.gov/priorities/opioid-overdose-prevention/naloxone-advisory.html.

103. WBUR Here & Now, "Here's What West Virginia Is Doing to Address the Opioid Crisis," *WBUR: Here & Now* (audio blog), May 11, 2018, https://www.wbur.org/hereandnow/2018/05/11/opioid-crisis-west-virginia.

104. Jan Rader, phone interview with author, March 13, 2019.

105. Lynh Bui, Rachel Weiner, and Justin Jouvenal, "'I Can't Breathe,' Freddie Gray Told Baltimore Police Officer, Prosecutor Says," *Washington Post*, December 2, 2015, https://www.washingtonpost.com/local/public-safety/opening-statements-to-begin-in-trial-of-officer-charged-in-freddie-grays-death/2015/12/02/b3c01ddc-9853-11e5-94f0-9eeaff906ef3_story.html?noredirect=on&utm_term=.dcde70f49829.

106. German Lopez, "The Baltimore Protests over Freddie Gray's Death, Explained," *Vox*, August 18, 2018, https://www.vox.com/2016/7/27/18089352/freddie-gray-baltimore-riots-police-violence.

107. John Woodrow Cox, Lynh Bui, and DeNeen L. Brown, "Who Was Freddie Gray? How Did He Die? And What Led to the Mistrial in Baltimore?" *Washington Post*, December 16, 2015, https://www.washingtonpost.com/local/who-was-freddie-gray-and-how-did-his-death-lead-to-a-mistrial-in-baltimore/2015/12/16/b08df7ce-a433-11e5-9c4e-be37f66848bb_story.html?utm_term=.f33f35cfd07d.

108. Doug Donovan and Mark Puente, "Some Local Leaders Call for Justice Department to Probe Freddie Gray Death," *Baltimore Sun*, April 20, 2015, https://www.baltimoresun.com/news/investigations/bs-md-gray-doj-review-20150420-story.html.

109. Daniel Grinberg, "Tracking Movements: Black Activism, Aerial Surveillance, and Transparency Optics," *Media, Culture & Society* 41, no. 3 (November 22, 2018): 294–316, doi:10.1177/0163443718810921, 294–295.

110. Kevin Rector, "Charges Dropped, Freddie Gray Case Concludes with Zero Convictions against Officers," *Baltimore Sun*, July 27, 2016, https://www.baltimoresun.com/news/maryland/freddie-gray/bs-md-ci-miller-pretrial-motions-20160727-story.html.

111. Mark Puente, "Undue Force," *Baltimore Sun*, September 28, 2014, http://data.baltimoresun.com/news/police-settlements/.

112. Joy Jenkins and J. David Wolfgang, "A Place to Protest," *Journalism Practice* 11, no. 8 (September 2017): 960–979, doi:10.1080/17512786.2016.1209976, 960.

113. Ryan J. Gallagher et al., "Divergent Discourse between Protests and Counter-protests: #BlackLivesMatter and #AllLivesMatter," *PLoS ONE* 13, no. 4 (April 18, 2018): 1–23, https://journals.plos.org/plosone/article?id=10.1371/journal.pone.0195644, 2.

114. Morgan Eichensehr and Daniel Popper, "How the Media Covered the Baltimore Riots," *American Journalism Review*, April 28, 2015, http://ajr.org/2015/04/28/how-the-media-covered-baltimore-riots/; Grinberg, "Tracking Movements," 1.

115. Joy Leopold and Myrtle P. Bell, "News Media and the Racialization of Protest: An Analysis of Black Lives Matter Articles," *Equality, Diversity and Inclusion: An International Journal* 36, no. 8 (2017): 720–735, doi:10.1108/edi-01-2017-0010, 720.

116. Kim Fridkin et al., "Race and Police Brutality: The Importance of Media Framing," *International Journal of Communication* 11 (2017): 3394–3414, https://ijoc.org/index.php/ijoc/article/view/6950.

117. Marilyn Ness, phone interview with author, March 21, 2019.

118. Marilyn Ness, phone interview with author, March 21, 2019.

119. Max Weiss, "Filmmaker Discusses Three-Year Process of Making Charm City Documentary," *Baltimore Magazine*, October 10, 2018, https://www.baltimoremagazine.com/2018/10/10/charm-city-filmmaker-marilyn-ness-discusses-three-year-process-creating-documentary.

120. Matthew Carey, "Director Marilyn Ness Revisits Troubled Baltimore in Oscar Contender 'Charm City,' Says It Was Like 'The Wire 2.0,'" *Deadline Hollywood*, January 1, 2019,

https://deadline.com/2019/01/charm-city-marilyn-ness-alex-long-baltimore-oscar-the-wire-1202527790/.

121. *Charm City*, dir. Marilyn Ness (USA: Big Mouth Productions, PBS Distribution, 2018), film.
122. Max Weiss, "Movie Review: Charm City," *Baltimore Magazine*, October 12, 2018, https://www.baltimoremagazine.com/2018/10/12/movie-review-charm-city.
123. Marilyn Ness, phone interview with author, March 21, 2019.
124. Charles Bramesco, "Charm City: The Documentary on Baltimore's Three Most Violent Years," *The Guardian*, October 17, 2018, https://www.theguardian.com/film/2018/oct/17/charm-city-baltimore-marilyn-ness-film.
125. *Charm City*, dir. Marilyn Ness.
126. Marilyn Ness, phone interview with author, March 21, 2019.
127. Carey, "Director Marilyn Ness Revisits Troubled Baltimore."
128. "Charm City," PBS: Independent Lens, accessed May 1, 2019, http://www.pbs.org/independentlens/films/charm-city/.
129. "Charm City Baltimore Pilot Impact and Engagement Plan" (2018), 3, 9–12; provided to the author by *Charm City* director Marilyn Ness.
130. Marilyn Ness, phone interview with author, March 21, 2019.
131. Marilyn Ness, phone interview with author, March 21, 2019.
132. Lester Davis, "City Policing Set for Reform: Consent Decree between Baltimore and the DOJ Sets Reform Agenda for City Police," *Baltimore Sun*, January 15, 2017, http://digitaledition.baltimoresun.com/tribune/article_popover.aspx?guid=78419231-f736-4b7c-9095-388dec189581.
133. Marilyn Ness, phone interview with author, March 21, 2019.

Chapter 7

1. Simon Kilmurry, phone interview with author, March 25, 2019.
2. "The Invisible War," ITVS, accessed March 21, 2019, https://itvs.org/films/invisible-war.
3. Mark Jenkins, "'Invisible War' Documentary Examines Rape in the Military," *Washington Post*, June 21, 2012, https://www.washingtonpost.com/entertainment/movies/invisible-war-documentary-examines-rape-in-the-military/2012/06/21/gJQAcGqhtV_email.html.
4. United States, Department of Defense, Pentagon, *Department of Defense Annual Report on Sexual Assault in the Military*, by Chuck Hagel (Washington, DC: Department of Defense, 2012), 28, May 7, 2013, https://archive.nytimes.com/www.nytimes.com/interactive/2013/05/08/us/politics/08military-doc.html; Chuck Hagel, *Department of Defense Annual Report on Sexual Assault in the Military*, PDF, Washington, DC: Department of Defense, 2012.
5. Kirby Dick, "The Invisible War Trailer," *Vimeo*, November 30, 2011, https://vimeo.com/32929190.
6. Jenkins, "'Invisible War' Documentary Examines Rape."
7. BRITDOC, *The Invisible War: The Impact Field Guide & Toolkit*, PDF, London: BRITDOC, https://impactguide.org/static/library/InvisibleWar.pdf.
8. Kirby Dick, phone interview with author, March 16, 2019.
9. Jenkins, "'Invisible War' Documentary Examines Rape."
10. *The Invisible War*, dir. Kirby Dick (USA: Cinedigm, 2012), film, May 13, 2013, http://www.pbs.org/independentlens/videos/the-invisible-war/.

11. BRITDOC, *The Invisible War*.

12. *Testimony on Sexual Assaults in the Military: Hearing before the Subcommittee on Personnel of the Committee on Armed Services, United States Senate*, 113th Cong. (2013); Matt Laslo, "Senator Kirsten Gillibrand Proposes New Military Sexual Assault Bill," *WRVO Public Media* (audio blog), March 3, 2014, https://www.wrvo.org/post/senator-kirsten-gillibrand-proposes-new-military-sexual-assault-bill.

13. Laslo, "Senator Kirsten Gillibrand Proposes."

14. Joie Tyrrell, "Gillibrand: Reform How Military Sex-assault Cases Are Handled," *Newsday*, November 16, 2017, https://www.newsday.com/news/nation/military-sexual-assault-gillibrand-1.15004968.

15. "Military Justice Improvement Act," Kirsten Gillibrand, United States Senator for New York, https://www.gillibrand.senate.gov/mjia.

16. Kirby Dick, phone interview with author, March 16, 2019.

17. Kirby Dick, phone interview with author, March 16, 2019.

18. Kirby Dick, phone interview with author, March 16, 2019.

19. Dmitry Epstein, Cynthia Farina, and Josiah Heidt, "The Value of Words: Narrative as Evidence in Policy Making," *Evidence & Policy: A Journal of Research, Debate and Practice* 10, no. 2 (2014): 243–258, doi:10.1332/174426514x13990325021128; Jeff Niederdeppe, Sungjong Roh, and Caitlin Dreisbach, "How Narrative Focus and a Statistical Map Shape Health Policy Support among State Legislators," *Health Communication* 31, no. 2 (2015): 242–255, doi:10.1080/10410236.2014.998913.

20. David Whiteman, "Out of the Theaters and into the Streets: A Coalition Model of the Political Impact of Documentary Film and Video," *Political Communication* 21, no. 1 (2004): 51–69, doi:10.1080/10584600490273263-1585; Barbara Abrash and David Whiteman, "The Uprising of 34: Filmmaking as Community Engagement," *Wide Angle* 21, no. 2 (1999): 87–99, doi:10.1353/wan.1999.0027; James McEnteer, *Shooting the Truth: The Rise of American Political Documentaries*, annotated ed. (Santa Barbara, CA: Praeger, 2005).

21. Christian Christensen, "Political Documentary, Online Organization and Activist Synergies," *Studies in Documentary Film* 3, no. 2 (2009): 77–94, doi:10.1386/sdf.3.2.77/1; Ion Bogdan Vasi et al., "'No Fracking Way!' Documentary Film, Discursive Opportunity, and Local Opposition against Hydraulic Fracturing in the United States, 2010 to 2013," *American Sociological Review* 80, no. 5 (2015): 934–959, doi:10.1177/0003122415598534.

22. Paul A. Sabatier, "Toward Better Theories of the Policy Process," *PS: Political Science and Politics* 24, no. 2 (June 1991): 147-156, doi:10.2307/419923, 148.

23. "Sin by Silence: A Documentary about Domestic Violence," Sin by Silence, accessed May 1, 2019, http://www.sinbysilence.com/.

24. Olivia Klaus, phone interview with authors, May 8, 2017.

25. Gloria Hillard, "Domestic Abuse Victims Get Chance at Freedom," NPR (audioblog), October 5, 2012, https://www.npr.org/2012/10/05/162169484/jailed-domestic-abuse-victims-get-chance-at-freedom.

26. Olivia Klaus, phone interview with authors, May 8, 2017.

27. "Governor Signs Both Sin by Silence Bills: Justice for Incarcerated Victims of Domestic Violence Finally at Hand," the Sin by Silence Bills, October 2, 2012, http://legislation.sinbysilence.com/lastest-news-updates/governor-signs-both-sin-by-silence-bills.

28. "Case Study: Sin by Silence," Fledgling Fund, accessed May 1, 2019, http://www.thefledglingfund.org/impact-resources/sin-by-silence/.

29. Aharris, "Investigation Discovery Breaks the Silence Surrounding Domestic Violence with 'Sin by Silence' & NNEDV," *Discovery Blog* (blog), October 11, 2011, https://corporate.discovery.com/blog/2011/10/11/investigation-discovery-breaks-the-silence-surrounding-domestic-violence/.
30. Olivia Klaus, phone interview with authors, May 8, 2017.
31. Olivia Klaus, phone interview with authors, May 8, 2017.
32. Olivia Klaus, phone interview with authors, May 8, 2017.
33. Fiona Ma, phone interview with authors, May 8, 2017.
34. "AB 1593 Facts & Summary," the Sin by Silence Bills, accessed May 1, 2019, http://legislation.sinbysilence.com/ab-1593/ab-1593-facts.
35. "AB 1593 Facts & Summary," the Sin by Silence Bills.
36. Fiona Ma, phone interview with authors, May 8, 2017.
37. Fiona Ma, phone interview with authors, May 8, 2017.
38. Olivia Klaus, phone interview with authors, May 8, 2017.
39. "Governor Signs Both Sin by Silence Bills: Justice for Incarcerated Victims of Domestic Violence, Finally at Hand," the Sin by Silence Bills, October 2, 2012, http://legislation.sinbysilence.com/lastest-news-updates/governor-signs-both-sin-by-silence-bills.
40. "Governor Signs Both Sin by Silence Bills."
41. "Governor Signs Both Sin by Silence Bills."
42. Brenda Clubine, phone interview with authors, June 7, 2017.
43. Olivia Ma, "Every Voice Matters: Domestic Violence Prevention," *Huffington Post*, September 29, 2017, https://www.huffingtonpost.com/entry/every-voice-mattersdomestic-violence-prevention_us_59cecec6e4b034ae778d4a8a.
44. "About the Film," Semper Fi: Always Faithful, accessed May 1, 2019, http://semperfialwaysfaithful.com/film/.
45. Jerry Ensminger, phone interview with authors, December 11, 2015.
46. Manuel Roig-Franzia and Catharine Skipp, "Tainted Water in the Land of Semper Fi," *Washington Post*, January 28, 2004, https://www.washingtonpost.com/archive/politics/2004/01/28/tainted-water-in-the-land-of-semper-fi/7aece962-26b6-44b2-96ec-8d58126435b4/?noredirect=on&utm_term=.f4d409b6bfc3.
47. Rachel Libert, phone interview with authors, December 2, 2015.
48. Dick Frandsen, phone interview with authors, March 29, 2016.
49. Jerry Ensminger, phone interview with authors, December 11, 2015.
50. Heather White, phone interview with authors, November 15, 2015.
51. Dick Frandsen, phone interview with authors, March 29, 2016.
52. "Semper Fi: Always Faithful, the Movie," Facebook, accessed January 2, 2019, https://www.facebook.com/semperfimovie/.
53. "About the Film," Semper Fi: Always Faithful, accessed May 1, 2019, http://semperfialwaysfaithful.com/film/.
54. Franco Ordonez and Barbara Barrett, "Obama Signs Law Giving Health Care to Lejeune Tainted Water Victims," *McClatchy DC*, August 6, 2012, https://www.mcclatchydc.com/news/politics-government/article24734458.html.
55. Ordonez and Barrett, "Obama Signs Law."
56. Jerry Ensminger, phone interview with authors, December 11, 2015.
57. Libby Spears and Nishima Chudasama, phone interview with authors, December 8, 2015.

58. Jennifer Conley, "Special Screening of the Documentary 'Playground,'" *I Live in Dallas* (blog), October 27, 2009, https://www.iliveindallas.com/special-screening-of-the-documentary-playground/.

59. "Playground: The Child Sex Trade in America," Nest Foundation, accessed January 2, 2019, https://www.nestfoundation.org/playground.

60. "Nest Foundation," Nest Foundation, accessed January 2, 2019, https://www.nestfoundation.org/.

61. Libby Spears and Nishima Chudasama, phone interview with authors, December 8, 2015.

62. Libby Spears and Nishima Chudasama, phone interview with authors, December 8, 2015.

63. *In Our Own Backyard: Child Prostitution and Sex Trafficking in the United States: Hearing Before the Subcommittee on Human Rights and the Law of the Committee on the Judiciary, United States Senate*, 111th Cong. (2010).

64. Libby Spears and Nishima Chudasama, phone interview with authors, December 8, 2015.

65. Domestic Minor Sex Trafficking Deterrence and Victims Support Act of 2011, S. 596, 112th Cong. (2011).

66. Justice for Victims of Trafficking Act of 2015, Pub. L. No. 114–22 § 101, 129 Stat. 227 (2015).

67. Libby Spears and Nishima Chudasama, phone interview with authors, December 8, 2015.

68. Carol Smolenski, phone interview with authors, March 11, 2016.

69. "Safe Harbors Initiative," Advocates for Human Rights, http://www.theadvocatesforhumanrights.org/safe_harbors_initiative.

70. Polaris Project, *Human Trafficking Issue Brief: Safe Harbor, Fall 2015*, PDF, Polaris, 2015.

71. Carol Smolenski, phone interview with authors, March 11, 2016.

72. Sarah Wasch et al., *An Analysis of Safe Harbor Laws for Minor Victims of Commercial Sexual Exploitation: Implications for Pennsylvania and Other States*, report, The Field Center for Children's Policy, Practice & Research, University of Pennsylvania (Philadelphia: University of Pennsylvania, 2016), March 11, 2016, https://fieldcenteratpenn.org/wp-content/uploads/2013/05/SafeHarborWhitePaperFINAL.pdf.

73. Sarah Wasch et al., *An Analysis of Safe Harbor Laws for Minor Victims*, Polaris Project, *Human Trafficking Issue Brief: Safe Harbor Fall 2015*, PDF, Polaris, 2015.

74. Polaris Project, *2013 Analysis of State Human Trafficking Laws*, DOCX, Polaris, 2013.

75. Joel Shapiro, phone interview with authors, January 8, 2016.

76. Carol Smolenski, phone interview with authors, March 11, 2016.

77. Carol Smolenski, phone interview with authors, March 11, 2016.

78. Sabatier, "Toward Better Theories of the Policy Process."

79. Epstein et al., "The Value of Words: Narrative as Evidence in Policy Making," 251.

Chapter 8

1. Laura Poitras, phone interview with author, July 30, 2019.

2. Lauren C. Williams, "'CitizenFour' Documaker Laura Poitras Talks Snowden and Responsible Journalism in the Digital Age," interview, ThinkProgress (blog), October 24, 2014, https://thinkprogress.org/citizenfour-documaker-laura-poitras-talks-snowden-and-responsible-journalism-in-the-digital-age-51545968ce90/#.1lxuhz1ba.

3. Laura Poitras, phone interview with author, July 30, 2019.

4. Laura Poitras, "The Program," *New York Times*, August 22, 2012, https://www.nytimes.com/2012/08/23/opinion/the-national-security-agencys-domestic-spying-program.html.

5. Williams, "'CitizenFour' Documaker Laura Poitras Talks Snowden."

6. Laura Poitras, phone interview with author, July 30, 2019.

7. Laura Poitras, phone interview with author, July 30, 2019.

8. Lisa Parks, "Cover Your Webcam: Unencrypting Laura Poitras's Citizenfour," *Film Quarterly* 68, no. 3 (2015): 11–16, doi:10.1525/fq.2015.68.3.11, 11.

9. Matt Patches, "From Inside the Snowden Saga: How Laura Poitras Covertly Shot Her New Film, *Citizenfour*," *Vanity Fair*, October 23, 2014, https://www.vanityfair.com/hollywood/2014/10/laura-poitras-citizen-four.

10. Steve Pond, "Edward Snowden Doc Director on Taking 'Staggering' Risks, Angering Powerful People," TheWrap, October 22, 2014, accessed May 1, 2019, https://www.thewrap.com/edward-snowden-doc-director-on-taking-staggering-risks-angering-powerful-people/.

11. Daniel Grinberg, "Troubling Histories: Re-viewing Documentary Production and Surveillance through the Freedom of Information Act," *Media, War & Conflict* (2018): 1–23, doi:10.1177/1750635218784966, 2.

12. Parks, "Cover Your Webcam," 14–15.

13. Laura Poitras, phone interview with author, July 30, 2019; Pond, "Edward Snowden Doc Director on Taking 'Staggering' Risks."

14. Georg Szalai, "Edward Snowden Doc to Get U.K. Premiere at London Film Festival," *Hollywood Reporter*, September 17, 2014, https://www.hollywoodreporter.com/news/edward-snowden-doc-get-uk-733683.

15. "Awards," CITIZENFOUR, https://citizenfourfilm.com/awards;

16. Cara Mertes, "CITIZENFOUR: Filmmaking as an Act of Justice," review, *Equals Change Blog* (blog), February 23, 2015, https://www.fordfoundation.org/ideas/equals-change-blog/posts/citizenfour-filmmaking-as-an-act-of-justice/.

17. Williams, "'CitizenFour' Documaker Laura Poitras Talks Snowden."

18. Pond, "Edward Snowden Doc Director on Taking 'Staggering' Risks."

19. Laura Poitras, phone interview with author, July 30, 2019.

20. Grinberg, "Troubling Histories: Re-viewing Documentary Production," 13.

21. Pond, "Edward Snowden Doc Director on Taking 'Staggering' Risks."

22. "About Field of Vision," Field of Vision, https://fieldofvision.org/about.

23. Charlotte Cook, in-person interview with author, May 17, 2019.

24. Ricardo Lopez, "Field of Vision Launches Fellowship Program for Rising Documentary Filmmakers," *Variety*, February 6, 2018, https://variety.com/2018/film/news/field-of-vision-fellowship-1202689240/.

25. Keith O'Brien, "Joining Forces in the Name of Watchdog Journalism," Nieman Reports, Summer 2016, 18, https://niemanreports.org/articles/joining-forces/

26. Brant Houston, "The Future of Investigative Journalism," *Daedalus* 139, no. 2 (2010): 45–56, doi:10.1162/daed.2010.139.2.45, 47.

27. Charlotte Cook, in-person interview with author, May 17, 2019.

28. Houston, "The Future of Investigative Journalism," 45.

29. Charles Lewis, "Seeking New Ways to Nurture the Capacity to Report," Nieman Reports, March 15, 2008, https://niemanreports.org/articles/seeking-new-ways-to-nurture-the-capacity-to-report/.

30. Richard J. Tofel, *Non-Profit Journalism: Issues around Impact*, PDF, ProPublica, Learning for Action Group, Bill & Melinda Gates Foundation, 2013, 5.

31. Houston, "The Future of Investigative Journalism," 45.

32. David L. Protess et al., *The Journalism of Outrage: Investigative Reporting and Agenda Building in America* (New York: Guilford Press, 1991), vi.

33. Laura Poitras, phone interview with author, July 30, 2019.

34. Carrie Lozano, phone interview with author, March 25, 2019.

35. Patricia Aufderheide, *Dangerous Documentaries: Reducing Risk When Telling Truth to Power*, PDF, Washington: Center for Media & Social Impact, February 2015, 6.

36. Aufderheide, *Dangerous Documentaries*, 6.

37. Renita Coleman and Lee Wilkins, "The Moral Development of Journalists: A Comparison with Other Professions and a Model for Predicting High Quality Ethical Reasoning," *Journalism & Mass Communication Quarterly* 81, no. 3 (2004): 511–527, doi:10.1177/107769900408100304.

38. Theodore L. Glasser and James S. Ettema, "Investigative Journalism and the Moral Order," *Critical Studies in Mass Communication* 6, no. 1 (1989): 1–20, doi:10.1080/15295038909366728.

39. James S. Ettema and Theodore L. Glasser, "Narrative Form and Moral Force: The Realization of Innocence and Guilt through Investigative Journalism," *Journal of Communication* 38, no. 3 (1988): 8–26, doi:10.1111/j.1460-2466.1988.tb02057.x.

40. Carrie Lozano, phone interview with author, March 25, 2019.

41. Caty Borum Chattoo and Bill Harder, *The State of the Documentary Field: 2018 Study of Documentary Professionals*, PDF, Washington, DC: Center for Media & Social Impact, September 2018.

42. Carrie Lozano, phone interview with author, March 25, 2019.

43. Grinberg, "Troubling Histories: Re-viewing Documentary Production."

44. Carrie Lozano, phone interview with the author, March 25, 2019.

45. Grinberg, "Troubling Histories: Re-viewing Documentary Production," 11.

46. Grinberg, "Troubling Histories: Re-viewing Documentary Production," 12.

47. "Festival Overview," Double Exposure Investigative Film Festival and Symposium, https://doubleexposurefestival.com/the-festival/.

48. Greg Evans, "IDA Grants $850G To 11 Documentaries; 'Blue Wall,' 'Hazing' among Picks," *Deadline*, October 20, 2017, https://deadline.com/2017/10/ida-international-documentary-association-grants-blue-wall-hazing-1202191529/.

49. Simon Kilmurry, phone interview with author, March 25, 2019.

50. *Southwest of Salem: The Story of the San Antonio Four*, dir. Deborah S. Esquenazi (USA: Motto Pictures, Naked Edge Films, 2016), film.

51. *Southwest of Salem: The Story of the San Antonio Four*.

52. *Southwest of Salem: The Story of the San Antonio Four*.

53. Maurice Possley, "Elizabeth Ramirez," Innocence Project of Texas, November 23, 2016, https://innocencetexas.org/cases/elizabeth-ramirez.

54. *Southwest of Salem: The Story of the San Antonio Four*.

55. *Southwest of Salem: The Story of the San Antonio Four*.

56. *Southwest of Salem: The Story of the San Antonio Four*.

57. Possley, "Elizabeth Ramirez," 2016.

58. Possley, "Elizabeth Ramirez," 2016.

59. *Southwest of Salem: The Story of the San Antonio Four.*

60. Michelle Mondo, "Did These Women Molest Two Girls?" *San Antonio Express-News*, December 21, 2010, https://www.mysanantonio.com/news/local_news/article/Did-these-womenmolest-two-girls-908873.php.

61. Deborah S. Esquenazi, phone interview with author, April 4, 2019.

62. Deborah S. Esquenazi, phone interview with author, April 4, 2019.

63. *Southwest of Salem: The Story of the San Antonio Four.*

64. John DeFore, "'Southwest of Salem: The Story of the San Antonio Four': Film Review," *Hollywood Reporter*, August 22, 2016, https://www.hollywoodreporter.com/review/southwest-of-salem-the-story-of-the-san-antonio-four-921741.

65. Matt Barone, "Justice for Some, Not All: The Powerful Story Behind the Can't-Miss Documentary SOUTHWEST OF SALEM," Tribeca, https://www.tribecafilm.com/stories/tribeca-film-festival-documentary-southwest-of-salem-san-antonio-four-deborah-esquenazi-interview.

66. Bridgette Dunlap, "Inside Case behind Wrongful Conviction Doc 'Southwest of Salem,'" *Rolling Stone*, October 13, 2016, https://www.rollingstone.com/culture/culture-features/inside-case-behind-wrongful-conviction-doc-southwest-of-salem-117090/.

67. Michael Hall, "The San Antonio 4 Are Finally Free," *Texas Monthly*, November 19, 2013, https://www.texasmonthly.com/the-daily-post/the-san-antonio-4-are-finally-free/.

68. "About," Southwest of Salem, accessed May 3, 2019, http://www.southwestofsalem.com/about-2.

69. Hanh Nguyen, "San Antonio Four: ID's 'Southwest of Salem' Doc Seeks Viewers' Help for Exoneration," *IndieWire*, August 2, 2016, https://www.indiewire.com/2016/08/san-antonio-four-southwest-of-salem-documentary-id-exoneration-1201712346/.

70. *Southwest of Salem: The Story of the San Antonio Four.*

71. Deborah S. Esquenazi, phone interview with author, April 4, 2019; Nguyen, "San Antonio Four: ID's 'Southwest of Salem' Doc."

72. Allen Cone, "'San Antonio 4' Exonerated by Texas' Top Court," *United Press International*, November 25, 2016, https://www.upi.com/Top_News/US/2016/11/25/San-Antonio-4-exonerated-by-Texas-top-court/9191480080238/.

73. Deborah S. Esquenazi, phone interview with author, April 4, 2019.

74. Deborah S. Esquenazi, phone interview with author, April 4, 2019.

75. Deborah S. Esquenazi, phone interview with author, April 4, 2019.

76. Deborah S. Esquenazi, phone interview with author, April 4, 2019.

77. Deborah S. Esquenazi, phone interview with author, April 4, 2019.

78. Jeanne Theoharris, "Comey Says Fbi's Surveillance of Mlk Was 'Shameful'—But Comey's Fbi Targeted Black Activists and Muslim Communities Anyway," *The Intercept*, April 24, 2018, https://theintercept.com/2018/04/24/james-comey-mlk-martin-luther-king-surveillance-muslims/.

79. Theoharris, "Comey Says Fbi's Surveillance."

80. "COINTELPRO," FBI Records: The Vault, May 5, 2011, https://vault.fbi.gov/cointel-pro; Charles E. Jones, "The Political Repression of the Black Panther Party 1966–1971," *Journal of Black Studies* 18, no. 4 (June 1988): 415–434, doi:10.1177/002193478801800402; David P. Hadley, "America's 'Big Brother': A Century of U.S. Domestic Surveillance," *Origins* 7, no. 3 (December 2013), December 2013, http://origins.osu.edu/article/americas-big-brother-century-us-domestic-surveillance.

81. Nelson Blackstock, *Cointelpro: The FBI's Secret War on Political Freedom*, 3rd ed. (New York: Pathfinder Press, 1988).

82. Jeffrey O. G. Ogbar, "The FBI's War on Civil Rights Leaders," *Daily Beast*, January 16, 2017, https://www.thedailybeast.com/the-fbis-war-on-civil-rights-leaders.

83. Sara Kamali, "Informants, Provocateurs, and Entrapment: Examining the Histories of the FBI's PATCON and the NYPD's Muslim Surveillance Program," *Surveillance & Society* 15, no. 1 (2017): 68–78, doi:10.24908/ss.v15i1.5254, 69.

84. Karl N. Llewellyn, "Some Realism about Realism: Responding to Dean Pound," *Harvard Law Review* 44, no. 8 (June 1931): 1222–1264, doi:10.2307/1332182, 1222.

85. Barton Gellman and Sam Adler-Bell, "The Disparate Impact of Surveillance," Century Foundation, December 21, 2017, https://tcf.org/content/report/disparate-impact-surveillance/?agreed=1.

86. Noor Zafar and Neema Singh Guliani, "How to Shine a Light on U.S. Government Surveillance of Americans," *ACLU* (blog), February 6, 2019, https://www.aclu.org/blog/national-security/privacy-and-surveillance/how-shine-light-us-government-surveillance-americans.

87. Jesse J. Norris and Hanna Grol-Prokopczyk, "Racial and Other Sociodemographic Disparities in Terrorism Sting Operations," *Sociology of Race and Ethnicity*, 2018: 416–431, doi:10.1177/2332649218756136, 416.

88. Kamali, "Informants, Provocateurs, and Entrapment."

89. Matt Apuzzo and Adam Goldman, "With CIA Help, NYPD Moves Covertly in Muslim Areas," *Seattle Times*, August 25, 2011, https://www.seattletimes.com/seattle-news/politics/with-cia-help-nypd-moves-covertly-in-muslim-areas/.

90. David Crary, "AP Series about NYPD Surveillance Wins Pulitzer," *Associated Press*, April 16, 2012, https://www.ap.org/ap-in-the-news/2012/ap-series-about-nypd-surveillance-wins-pulitzer.

91. Kamali, "Informants, Provocateurs, and Entrapment," 68.

92. Patrik Jonsson, "Muslim Group Sues FBI over Surveillance at California Mosques," *Christian Science Monitor* (Boston), February 23, 2011, https://search-proquest-com.proxyau.wrlc.org/docview/853347316?accountid=8285.

93. *The Feeling of Being Watched*, dir. Assia Boundaoui (USA: Impact Partners, Multitude Films, Naked Edge Films, 2018), film.

94. *The Feeling of Being Watched*.

95. Assia Boundaoui, phone interview with author, April 17, 2019.

96. Noreen S. Ahmed-Ullah et al., "Hard-liners Won Battle for Bridgeview Mosque," *Chicago Tribune*, February 8, 2004, https://www.chicagotribune.com/news/chi-0402080265feb08-story.html.

97. Michael E. Deutsch and Erica Thompson, "Secrets and Lies: The Persecution of Muhammad Salah (Part I)," *Journal of Palestine Studies* 37, no. 4 (Summer 2008): 38–58, http://dx.doi.org.proxyau.wrlc.org/10.1525/jps.2008.37.4.38, 51.

98. *The Feeling of Being Watched*.

99. *The Feeling of Being Watched*.

100. Tanvi Misra, "When Your Block Is Being Watched," CityLab, October 18, 2018, https://www.citylab.com/equity/2018/10/when-your-block-being-watched/573157/.

101. Assia Boundaoui, phone interview with author, April 17, 2019.

102. "Screenings," The Feeling of Being Watched, accessed April 20, 2019, http://www. feelingofbeingwatched.com/screenings.

103. Jessica Devaney, phone interview with author, April 22, 2019.

104. Anya Rous, phone interview with author, April 24, 2019.

105. "The Feeling of Being Watched," POV, accessed May 1, 2019, https://www.pbs.org/pov/ feelingofbeingwatched/.

106. Assia Boundaoui, phone interview with author, April 17, 2019.

107. Jackie Spinner, "Q&A: Filmmaker on FBI Surveillance of Her Neighborhood and the Fight for the Records That Prove It," *Columbia Journalism Review*, August 16, 2017, https://www.cjr.org/united_states_project/the-feeling-of-being-watched-assia-boundaoui.php.

108. Assia Boundaoui, phone interview with author, April 17, 2019.

109. Assia Boundaoui, phone interview with author, April 17, 2019.

110. Assia Boundaoui, phone interview with author, April 17, 2019.

111. Patrick E. Croke and Sidley Austin LLP, *Vulgar Betrayal*, PDF, Chicago, June 26, 2017, https://www.courthousenews.com/wp-content/uploads/2017/06/VulgarBetrayal. pdf.

112. Assia Boundaoui, phone interview with author, April 17, 2019.

113. Assia Boundaoui, phone interview with author, April 17, 2019.

114. Alan Goforth, "Mapping the Documentary-Journalism Landscape: Collaborative Project Connects Filmmakers with Journalism Resources," International Documentary Association, March 6, 2018, https://www.documentary.org/feature/mapping-documentary-journalism-landscape-collaborative-project-connects-filmmakers; "Mapping the Documentary-Journalism Landscape," Jonathan B. Murray Center for Documentary Journalism at the University of Missouri, https://docjournalism.com/ map/.

115. Steven Maras, "The View from Nowhere," in *Objectivity in Journalism (Key Concepts in Journalism)* (Cambridge, UK: Polity, 2013), 77–81.

116. Assia Boundaoui, "POV vs. Objectivity," *Documentary* Magazine, February 19, 2019, https://www.documentary.org/blog/pov-vs-objectivity.

Chapter 9

1. Tabitha Jackson, phone interview with author, May 20, 2019.

2. Mandalit Del Barco, "The Documentary Is In—and Enjoying—an 'Undeniable Golden Age,'" NPR, February 19, 2019, https://www.npr.org/2019/02/19/696036323/ the-documentary-is-in-and-enjoying-an-undeniable-golden-age.

3. Victor Pickard, "The Violence of the Market," *Journalism* 20, no. 1 (January 2019): 154–158, https://doi.org/10.1177/1464884918808955, 154.

4. Simon Kilmurry, email correspondence with author, September 2, 2019.

5. John Corner, "Performing the Real: Documentary Diversions," *Television & New Media* 3, no. 3 (August 2002): 255–269, doi:10.1177/152747640200300302, 263.

6. Matthew Hindman, *The Internet Trap: How the Digital Economy Builds Monopolies and Undermines Democracy* (Princeton: Princeton University Press, 2018), 14.

7. Nick Couldry, Sonia M. Livingstone, and Tim Markham, *Media Consumption and Public Engagement: Beyond the Presumption of Attention* (London: Palgrave Macmillan, 2010), 16.

8. Couldry, Livingstone, and Markham, *Media Consumption and Public Engagement,* 37.

9. Henry Jenkins, *By Any Media Necessary: The New Youth Activism*, ed. Henry Jenkins et al. (New York: New York University Press, 2016), 3.

10. Renee Tajima-Peña, "#DocsSoWhite: A Personal Reflection," *Documentary Magazine,* August 30, 2016, https://www.documentary.org/feature/docssowhite-personal-reflection.

11. Caty Borum Chattoo and Bill Harder, "The State of the Documentary Field: 2018 Survey of Documentary Professionals," *Center for Media & Social Impact*, 2018, https://cmsimpact. org/report/state-documentary-field-2018-study-documentary-professionals/ .

12. Tajima-Peña, "#DocsSoWhite."

13. Caty Borum Chattoo, "Oscars So White: Gender, Racial, and Ethnic Diversity and Social Issues in U.S. Documentary Films (2008–2017)," *Mass Communication and Society* 21, no. 3: 368–394, https://doi.org/10.1080/15205436.2017.1409356, 381–384.

14. Borum Chattoo, "Oscars So White," 380.

15. Borum Chattoo, "Oscars So White," 387.

16. Caty Borum Chattoo, Patricia Aufderheide, Kenneth Merrill, and Modupeola Oyebolu, "Diversity on U.S. Public and Commercial TV in Authorial and Executive-Produced Social-Issue Documentaries," *Journal of Broadcasting & Electronic Media* 62, no. 3 (July 2018): 495–513, https://doi.org/10.1080/08838151.2018.1451865.

17. Caty Borum Chattoo, Patricia Aufderheide, Michele Alexander, and Chandler Green, "American Realities on Public Television: Analysis of Independent Television Service's Independent Documentaries, 2007–2016," *International Journal of Communication*, 12 (March 2018): 1541–1568, https://ijoc.org/index.php/ijoc/article/view/7826/2314, 1541.

18. Tajima-Peña, "#DocsSoWhite."

19. Sandie Viquez Pedlow, phone interview with author, June 4, 2019.

20. Leo Chiang, email correspondence with author, May 16, 2019.

21. "Who We Are," A-Doc, accessed May 1, 2019, https://a-doc.org/.

22. S. Leo Chiang, email interview correspondence with author, May 23, 2019.

23. Brown Girls Doc Mafia, accessed May 1, 2019, https://browngirlsdocmafia.com/.

24. Erik Pederson, "Brown Girls Doc Mafia Names Board of Directors," *Deadline*, December 14, 2018, https://deadline.com/2018/12/brown-girls-doc-mafia-names-board-of-directors-1202520298/.

25. Pederson, "Brown Girls Doc Mafia Names Board."

26. Iyabo Boyd, interview with author, May 16, 2019.

27. Iyabo Boyd, interview with author, May 16, 2019.

28. James LeBrecht, "A Place at the Table: Doc Filmmakers with Disabilities on Building Careers and Disproving Stereotypes," *Documentary Magazine*, January 8, 2018, https://www.documentary.org/feature/place-table-doc-filmmakers-disabilities-building-careers-and-disproving-stereotypes.

29. Jim LeBrecht, phone interview with author, May 13, 2019.

30. Dino-Ray Ramos, "International Documentary Association Announces Keynotes for Getting Real Conference," *Deadline*, June 25, 2018, https://deadline.com/2018/06/international-documentary-association-keynote-speakers-getting-real-conference-1202417134/.

31. Jim LeBrecht, phone interview with author, May 14, 2019.

32. Sonya Childress, "Beyond Empathy," *Fireligtht Media* (blog), March 20, 2017, https://medium.com/@firelightmedia/beyond-empathy-ad6b5ad8a1d8.

33. Anita Varma, "When Empathy Is Not Enough," *Journalism Practice* 13, no. 1 (2019): 105–121, https://doi.org/10.1080/17512786.2017.1394210, 105.

34. Rebecca Krefting, *All Joking Aside: American Humor and Its Discontents* (Baltimore: Johns Hopkins University Press, 2014), 18.

35. Beatrice Verhoeven and Matt Donnelly, "Why Amazon, Netflix Ghosted Sundance Sales after Dominating Last Year," *The Wrap*, January 31, 2018, https://www.thewrap.com/sundance-sales-market-amazon-and-netflix-ghost-film-festival/.

36. Verhoeven Donnelly, "Why Amazon, Netflix Ghosted Sundance."

37. Anthony Kaufman, "Netflix and Amazon Aren't Buying Documentaries, but the Non-Fiction Market Is Booming Anyway," *IndieWire*, April 17, 2018, https://www.indiewire.com/2018/04/netflix-amazon-documentary-market-tribeca-hot-docs-1201953235/.

38. Kaufman, "Netflix and Amazon Aren't Buying Documentaries."

39. Anthony Kaufman, "Documentary Business Reveals Widening Gap between Rich and Poor," *IndieWire*, May 8, 2019, https://www.indiewire.com/2019/05/documentary-market-sales-netflix-1202132285/.

40. Kaufman, "Documentary Business Reveals Widening Gap."

41. Kaufman, "Netflix and Amazon Aren't Buying Documentaries."

42. John Corner, "Performing the Real: Documentary Diversions," *Television & New Media* 3, no. 3 (August 2002): 255–267, doi:10.1177/152747640200300302, 267.

43. Charlotte Cook, in-person interview with author, May 17, 2019.

44. Ava DuVernay (@ava), "One of the things I value about Netflix is that it distributes black work far/wide. 190 countries will get WHEN THEY SEE US. Here's a promo for South Africa. I've had just one film distributed wide internationally. Not SELMA. Not WRINKLE. It was 13TH. By Netflix. That matters," Twitter, (@ava), March 3, 2019, https://twitter.com/ava/status/1102236624895655936?lang=en.

45. Tre'vell Anderson, "'Strong Island' Director Yance Ford Has Already Made Oscars History," *Los Angeles Times*, March 4, 2018, https://www.latimes.com/entertainment/la-et-oscars-2018-90th-academy-awards-strong-island-director-yance-ford-has-1520166441-htmlstory.html.

46. Anne Thompson, "Netflix Picks Release Date for Obamas' First Oscar Contender, 'American Factory'—Exclusive," *IndieWire*, June 26, 2019, https://www.indiewire.com/2019/06/netflix-obamas-american-factory-lands-oscar-release-date-1202152917/; Hannah Yasharoff and Carly Mallenbaum, "'American Factory,' first title from Barack, Michelle Obama's production company, wins Oscar," *USA Today*, February 10, 2020, https://www.usatoday.com/story/entertainment/movies/oscars/2020/02/09/oscars-2020-barack-michelle-obama-american-factory-wins/4710543002/

47. POV, "Roll Red Roll Press Kit," accessed September 29, 2019, https://www.pbs.org/pov/roll-red-roll-press-kit/; "About," Roll Red Roll, accessed September 29, 2019, https://rollredrollfilm.com/about/.

48. Lauren Wissot, "Courage under Fire Award: Stephen Maing and the NYPD 12," *Documentary Magazine*, November 14, 2018, https://www.documentary.org/online-feature/courage-under-fire-award-stephen-maing-and-nypd-12.

49. THR Staff, "News & Documentary Emmys: 2019 Winners," *Hollywood Reporter*, September 24, 2019, https://www.hollywoodreporter.com/lists/news-documentary-emmys-2019-winners-1238686.

50. Anne Thompson, "Amazon Rules Sundance, Spending $41 Million as Traditional Distributors Lie Low," *IndieWire*, January 31, 2019, https://www.indiewire.com/2019/01/sundance-market-amazon-studios-netflix-hbo-platforms-1202039431/.

51. Greg Evans, "IDA Grants $850G to 11 Documentaries; 'Blue Wall,' 'Hazing' among Picks," *Deadline*, October 20, 2017, https://deadline.com/2017/10/ida-international-documentary-association-grants-blue-wall-hazing-1202191529/.

52. Greg Evans, "Hulu Acquires Bing Liu's 'Minding the Gap'; Doc Nabbed Sundance Jury Award," *Deadline*, June 5, 2018, https://deadline.com/2018/06/hulu-bing-liu-minding-the-gap-documentary-acquisition-1202403812/.

53. Kate Nash, Craig Hight, and Catherine Summerhayes (eds.), *New Documentary Ecologies* (London: Palgrave Macmillan, 2014), 1–2.

54. "Tribeca Immersive," Tribeca Film Festival, accessed June 1, 2019, https://www.tribecafilm.com/immersive.

55. "New Frontier," Sundance Institute, accessed June 1, 2019, https://www.sundance.org/newfrontier10.

56. "About," MIT Open Documentary Lab, accessed June 1, 2019, http://opendoclab.mit.edu/about-3/.

57. "About IF/Then Shorts," Tribeca Film Institute, accessed June 1, 2019, https://www.tfiny.org/pages/about_if_then_short_documentary_program.

58. Ingrid Kopp, "Building It as We Go," Immerse (blog), May 20, 2019, https://immerse.news/building-it-as-we-go-226f24086e86.

59. "Indie Lens StoryCast," Independent Lens, accessed June 1, 2019, http://independentlens.s3.amazonaws.com/indie-lens-storycast/indie_lens_storycast_epk.pdf.

60. Janko Roettgers, "PBS POV Spark Announces Immersive Films, Instagram Stories," *Variety*, April 16, 2019, https://variety.com/2019/digital/news/pbs-pov-spark-announces-immersive-films-instagram-stories-1203190615/amp/?__twitter_impression=true.

61. Caty Borum Chattoo and Bill Harder, "The State of the Documentary Field: 2018 Survey of Documentary Professionals," *Center for Media & Social Impact*, 2018, https://cmsimpact.org.

62. Borum Chattoo and Harder, "The State of the Documentary Field."

63. Ken Jacobson, "The Documentary Sustainability Movement: A Work in Progress," *Documentary Magazine*, August 30, 2018, https://www.documentary.org/feature/documentary-sustainability-movement-work-progress.

64. National Endowment for the Arts, *State of the Field: A Report from the Documentary Sustainability Summit*, 2017, https://www.arts.gov/publications/state-field-report-documentary-sustainability-summit.

65. Alan Goforth, "The Road to Sustainability: Midwest Summit Participants Continue Journey to a Viable Future," *Documentary Magazine*, March 26, 2018, https://www.documentary.org/online-feature/road-sustainability-midwest-summit-participants-continue-journey-viable-future.

66. AFI Docs, "Thank you to Corporation for Public Broadcasting for supporting today's Localism Works Convening designed to support & strengthen local filmmaking communities," *Facebook*, June 21, 2019, accessed September 29, 2019, https://www.facebook.com/AFIDocs/posts/thank-you-to-corporation-for-public-broadcasting-for-supporting-todays-localism-/10158725965209741/.

67. Rebecca Day (and opening editorial note from the International Documentary Association, "Mental Health: A Crisis in Our Community," *Documentary Magazine*, August 24, 2019, https://www.documentary.org/online-feature/mental-health-crisis-our-community.

68. "Viewpoint: NYC Doc Producers Call for 'A Little Respect,'" RealScreen, September 27, 2016, http://realscreen.com/2016/09/27/viewpoint-nyc-doc-producers-call-for-a-little-respect/; Beth Levison, "Documentary Producers Alliance Unveils Crediting Guidelines," *Documentary Magazine*, January 15, 2019, https://www.documentary.org/feature/documentary-producers-alliance-unveils-crediting-guidelines.

69. Documentary Producers Alliance, accessed June 1, 2019, https://www.documentary-producersalliance.com/.

70. Documentary Producers Alliance, "A Guide to Best Practices in Documentary Crediting," January 2019, https://static1.squarespace.com/static/5c06c490c3c16a8aca5649d8/t/5c4a90bbf950b7df1953babf/1548390589082/DPACreditingGuidelines.pdf.

71. Andrew Cox, "What Are Communities of Practice? A Comparative Review of Four Seminal Works," *Journal of Information Science* 31, no. 6 (December 2005): 527–540, doi:10.1177/0165551505057016.

72. The D-Word, accessed June 1, 2019, https://www.d-word.com/.

73. Peter Dahlgren, "Reconfiguring Civic Culture in the New Media Milieu," in *Media and the Restyling of Politics: Consumerism, Celebrity and Cynicism*, ed. John Corner (Thousand Oaks, CA: Sage, 2003), 156.

74. Jenkins, *By Any Media Necessary*, 17.

75. Patricia Aufderheide, "Perceived Ethical Conflicts in US Documentary Filmmaking: A Field Report," *New Review of Film and Television Studies* 10, no. 3 (2012): 362–386, https://dx.doi.org/10.1080/17400309.2012.691248, 382.

76. Tabitha Jackson, phone interview with author, May 20, 2019.

About the Author

Caty Borum Chattoo is executive director of the Center for Media & Social Impact (CMSI), an innovation lab and research center at American University that creates, showcases, and studies media for social change; and assistant professor at the AU School of Communication in Washington, DC. She is the co-author of *A Comedian and An Activist Walk into a Bar: The Serious Role of Comedy in Social Justice* (University of California Press, 2020), with Lauren Feldman. As a documentary producer, her films and TV programs have screened in the US and abroad. Borum Chattoo's peer-reviewed research about the intersection of entertainment storytelling, creativity, and social change is featured in *Journal of Communication; Journalism; Media, Culture & Society; Journal of Broadcasting & Electronic Media; Mass Communication and Society; International Journal of Communication*, and others. Borum Chattoo serves on the board of directors of Kartemquin Films and Working Films, and on the East Coast advisory board of the George Foster Peabody Awards.

Index